THE GALVANIZED YANKEES

The Galvanized Yankees

By
Dee Brown

University of Nebraska Press
Lincoln and London

Library of Congress Cataloging-in-Publication Data
Brown, Dee Alexander.
  The galvanized Yankees.
  Reprint. Originally published: Urbana: University
of Illinois Press, 1963.
  1. Indians of North America—Wars—1862–1865.
2. Indians of North America—Great Plains—Wars.
3. United States. Army—Military life. 4. United
States—History—Civil War, 1861–1865—Prisoners and
prisons. I. Title.
E83.863B7 1985   978'.02   85-23219
ISBN 0-8032-6075-X (pbk.)

Reprinted by arrangement with Dee Brown,
represented by Literistic, Ltd.

Originally published in 1963 by the University of Illinois Press, Urbana

Contents

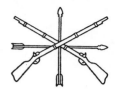

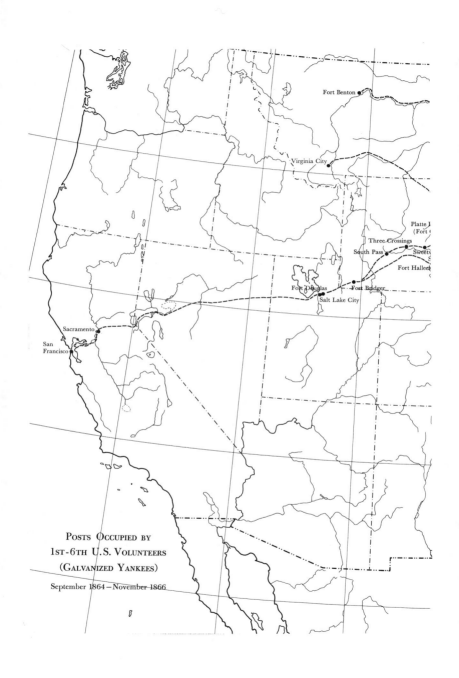

Fort Benton

Virginia City

Platte [
(Fort

Three Crossings
South Pass   Sweet
                    Fort Hallec

Fort Douglas   Fort Bridger
         Salt Lake City

Sacramento

San
Francisco

Posts Occupied by
1st-6th U.S. Volunteers
(Galvanized Yankees)

September 1864 – November 1866

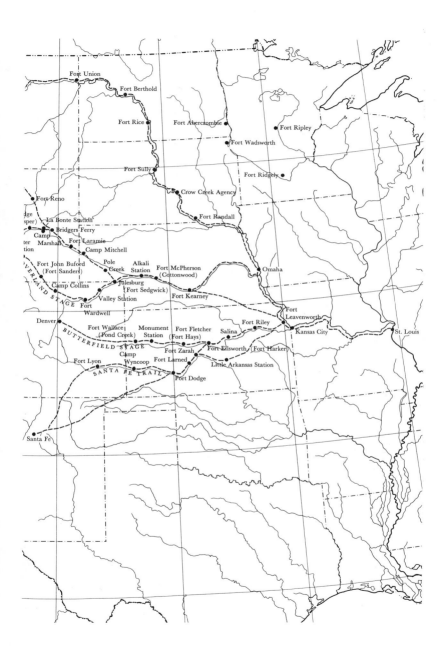

Fort Union

Fort Berthold

Fort Rice

Fort Abercrombie

Fort Ripley

Fort Wadsworth

Fort Sully

Fort Ridgely

Crow Creek Agency

Fort Reno

Fort Randall

dge
sper)   La Bonte Station

Bridgers' Ferry

Camp
Marshall   Fort Laramie
ter
tion   Camp Mitchell

Pole
Fort John Buford   Creek   Alkali
(Fort Sanders)   Station   Fort McPherson
                                                  (Cottonwood)   Omaha

Camp Collins   Julesburg
                       (Fort Sedgwick)
              Valley Station
              Fort   Fort Kearney
              Wardwell

Denver

Fort Wallace   Monument   Salina
(Pond Creek)   Station   Fort Fletcher
                                       (Fort Hays)

Fort Riley   Fort
                    Leavenworth

Kansas City   St. Louis

BUTTERFIELD STAGE

OVERLAND STAGE

Camp   Fort Zarah   Fort Ellsworth (Fort Harker)
Fort Lyon   Wyncoop   Fort Larned
                                    Fort Dodge   Little Arkansas Station

SANTA FE TRAIL

Santa Fe

I

Introduction

From the Cannon Ball River in Dakota up the muddy Missouri to Montana; along the Platte, the Sweetwater, the Powder, and other watercourses of the Great Plains and the Rockies; on the Oregon Trail and the Santa Fe Trail; out through South Pass and the Wasatch Mountains to the Salt Lake country of the Mormons; in camps and cantonments and a score or more forts—Kearney, Rice, Reno, Union, Laramie, Bridger; at ranche stops of the Overland Stage; in cedar-and-adobe huts of the Pacific Telegraph Line; everywhere on the Western frontier in those last days of the Civil War and the hard months after it ended, some 6,000 Americans served as outpost guardians for the nation that at one time or another each had sought to destroy.

These were the Galvanized Yankees, former soldiers of the Confederate States of America, who had worn gray or butternut before they accepted the blue uniform of the United States Army in exchange for freedom from prison pens where many of them had endured much of the war. Sent to the Western frontier so they would not meet their former comrades in battle, they soon found a new foe, the Plains Indian.

Between September 1864 and November 1866 they soldiered across the West. Many of them died there—killed by Indians, scurvy, epidemic disease, wintry blizzards. Some of them deserted, although their rate of desertion was only slightly higher than in state volunteer regiments of the Union.*

Officially they were known as the United States Volunteers, six regiments recruited from prisons at Point Lookout, Rock Island, Alton, Camps Douglas, Chase, and Morton. Some were foreign-born, Irish and German predominating; some were native stock from the hill country of Tennessee, North Carolina, and Kentucky; a few were from the Old South plantation country, from Virginia to Louisiana. Each man had his own reasons for choosing this dubious route to freedom—desperation from dreary months of ignominious confinement, of watching comrades die by the hundreds in prison hospitals; a determination to survive by any means; disillusionment with the war; a genuine change of loyalty that was as emotional as religious conversion; a secret avowal to desert at the first opportunity; despair, optimism, perhaps cowardice. In that day there were no psychologists to interview these 6,000 Galvanized Yankees, to search their minds and record their inner fears and longings.

After a century they have been almost forgotten. At the end of service they were discharged at Forts Leavenworth and Kearney. They scattered with the winds, some choosing new names, new identities. In the Old West a man's past was his own business. It was the man who mattered, not what he had been.

One may conjecture upon their peacetime pursuits: solid citizens and gunfighters, cattlemen and rustler, miners and highwaymen. † The glories of the Civil and Indian wars were kept alive by local organizations, which held annual reunions for half a century or more, recounting personal feats of bravery, recording them for posterity. If the Galvanized Yankees met in reunions, they must have gathered anonymously. Few of them indulged in reminiscences. No Southern state would claim them; the Grand Army of the Republic forgot them. They were a lost legion, unhonored, unsung.

* Ella Lonn in *Desertion During the Civil War*, 1928, p. 226, estimates one desertion to each seven enlistments (about 13 per cent) in the Union Army during the war. Immediately following the war, desertion on the Western frontier ran considerably higher, sometimes to 50 per cent of a company. A random check of several Galvanized Yankee companies shows very low rates in some, very high rates in others, with an average of about 14 per cent.

† For an account of a Galvanized Yankee who became a successful Colorado newspaper publisher, see "No Windy Promises," by Barron B. Beshoar, *Denver Westerners Brand Book*, 1961, pp. 79-99.

Yet the record of the six regiments in the West is one in which any American could take pride. During the spring and summer of 1865, the 2nd and 3rd Regiments restored stage and mail service between the Missouri River and California, continually fighting off raiding Indians. They escorted supply trains along the Oregon and Santa Fe trails; they rebuilt hundreds of miles of telegraph line destroyed by Indians between Fort Kearney and Salt Lake City. They guarded the lonely dangerous stations of the telegraphers. In the autumn of 1865 and through most of 1866, the 5th and 6th Regiments assumed these same dangerous duties. Sometimes they carried the mail through themselves. Two companies of the 5th escorted Colonel James Sawyers' Wagon Road Expedition to Montana, and then served for almost a year as rearguard outposts at isolated Fort Reno. Six companies of the 6th Regiment were strung out across 500 miles of trails between Fort Kearney and Salt Lake City.

On the bitterly contested Minnesota frontier, the 1st Regiment helped keep hostile Sioux off the settlements; along the Missouri River the 1st and 4th Regiments manned five forts, were engaged in numerous skirmishes, fought gallantly in one bloody battle. In the autumn of 1865, four companies of the 1st marched out upon the Kansas plains to open a new stage route, and endured a winter of Indian attacks, starvation, and blizzard marches.

There were Galvanized Yankees in Patrick Connor's Powder River Expedition; they fought on the Little Blue, the Sweetwater, at Midway, Fort Dodge, Platte Bridge. They guarded surveying parties for the Union Pacific Railroad; they searched for white women captured by hostile Indians. They knew Jim Bridger, Wild Bill Hickok, Buffalo Bill Cody, Spotted Tail, and Red Cloud, before the outside world had scarcely heard these now celebrated names. In the course of their military duties they found time to write poetry, to publish a newspaper. And at least one Galvanized Yankee achieved legendary fame in later life—Henry M. Stanley, who found Dr. Livingstone in Africa.

They went West in a time of great urgency. Thousands of Union soldiers were nearing the ends of their three-year voluntary enlistments, and draft calls were causing riots in Northern cities. Peace groups and Copperheads were inciting sedition and sabotage. A Presidential campaign was dividing the Union's purposes. Prices were soaring and morale was falling on the home front. Danger threatened from Canada, where small bands of Confederates plotted invasion. In Mexico, European adventurers were gathering around the French emperor, Maximilian, with dreams of severing the rich Western states and territories from a weakened United States.

Aware of dwindling forces in frontier forts, hostile Indian tribes had begun raiding as early as 1862, and by 1864 a full-scale Indian war was sweeping the Plains. Kansas, Nebraska, Iowa, Colorado, and Minnesota were thinly populated, and many of their young men had gone East to fight for the Union. Regiments were recalled, yet local territories could not supply enough troops to staff forts necessary for security, or to guard the long lines of sustenance and communication which held East and West together.

In mid-year of 1864, Fort Kearney on the Oregon Trail could muster only 125 men; Fort Laramie 90. Thirty-nine men held Fort Larned on the Santa Fe Trail. In late summer of that year the Overland Route was completely closed for a month; not a stagecoach or a wagon rolled; no telegraph messages could be sent over broken lines. Californians were cut off from the Eastern United States, except by sea passage around the Horn or over the Isthmus. Supplies, mail, and news for Coloradans had to come by boat to San Francisco and then overland from there.

Old-timers often described 1865 as "the bloody year on the Plains," and that was the year the Galvanized Yankees fanned out from the army's staging point at Fort Leavenworth along Western trails and rivers, to do their share of what had to be done. In personal and public records of that time and place, one can find frequent references to their presence.

Captain Eugene Ware of the 7th Iowa Cavalry:

I started back to Fort Kearney, along with a captain and six lieutenants of the 3rd U.S. Volunteers. These "United States Volunteers" as they were called, were soldiers recruited from the military prison-pens at Chicago and Rock Island, and were made up of men taken from the Southern Confederacy who were willing to go West and swear allegiance to the United States on the condition that they would not be requested to go South and fight their own brethren. They wanted to get out of prison, were tired of the war, didn't want to go back into the service, did not want any more of the Southern Confederacy, did not want to be exchanged, and were willing to go into the United States service for the purpose of fighting the Indians.[1]

William Darnell, Kansas bullwhacker: "At Fort Riley at this time [March 1865] there were some two hundred Confederate soldiers encamped a little below the fort on the Republican river. These men had been captured during the war, and had been paroled on condition they would go West and fight the Plains Indians who at this period were most troublesome. These Confederates were known in the West as 'galvanized soldiers' and at this time were waiting to be sent out to Fort Dodge."[2]

Surgeon William Waters, 18th U.S. Infantry: "Fort Bridger upon our arrival, was garrisoned by three companies of ex-rebel soldiers who enlisted in our army, when prisoners of war, for duty on the frontier, fighting Indians. These troops are styled officially U.S. Volunteers, but are more generally known as 'Galvanized Yankees,' a term that seemed not at all offensive to them."[3]

The Atchison (Kansas) *Press,* March 1, 1865: "During the week eight or ten companies of rebel prisoners, who have become dissatisfied with the rebel cause, taken the oath, and enlisted in Uncle Sam's service, passed through St. Joe on the way to Fort Kearney and other posts along the line from there to Denver, to fight the Indians who are now holding high carnival along the route."[4]

Chaplain Thomas J. Ferril, 16th Kansas Cavalry: "Some of these recruits [with Connor's Expedition] were called 'galvanized Yankees,' that is, Confederate prisoners who were enlisted from northern prisons, willing to fight Indians on the condition that they would not be sent south against their former comrades in the Confederacy."[5]

William Mackey, Fort Larned blacksmith: "About this time there was a company that came to the post, I don't know where from, we called the 'galvanized company.' "[6]

At first the Galvanized Yankees were received with skepticism, suspicion, open dislike. Few commanders in the West believed that former Confederates would make good soldiers, and when some of the Southerners deserted in their first days of service, the doubting commanders condemned the entire experiment, and asked that no more "Rebel regiments" be sent to their districts.

After a few months of trial on the frontier, however, attitudes changed. General Alfred Sully thought so highly of the 1st Regiment's "well-disciplined troops" that he requested more companies be sent to his hard-pressed posts in Dakota. When they were not forthcoming he went to Chicago himself and enlisted another regiment from prisoners at Camp Douglas. He lost these men to General Grenville Dodge, who needed them on the Plains in 1865. Dodge afterwards declared that his five regiments of U.S. Volunteers "recruited from the rebel prisoners . . . had to be depended upon mostly for taking care of all the country west of the Lakes— the Overland routes on the Plains, to man the posts on the Upper Missouri and Mississippi rivers, and for escorts for surveying parties." They formed more than half the forces he was given to reopen travel and communication lines which had been closed by Indians.[7]

In the autumn of 1864 General John Pope, directing military operations on the frontier, was highly dubious of enlisted Confederate prisoners. By June of 1865, however, he was pleading with Washington not to muster these men out of service. "There are in this division the 1st, 2nd, 3rd, 4th, 5th, and four companies of the 6th U.S. Volunteers. . . . They are stationed along the Overland routes across the plains, and at remote stations in the Indian country from St. Paul to the Rocky Mountains. I cannot now replace them." Pope was able to retain most of his Galvanized Yankees until autumn, when enlistment terms for the 2nd and 3rd Regiments expired. On October 10, he requested authorization from General Grant to re-enlist the men of the 2nd and 3rd into a consolidated regiment. The state troops, Pope explained, had enlisted only for the duration of the Civil War and were "dissatisfied and mutinous and are even now rapidly deserting." On the other hand, the 2nd and 3rd Galvanized Yankees were "good soldiers, in good discipline, and unless I can reorganize them at once I fear we shall have great difficulty on the plains."[8]

Surgeon Stephen P. Yeomans, 7th Iowa Cavalry, who was assigned to the 1st and 4th U.S. Volunteers in August 1865, said they were a much better class of men than he had expected to find. "They have been schooled in the most thorough discipline in both armies, and are brave even to recklessness. I have met with no troops whose deportment toward officers as well as each other was more gentlemanly, none who exhibited as much neatness in their personal appearance, none who discharged their duties with greater cheerfulness and alacrity, nor any less addicted to the camp vices of drunkenness, profanity and vulgarity."[9]

When a battalion of the 6th Regiment arrived at Camp Douglas, Utah, in October 1865, an officer of the California Volunteers saluted them in the post newspaper: "They are a splendid looking lot of men; and have the reputation of being intelligent, disciplined and thorough soldiers." Later he wrote an editorial about them: "The men who have fought bravely against the Union cause have shaken hands with the men who have fought for it, and 'the Union one and undivided' is again their joint motto. It is the policy of the truly brave to forget past differences, which the soldiers of Camp Douglas, who are now a mixed class, will endeavor to do. During the war they fought on opposite sides, but they are all members of the one family of Americans."[10]

In June 1865, Enoch G. Adams, Captain of B Company, 1st Regiment, and commander of troops at Fort Rice, defended his Galvanized Yankees when there were still doubts as to their loyalty: "Their whole course and behavior has displayed that unadulterated patriotism was the only motive that urged them on. . . . Many have laid down their lives at the beck of disease, some have been murdered by the arrow of the savage, and with but few exceptions, living or dead, have been true to their trust." Later, in October, as his men were preparing to leave Dakota Territory for mustering out, Captain Adams expressed the belief that the U.S. Volunteers were "the first fruits of a re-united people . . . the link between the North and the South."[11]

Undoubtedly one of the main reasons for the success or failure of individual companies of the Galvanized Yankees was the quality of the officers. Excepting a very few, they were Union Army men with some battlefield experience, and in general they were ambitious, energetic, and young. ("Most of them are boys," General Sully commented when the 4th Regiment's officers reported for duty in his district.) Captain Ware of the 7th Iowa Cavalry said the officers of the 3rd Regiment he met at Fort Kearney were all of "undoubted courage and ability, who had been selected from among the capable sergeants of the State regiments. . . . They were as intelligent and capable a lot of young men as you could hope to find; in fact, they were selected from the best, and averaged up much higher and better than the usual run of volunteer lieutenants."[12]

Among the six colonels was one West Point graduate, Henry E. Maynadier, who had soldiered in the West before the war. He was regular army, but like most native Virginians who remained loyal he was given assignments outside the Eastern theater of war.

Maynadier commanded the 5th Regiment, most of the time from Fort Laramie, which was the center of action in 1865-66. Andrew Patrick Caraher commanded the 2nd Regiment. A native of Ireland, Caraher had won citations at Fredericksburg and Gettysburg. Christopher McNally, an Englishman, commanded the 3rd Regiment; he had seen action in the early months of war in the far Southwest, was cited for gallantry at Mesilla, New Mexico. Charles Dimon of the 1st Regiment started his career as a private in a Massachusetts unit, moving rapidly up in rank as a protégé of General Benjamin Butler, who gave him the colonelcy of the 1st. Charles Thornton of the 4th Regiment had been an officer in the 12th Maine. Carroll Potter of the 6th Regiment was another New Englander, with a year and a half of training at West Point.

Two company commanders later achieved some reputation with the Indian-fighting cavalry. Leopold Parker of the 4th Regiment was with General Ranald Mackenzie's famed raiders along the Texas border, serving for several years as Mackenzie's adjutant. Thomas McDougall of the 5th Regiment became a major in Custer's 7th Cavalry; he was in command of the pack train at the Little Big Horn and survived the massacre. Washington Matthews, assistant surgeon to the 4th Regiment, later became a noted ethnologist and anthropologist, an authority on the Navajo Indians. Chaplain Alpha Wright of the 2nd Regiment liked frontier duty so well that after the Galvanized Yankees were mustered out he remained at Fort Laramie for several years as post chaplain, his name frequently appearing in later chronicles of that crossroads of the West.

How was it that the sobriquet came into being? Who first used the words "Galvanized Yankees?" And when? Probably no one can say for certain. All sorts of appellations bearing the word "Yankee" were in vernacular use during most of the war. In border states where allegiances were divided, local Confederates referred to neighbors on the Federal side as "Home-made Yankees." In northern prisons, soldiers of the Invalid Corps serving as guards were called "Condemned Yankees" by their Confederate captives because they wore the insignia "I. C.," which in the quartermaster department meant "inspected and condemned." And "Damn Yankees" of course has survived to become a part of the American language.[13]

Evidence indicates that "Galvanized Yankees" was first used to designate any captured Union soldier who turned Confederate. Warren Lee Goss and Melvin Grigsby, who wrote of their experiences at Andersonville, both used the term with this meaning.[14] As late as March 5, 1865, General Dodge referred to some "galvanized Yankees" in prison at Alton, identifying them as former Union men "taken prisoners by the enemy during the last year, and who to avoid starvation and death" enlisted in the Confederate Army, "and who in the recent raid deserted on the approach of our forces to us."[15] As the expression came into use, however, it was applied by Confederates to any one who took the oath of allegiance to the Union, and even to Union sympathizers in the South.

General Benjamin Butler, who was instrumental in recruiting the 1st Regiment under President Lincoln's direction, referred to the recruits as "repentant rebels, whom a friend of mine calls *transfugees*."[16] In most of the early official communications they were described simply as "rebel prisoners" or "deserters," terms which soon became inapplicable and were resented by the men themselves. When the U.S. Volunteers first arrived on the frontier, the phrase "white-washed Rebels" was sometimes used by their fellow soldiers from the Western state regiments.

It was Samuel Bowles who defined with exactness the present meaning of Galvanized Yankees and made it stick by dispatching a story to his widely quoted newspaper, the *Springfield* (Mass.) *Republican*. From Fort Kearney, Nebraska, May 24, 1865, Bowles wrote: "Among the present limited number of troops on the Plain are two regiments of infantry, all from the rebel army. They have cheerfully re-enlisted into the federal service. . . . They are known in the army as 'white-washed rebs,' or as they call themselves 'galvanized Yankees.' "[17]

American nomenclature, however, has a shifting quality, and during the remaining year and a half they served in the West, the Galvanized Yankees were referred to in common speech not only by that name but as galvanized infantry, enlisted prisoners, Rebels, former Rebels, and of course, U.S. Volunteers. In all official communications they were U.S. Volunteers, and the longer the regiments served, the fewer were the references to their origin.

It is not easy to visualize the enormous spread of frontier where these 6,000 men marched and fought and endured the tedium of garrison duties. From Fort Kearney to Julesburg. From Julesburg to Laramie and along the Sweetwater through South Pass to Utah. From Julesburg up the South Platte to Denver, by Cache La Poudre to the Laramie Plains and Fort Bridger. From Fort Randall up past Sully to Rice, Berthold and Union. From Fort Ellsworth to Dodge and Fort Lyon to Santa Fe.

They made themselves a part of all the raw and racy names on that wild land of buffalo and Indians—Cottonwood Springs and Three Crossings, Lodgepole and Alkali Station, Medicine Creek and Sleeping Water, Fort Zarah and White Earth River, St. Mary's, Fort Wicked, Laughing Wood, Soldier Creek, Rabbit Ear Mound, Dead Man's Ranche, and the Lightning's Nest.

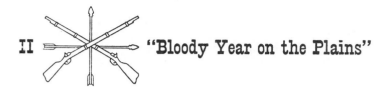

II   "Bloody Year on the Plains"

1

The "two regiments of infantry, all from the rebel army," which Samuel Bowles reported as being on the Plains in May 1865, were the 2nd and 3rd U.S. Volunteers, and those soldiers whom he met personally were in Companies A and B of Colonel Christopher McNally's 3rd Regiment, stationed at Fort Kearney. Scarcely a month earlier, the man primarily responsible for their presence on the frontier, Abraham Lincoln, had died by the hand of an assassin.

It had been a matter of politics back in late September 1864, when Lincoln was engaged in his presidential campaign against George B. McClellan. The race looked close then, particularly in the Eastern states, where McClellan was popular. Resentment was rising against the administration because of draft calls and conscription laws. Pennsylvania, for example, had sent almost a quarter of a million men to war, and in order to keep enough able-bodied breadwinners at home, was paying heavy bounties for substitutes. By late 1864 acceptable substitutes were not easy to come by.

When two Pennsylvania politicians approached Lincoln with a plan to use Confederate prisoners of war as substitutes, the President listened with a willing ear. His opponent, McClellan, was a Pennsylvanian, and Lincoln believed he needed that state to win re-election. Any move which would gain votes in Pennsylvania was good politics.

The visitors from Meadville, Pennsylvania, were Lieutenant-

Colonel Henry S. Huidekoper of the 150th Pennsylvania Volunteers and Judge S. Newton Pettis. On September 1, Lincoln wrote
a note for Colonel Huidekoper:

It is represented to me that there are at Rock Island, Ill., as rebel
prisoners of war, many persons of Northern and foreign birth, who are
unwilling to be exchanged and sent South, but who wish to take the oath
of allegiance and enter the military service of the Union.

Colonel Huidekoper, on behalf of the people of some part of Pennsylvania, wishes to pay the bounties the Government would have to pay to
proper persons of this class, have them enter the service of the United
States, and be credited to the localities furnishing the bounty money. He
will therefore proceed to Rock Island, ascertain the names of such persons
(not including any who have attractions southward), and telegraph them
to the Provost-Marshal-General here, whereupon direction will be given
to discharge the persons named upon their taking the oath of allegiance;
and then, upon the official evidence being furnished that they shall have
been duly received and mustered into the service of the United States,
their number will be credited as may be directed by Colonel Huidekoper.[1]

A few days later Huidekoper and Pettis journeyed to Rock
Island prison to start the process of converting Confederates to
Yankees. In the meantime, however, Lincoln's Secretary of War,
Edwin M. Stanton, had refused to pass his chief's informal order
into official channels so that the commandant at Rock Island had
no military authority to begin actual enlistments. Learning of this
on September 20, Lincoln sent another copy of the Huidekoper
note with an endorsement to Stanton. Again the balky Secretary
refused to act, and Lincoln had to go personally to the War Department and explain the political realities, after which he insisted
that the order be executed immediately.[2]

During this interview, Stanton must have told the President
that he had refused to act because General Grant was in strong
opposition to enlisting Confederate prisoners into the Union Army.
In the early months of 1864, Stanton, Lincoln, and General Benjamin Butler had quietly organized the 1st U.S. Volunteers from
prisoners at Point Lookout, Maryland, but Grant thus far had refused to use them for anything but minor guard duties around
Norfolk. (The story of the 1st U.S. Volunteers in the West is told
in Chapter IV.)

Following the interview, Lincoln felt obliged to send an explanation to his chief general:

I send this as an explanation to you and to do justice to the Secretary
of War. I was induced, upon pressing application, to authorize the agents

of one of the districts of Pennsylvania to recruit in one of the prison depots in Illinois, and the thing went so far before it came to the knowledge of the Secretary that, in my judgment, it could not be abandoned without greater evil than would follow its going through. I did not know at the time that you had protested against that class of thing being done, and I now say that while this particular job must be completed no other of the sort will be authorized without an understanding with you, if at all. The Secretary of War is wholly free of any part in this blunder.

Yours, truly
A. Lincoln.[3]

On that same day, September 22, the President arranged for one of his favorite young officers, Captain Henry R. Rathbone, to be sent out to Rock Island to make a special inspection of the persons to be enlisted. Lincoln trusted Rathbone's judgment and ability to get things done. (A few months later he chose Rathbone as a protector when he attended Ford's Theater, but on that last mission, Rathbone failed the President.)

Now that the plan was in motion, Lincoln left the details to the War Department. On September 25, Stanton queried Grant for suggestions:

The President some time ago authorized a regiment of prisoners of war at Rock Island to be enlisted into our service. He has written you a letter of explanation. It was done without my knowledge and he desires his arrangement to be carried into effect. The question now arises, how shall they be organized, officered, and assigned to duty? Shall they be formed into one regiment by companies as other troops, or assigned in companies or squads to other organizations? Please favor me with your views on the subject. . . .[4]

Grant replied that same day, succinctly and to the point:

Your dispatch in relation to the organization of troops from prisoners of war is just received. I would advise that they be placed all in one regiment and be put on duty either with Pope [on the Northwest frontier] or sent to New Mexico.[5]

Grant's decision made it much easier for Rathbone to recruit prisoners who might object to enlisting to fight against former comrades-in-arms, but Rathbone was still bound by Lincoln's order to enlist only persons of Northern or foreign birth, and after he had reached Rock Island he discovered that a large majority of prospective recruits were discouraged Southerners. Early in October, Lincoln was again brought into the scheme because of the restrictions in his original note to Colonel Huidekoper. After considering the matter, Lincoln wrote a new memorandum:

. . . It is proposed to change this so that the ascertainment of names, examination and mustering can all be gone through with there, under the supervision of Colonel Johnson [Andrew J. Johnson, commanding at Rock Island] and Captain Rathbone, thus saving much time and trouble. It is also proposed that the restriction in the President's order limiting the recruits to persons of foreign and Northern birth be removed, and that the question of good faith on the part of those offering to enlist be left to the judgment and the discretion of Col. Johnson and Col. Caraher [Andrew P. Caraher, later commander of the 2nd U. S. Volunteers]. The limit of the whole not to exceed 1,750 men.[6]

As a result of these new instructions, recruiting among the prisoners at Rock Island went smoothly throughout October. For their various reasons—despair, optimism, disillusionment—many Southerners took the oath and signed up for frontier service.

Colonel Johnson separated the recruits from the other prisoners with a high board fence, crowding them temporarily into 16 small barracks. This area was immediately dubbed the "calf pen," the main area of the prison being known as the "bull pen." One of the prisoners, J. W. Minnich, said that "some of the men who went into the 'calf pen' gave evidence of a desire to help some comrade who would remain true to his cause, and communications were soon established and chunks of meat and bread would find their way over the fence without wings, though flying. . . . Headquarters soon dropped on to it, and a guard was put on the beat between the fence. . . ."[7]

The total number of recruits reached 1,797, slightly in excess of Lincoln's authorized 1,750, quite enough for two regiments. According to Minnich, hunger was a prime factor in the ease of recruitment. Rations had been cut, and packages of food were no longer permitted to be received from outside. "The authorities had opened a recruiting office," he said, "holding out the bribe of 'full rations' to complaining stomachs, ostensibly on the grounds that there were many men among us who realized that they were engaged in a wrong cause and would gladly accept service with the loyal States under a guarantee that they should not be anywhere engaged against their former comrades, but be sent to the frontier to war against the Indians. . . ."[8]

Days and weeks passed and as winter came on the confined recruits spent their days shivering around barracks stoves, awaiting orders to be sent West. Johnson dispatched several urgent messages to Washington, reporting the situation and requesting instructions. "Their clothing is of the poorest description," he wrote. "As they are no longer prisoners of war, clothing cannot be issued to them from the prisoners' portion, and as they are not organized, clothing cannot be issued by the quartermaster. . . . These men are to be pitied, as they are under the same surveillance, owing to their being in prison, as the prisoners, and their conduct does not warrant this watchfulness."[9]

During the same weeks that Johnson was attempting to prod the War Department into issuing orders which would send these recruits on their way, General Pope was desperately seeking troops to man his far-flung frontier posts.

At last, on February 6, 1865, the slow-moving military bureaucracy brought supply and demand together, and Pope was authorized to organize the Rock Island volunteers into two regiments and appoint officers to command them. "The officers appointed," the order specified, "must be in the service now, or have been honorably discharged. So far as can be done, they should be men familiar with frontier life."[10]

Pope wasted no time in issuing his orders. He sent General Alfred Sully to Chicago, and within two weeks the long-suffering U.S. Volunteers were organized, uniformed, and staffed with officers. Between February 20 and 24, various companies of the 2nd Regiment moved by rail to Fort Leavenworth. The following week, companies of the 3rd Regiment made the same journey, and in the last days of February the Galvanized Yankees, wearing unaccustomed blue uniforms, were drilling with arms and awaiting orders to march into the turbulent land of the Plains Indians.[11]

From army scouts, stage drivers, bullwhackers, and soldiers who had been out on the Plains during the winter, these former Confederates heard that life would be dangerous indeed anywhere west of Forts Riley and Kearney. The Leavenworth newspapers informed them that this was "no Indian scare but a bloody Indian war in reality."

The raids of late summer 1864, they were told, had quieted down for a while after General Samuel R. Curtis led a few regiments on a thousand-mile march up the Platte and then back to Leavenworth over the Santa Fe Trail. Ben Holladay of the Overland Stage had made a cautious inspection tour, and promised to run his coaches again if the government would furnish military guards and escorts. The government, being anxious to keep travel and communications open, assured Holladay of its cooperation; the overland mail contract was renewed for four years at the exorbitant rate of $750,000 per annum; and orders went out to military commanders to assist in reopening the routes.[12]

Schedules were just beginning to run smoothly again when Colonel J. M. Chivington and his Colorado cavalrymen rode out to teach the Cheyennes a lesson in their winter camp at Sand Creek. What followed on November 29, 1864, was the Sand Creek Massacre, and the Cheyennes were soon boiling all over the Plains, eager for revenge.

With Sioux and Arapaho allies, the Cheyennes concentrated along the South Platte and Sweetwater, raiding and plundering over a distance of 400 miles, burning Julesburg and many road ranches, ripping out miles of telegraph line. With their Southern allies—the Comanches and Kiowas—they attacked trains, posts, and escorts along the Santa Fe Trail.

Once again in Denver and Santa Fe there was panic; merchants raised the price of scarce goods. No trains would cross the Plains to bring food and clothing, hardware and ammunition.

About the same time that the 2nd and 3rd U.S. Volunteers were preparing to march west from Fort Leavenworth—March 1865—a few heavily armed wagon trains were beginning to move again. Joseph H. Taylor, a guard with one of the first trains to risk the journey from Julesburg to Fort McPherson, said the trail was "one continuous string of dead, both white men and Indians—dead stock, burned trains and ranches."[13] Flour, coffee and tea, tins of kerosene, bolts of cloth were scattered over the prairie. Naked and mutilated bodies, rotting where they had fallen, or charred in the ruins of burned cabins, lay unburied.

Those in authority knew that this repetition of the previous summer's scenes meant that henceforth the lines could be kept open only with strong and continuous military support. The job of seeing that this was done was assigned to General Grenville M. Dodge. The men who would face most of the dangers were the Galvanized Yankees.

Dodge started the 2nd Regiment marching toward Fort Riley on March 1, but he held the 3rd a few days longer at Fort Leavenworth because none of its field and staff officers and only a few of its company officers had reported for duty. On March 7, he ordered the 10 companies of the 3rd to assemble for a parade review March 9 in the garrison square and be prepared to "move immediately after en route for Fort Kearney where they will report to the commanding officer and await further orders."[14]

On March 9, however, no senior officer had yet reported, and departure was held up for two more days. The highest ranking officer was Lieutenant Lafayette E. Campbell of Company E, but Dodge decided he could not hold the regiment any longer than March 11; troops were needed too badly on the stage line west of Fort Kearney. They marched that morning under Lieutenant Campbell, with a few mule-drawn wagons, "well-armed and equipped, clothing, camp and garrison equipage . . . very deficient. . . . The weather and roads were very bad, but little transportation could be obtained and the march was very laborious."[15] At Fort Riley they found some of their old comrades of the 2nd Regiment still awaiting assignments along the Santa Fe Trail. They rested there for four days, picked up a few more officers, and on March 26 started Northwest for Fort Kearney.

· On April 9, some 800 weary former Confederates slogged the last mile into Fort Kearney, into a land totally strange to most of them—a barren sweep of country, somber, forbidding, gripped by a winter reluctant to give way to spring. But after the long 350-mile overland march, even the rotting cottonwood barracks of Kearney seemed like a sanctuary. Only two companies, however, would remain long at Fort Kearney.

The 3rd U.S. Volunteers were now in the Department of the Plains, under the command of a tough and impatient frontier campaigner, General Patrick E. Connor. On April 9 the telegraph line was open from Kearney to Denver, and Connor learned of the arrival of his new troops that same day. He immediately issued orders for the disposition of units of the 3rd Regiment. "Two companies at each of Kearney, Cottonwood, Julesburg, Junction, and Laramie. Headquarters of regiment will be at Julesburg."[16]

Further instructions followed in rapid succession from Connor's headquarters, orders which divided the regiment "in small parties of one non-commissioned officer and twelve privates each stationed at various points generally ten miles apart on the line of the Overland Mail Route for the purpose of guarding citizens and their property from attacks of hostile Indians." By the end of May the regiment was guarding 600 miles of road.[17]

Companies A and B, with headquarters at Fort Kearney, were

the first to move out to specific assignments, details from A guarding stations immediately west of the fort, details from B guarding stations to the east. On April 13, the remaining companies resumed march from Fort Kearney, and a hundred miles farther west, C and D were detached at Post Cottonwood. Some of the men of Captain Fritz Rehwinkel's Company D, which was to see considerable action, later marched back over part of this same route, distributing one sergeant and 10 men at each of Gilman's, Midway, Pennestein, and Miller's, all frequent targets for raiding Indians. Lieutenant William H. Bartlett's C Company drew the stations west of Cottonwood.

At Camp Rankin in Julesburg, just across the line in Colorado Territory, the 3rd Regiment established headquarters April 25, retaining Companies E and F. Half the men of each company were assigned to stage stations in the vicinity; the others were to assist in constructing a new post near Julesburg to be known as Fort Sedgwick.

Companies G and H marched another hundred miles west to Junction (later known as Camp Wardwell), which was in an area relatively free of Indian troubles in 1865.

Companies I and K journeyed up to Fort Laramie to enter into a series of dangerous adventures along the Pacific Telegraph Line. Acting under special orders from General Connor, these two companies left Laramie May 15. In addition to guard duties they were expected "to assist the telegraph operators to repair the line when required." Captain Henry Leefeldt established headquarters for K Company at Camp Marshall, 65 miles to the west. Captain A. Smith Lybe marched Company I to Three Crossings, distributing his men along the telegraph line at Sweetwater, St. Mary's, and South Pass, 300 miles west of Laramie. Company I would march farther, fight more Indians, and suffer more casualties than any other company of the 3rd Regiment.[18]

As warm weather brought green leaves to willows and cottonwoods along the streams of the Plains country, the Galvanized Yankees settled into their new routines. At each of their headquarters stations, they shared duties with units of various state volunteer cavalry regiments. Troopers of the 1st Nebraska were at Cottonwood and Fort Kearney; Colorado cavalrymen were at Junction. A detachment of the 7th Iowa and a company of that remarkable group of mounted Indians, the Pawnee Scouts under Captain

Frank North, operated out of the 3rd Regiment's headquarters at Julesburg. West of Fort Laramie along the North Platte and Sweetwater, the 11th Ohio Cavalry welcomed I and K Companies of the 3rd, and there may well have been some surprising reunions of former Confederate soldiers. The 11th Ohio carried several Galvanized Yankees on its rolls, mostly Kentuckians, some of whom had served under General John Morgan. (Their story is told in Chapter IX.)

The records show very little friction between state volunteers and the former prisoners of war from Rock Island. The state troopers had been serving for a long time; the Civil War back East had ended, and they were eager to be mustered out of service. Any replacements were welcomed. A soldier of the 11th Ohio, Lewis B. Hull, who was at Fort Laramie in May to pick up supplies, noted in his diary the good news of the arrival of "two companies 3rd U.S., enlisted rebels from Rock Island." He added that he "talked to rebels awhile," and seemed to accept their presence in U.S. uniforms as a matter of course.[19]

From their assigned posts along the Overland Stage Line, the U.S. Volunteers began accompanying the veteran cavalrymen on escort rides with stagecoaches. The bracing spring air, the big open sky, the wide rolling land, the sweet taste of freedom, must have erased any individual doubts they may have had of their decisions to exchange the confinement of prison life for frontier duty. They soon acquired the jaunty manners of their Western mentors; they learned to distinguish deer, antelope, and elk, gray wolves and coyotes; they marveled at the tremendous herds of buffalo; they learned the tricks of identifying at long distances the hostiles from the friendly Indians.

The system under which the army guarded stagecoaches and telegraph lines across the Plains developed from a plan advanced in the 1850's by Henry O'Rielly, a pioneer builder of telegraph lines. O'Rielly was the first to propose a line from the Missouri River to the Pacific Ocean, and although he later lost the contract to others, some of his suggestions for overcoming difficulties were adopted. Known as the "Stockade Routes Proposal," O'Rielly's plan was to open transcontinental military roads guarded by soldiers all the way across the West. Each detachment of soldiers would construct its own stockade "like frontier settlers, and a portion of its dragoons riding each way every day, as patrols, or sentinels, ten miles out and ten miles back—thus giving protection to travelers and settlers; while these patrols moving with military precision, could transmit an express letter-mail across our vast territories to the Pacific Ocean." As soon as these military routes were made secure, O'Rielly envisioned the construction of telegraph lines alongside the roads.[20]

When the Overland Stage Line began operation, the managers disregarded O'Rielly's military security plan, but they did establish stations all the way from Atchison, Kansas, to Salt Lake City, 10 to 12 miles apart. As O'Rielly had foreseen, Indian troubles soon developed, and the stations had to be fortified. Stage horses, being the sturdiest and swiftest steeds available, were considered great prizes by the Indians, and in a short time the stage line was asking for military escorts to ride "ten miles out and ten miles back," as originally proposed by O'Rielly.

Many of the stations were established at road ranches, which had been operating for years as crude taverns along the Western trails. In hostile Indian country, the owners built their ranches in the manner of an O'Rielly stockade so as to withstand raids. Along the Platte, ranche buildings were usually constructed of sod walls with roofs of timber and brush covered with more sod. Floors were often nothing more than tamped earth. The main house was divided into a living room, a storeroom, and a "pilgrim" room. Groceries and whiskey were sold in the store room, and travelers could spend the night in the pilgrim room. Around the ranche were stables and corrals where the owner's stock and relief teams for stagecoaches were confined.

Overland Stage stations varied considerably in size and quality of services, and were known along the line as "home" stations and "swing" stations. Every fifth or sixth stop was a home station, headquarters for blacksmiths, harness repairmen, carpenters, stock tenders, and coach drivers. Because several people lived there, a home station attracted additional establishments, such as stores, saloons, and dance halls. Soldiers escorting coaches always preferred assignments which brought them into a home station for the night. Life was livelier there than at a swing station, where two or three other soldiers and a single stock tender furnished the only human diversion, and there was usually nothing to do but read a yellow-backed novel or a month-old newspaper—that is, unless hostile Indians happened to be on the prowl.

On May 11, General Connor moved his headquarters from Denver to Julesburg, which he considered a better vantage point for planning his summer campaign against the hostiles. The move also brought him into position to view the behavior of his Galvanized Yankees at close hand. Colonel Christopher McNally reported for duty at Julesburg on May 12, and Connor gave him command of the post in addition to his duties as commander of the 3rd Regiment. Connor was Irish, McNally English, but they had similar military backgrounds, both having come up through the ranks during the Mexican War. McNally had seen seven years of hard service as an enlisted Mounted Rifleman, and he understood the enlisted man's viewpoint. He was still recovering from severe wounds received in Civil War actions in Arizona, but he entered immediately into the difficult task of commanding a regiment spread out over 600 miles of Western trails.

McNally's first report as post commander, on May 31, was routine: "During time in which I have been in command no scouting parties as such have been sent out. I have sent out several parties to discover if possible a supply of wood for the use of this camp. . . . My efforts somewhat successful, but not entirely satisfactory. . . . I now have a party of fifty men . . . out for the purpose above mentioned, under charge of Lieutenant Charles A. Small, Co. A, Pawnee Scouts."[21]

During May most of the action involving the 3rd Regiment was taking place far to the east of Julesburg, along the Platte Valley between Cottonwood and the Little Blue. As usual the coming of new grass heralded the beginnings of Cheyenne and Sioux raids from the North. A small war party struck a wagon train near Mulhally's Ranche on May 5; on the morning of May 12 a larger party raided corrals at Smith's Ranche near Midway.

In this latter attack, which lasted for some hours, detachments of Company D from Midway and Gilman's Station experienced their first Indian fighting. They drove the enemy off after inflicting several casualties, but the company also suffered casualties: Private J. W. Hall severely wounded; Sergeant Reel and Privates Carr and O'Ney slightly wounded.[22]

In response to calls for a surgeon to attend these wounded, an ambulance and escort of 18 Nebraska cavalrymen and five mounted men of Company C, 3rd U.S. Volunteers, left Cottonwood at 3:00 P.M., May 12. Arriving at Gilman's late in the day, the escort learned that another group of mounted men had crossed the Platte in pursuit of the Indians. After considering the matter, the lieutenant in command decided to join in the chase. Borrowing two pounds of bacon for each of his men from the station operator, the lieutenant then proceeded east along the road until Smith's Ranche came into view. Bidding farewell to the surgeon and the ambulance, the escort party turned and galloped for the river, where it soon picked up the hoofmarks of the other pursuit detachment.

Thus, for the first time Galvanized Yankees were out scouting on the Plains for hostile Indians. At the river bank they halted 10 minutes to secure arms and ammunition; it was 6:00 P.M. when they plunged into the treacherous currents of the Platte. By the time they crossed the mile-wide stream, night had fallen. Four horses failed to make it across, one drowning, the other three with their riders being sent back when they began to falter. A fifth horse was too exhausted to go on; its rider and the cavalryman who had lost his mount by drowning made a dark camp on the river bank, hoping to swim their way back across to Smith's Ranche at daylight.

The patrol was now reduced to 18 men—the five Galvanized Yankees still intact—and nearly all the ammunition was wet. Dry cartridges were pooled and redistributed, so that each man had 15 rounds. They rode on in the darkness, attempting to follow the trail of the troopers ahead of them, but by 11:00 P.M. they lost it, and made camp until dawn.

The night was very cold, and without fires the men shivered in their wet uniforms until light showed in the sky. After scattering in all directions, they picked up the trail again at 7:00 A.M., reformed and moved north in alternating walks and trots for 20 miles. By midmorning they were in a canyon, and scouts had to be sent up on the ridges.

Not being accustomed to long hours in the saddle or the exposure of the previous night, the five men of Company C were beginning to feel the effects of the hard march. They held on doggedly, but around noon one of them became too ill to go on. A man was assigned to return with him to Smith's Ranche, and the remaining 16 riders resumed march North.

Early in the afternoon they came out the head of the canyon on a high prairie, and soon lost the trail. Forming a line front, they spread out at hundred-yard intervals and moved on across the empty undulating land, searching for horse tracks. After five miles, they gave up the pursuit. Their canteens were empty, their bacon was gone, they were short of ammunition, and being 40 miles north of the Platte were vulnerable to attack. Swinging back southward, they reached the Platte during the night, crossed the next morning, and rode on to headquarters at Cottonwood.

On their first scouting mission, this little group of Galvanized Yankees found no Indians, but they did win the respect of the veteran frontiersmen with whom they had shared and endured adversities. They had proved they were soldiers who could ride with the best, and that was enough to satisfy the hardy Nebraskans.

A few days later, May 18, on the road east of Fort Kearney, another group of 3rd U.S. Volunteers ran squarely into a prowling band of wild bucks, and this time not all escaped with their lives. These men had been convalescents of various companies left at Fort Leavenworth when the regiment moved out on the Plains in March. On May 10 they left Leavenworth en route West to join their companies. The highest ranking soldier among them was Sergeant Jefferson Fields of C Company. For some reason—army red tape or carelessness—no arms were issued to them before departure. Had they marched a few days earlier they probably would have needed no weapons before they reached Fort Kearney, but they happened to enter the valley of the Little Blue just about the time several bands of hostiles came raiding from the North.

Sergeant Fields's detachment was accompanied by a six-mule wagon with a civilian teamster, and the men took turns riding and walking, testing their strength after long weeks of hospital confinement. They moved slowly up the Little Blue, and at 2:00 P.M. on May 18 they were two miles east of Elm Creek Station. That was where the Indians found them—15 bluecoats without a single rifle or revolver.

In later testimony, the number of Indians in the attacking party varied from 12 to 30; the one-sided fight happened so quickly that none of the Volunteers had time to make an accurate count. The Indians simply rode up, met no resistance, and decided to capture and plunder the loaded wagon.

In a matter of seconds, two soldiers were dead, six wounded. Some of the Indians carried U.S. Cavalry sabers, and they used them with savage effect. Washington Fulton, the civilian teamster who was one of the first to be wounded, told of how he watched helplessly while a soldier was struck with a saber, then knocked down, and scalped while still alive. "The Indian who had charge of the party attacking us wore buckskin leggings," Fulton added. "His hair was long and had some kind of fur attached to his back hair. He was the only Indian who had long hair; he also had a revolver. Two of the attacking party had short hair 'roached' on top of their heads. . . . One of them, the Indian who scalped the soldier, had a large scar over his eye; whether right or left eye I cannot say."

The scalped soldier was Private John W. Twyman of Company H, and he lived to tell about it. "I was attacked by one of them with a U.S. saber, who struck me three times, knocking me down. Then he returned to the party and another of them came to me and scalped me; then he hit me with his saber and left. They were dressed in buckskin clothing, so far as I could see, except the chief, or the one in charge, who was dressed in some kind of light robe or blanket thrown over his shoulders. . . . I think they did it in revenge for something, as they spoke of the whites breaking a treaty with them."

Private Peter J. Flynn, Company A, was wounded in the face and back, and then held in temporary captivity by an Indian dressed in black velvet pants with two rows of brass buttons down the outer seams. "He also wore fancy beadwork moccasins and fancy beadwork cap, with a light-colored blanket thrown carelessly over him," Flynn said. "He gave me an arrow, four crackers, and a canteen, and released me and told me to go."

Sergeant Fields, who had suffered a deep arrow wound in his left shoulder, was helpless to do anything other than order his men to leave the vicinity of the wagon and start down the road. The Indians, he said, "followed us about one-quarter of a mile, and then motioned at us and told us to go, and then returned to the wagon and commenced plundering. They left the wagon standing in the road, and cut to pieces all the harness, and drove off the mules, six in number."

Because they had been told in Leavenworth that they would pass through friendly Pawnee country, these badly mauled Southerners—who were still too new to the frontier to distinguish one tribesman from another—decided among themselves that their attackers were a band of clever, deceitful Pawnees.

"The arrows they had were Sioux and Cheyenne," Sergeant

Fields testified, "but I am of the opinion they were Pawnees as they were so anxious that we should keep some of the Sioux arrows." Peter Flynn also believed the attackers were Pawnees because the chief who captured him "seemed very anxious to impress upon my mind that he was a Cheyenne chief." Private Twyman, likewise was convinced that his scalp was in possession of a Pawnee "for the reason they were so anxious to impress upon us they were Cheyennes."

The teamster, Wash Fulton, would not commit himself. With pithy frontier irony he commented: "They said they were friendly Sioux."[23]

The attack on Sergeant Fields's party was no isolated incident. That same day Indians raided or attempted raids against almost every road ranche along the Little Blue. One of these parties had engaged an Overland stagecoach in a six-mile running fight. Because of a break in the telegraph line, news of the raids did not reach Fort Kearney, 35 miles away, until late the next day. The subdistrict commander, Colonel Robert R. Livingston, ordered two pursuit parties into the field—a company of Nebraska Cavalry under Captain Lee Gillette, and a company of Omaha Indian scouts under Captain Edwin W. Nash. Captain Gillette marched all night directly to Elm Creek Station. Captain Nash proceeded southward toward the Republican River country where it was believed the hostiles may have gone in search of buffalo.

Meanwhile in Leavenworth, General Dodge had learned of the attack on the U.S. Volunteers, and he immediately demanded an explanation from the post commander: "The men were without arms. They should not be sent out unarmed. Who sent them that way?"[24]

A reprimand for some obscure officer of the quartermaster no doubt followed this inquiry, but that was not the end of the incident on the Little Blue. On May 22, Lieutenant William H. Bartlett, commanding Company C from Post Cottonwood, sent an indignant report to Colonel McNally at Julesburg. "Among the killed," Bartlett wrote,

was Private William J. Mers of this company, and among the wounded beside [Sergeant Fields] was Private Rinaldo Hedges, also of this company. . . . The wounded are at Fort Kearney. Fields . . . states that before leaving Fort Leavenworth he made application for arms, but none were furnished him. In my opinion, the officer who ordered him away from Fort Leavenworth, unarmed as he was, to make a march of nearly 300 miles through a country known for the most part to be infested by a savage and barbarous enemy, and unaccompanied by any armed force whatever, committed a grievous error, and should be held to account for so flagrant a breach of humanity, not to say neglect of duty; and I beg leave to call the attention of the commanding officer of the regiment to the facts in the case, and respectfully request that he take the matter in hand and adopt such measures as will tend to attach the blame where it belongs, so that the guilty as well as the innocent may share in the sufferings caused by some unworthy official dignitary's mismanagement.[25]

McNally indorsed Bartlett's report over to General Connor, who in turn forwarded it to Colonel Livingston at Fort Kearney. But instead of requesting Leavenworth headquarters to seek out and court-martial an army officer, Livingston chose to place all blame upon the Indians. On May 26, Captain Nash returned to Kearney with his Omaha Scouts, and reported that he had encountered a band of Pawnee buffalo hunters who had five mules in their possession. Two of the mules were bay-colored with shaved tails, the exact description of those cut loose from Sergeant Fields's wagon. "The Pawnees seemed anxious to sell the two bay mules," Nash reported, "saying they had recently found them."

In his haste to affix blame and punishment upon Indians, Livingston informed General Connor that "evidence proves conclusively that the mules . . . were part of the team accompanying detachment 3rd U.S. Volunteers, attacked by Indians on the Little Blue. . . . The presence of the Pawnees on the road at the time of the attack, fixes the atrocious murder of our men on the Pawnees. . . . The trail found, the only one found, was a Pawnee trail."[26]

Connor's reaction was typical of that veteran Indian fighter's ruthless methods. He ordered Livingston to send an expedition to the Pawnee reservation with instructions to demand "the members of the tribe guilty of the murder of our soldiers, and in case of refusal, to arrest five of the chiefs or principal men, bring them to Fort Kearney where you will hold them securely and report your action to these headquarters."[27]

Before Livingston could make an investigation on the Pawnee reservation, Captain Gillette returned with information which virtually destroyed his commander's theory that the Pawnees were guilty. By coincidence, Gillette had encountered General Connor at Big Sandy Station (Connor was personally escorting several high government officials across the Plains) and the general had ordered Gillette to march directly to the Pawnee reservation and make a search. Gillette found no army mules or anything else identifiable with the plundering of Sergeant Fields's wagon. "From the evidence adduced, and my own observations," Gillette informed Livingston on June 2, "I can find nothing that directly implicates the Pawnees."[28]

Livingston, however, had already committed himself to General Connor, and he was determined to find some guilty Pawnees. With a considerable mounted force and the survivors of Sergeant Fields's detachment—including the convalescent wounded—he marched to the Pawnee reservation early in June. There he assembled the chiefs in council. The Pawnee leaders were polite but indignant. Had not their people been at peace with the white men for many moons? Were not the best of their young warriors serving with the bluecoats under Captain Frank North? Livingston told them he had brought along the soldier survivors of the party which had been attacked on the Little Blue. He wanted every adult male in the Pawnee Nation paraded before them so that the guilty might be identified and punished.

There is no record of the emotions of the young Southerners as they watched the Pawnees submit to this indignity, but some might have wondered at the inconsistency of this army—their army now—which had freed the slaves, yet treated friendly Indians as though they were incorrigible. All day long the Pawnees shuffled past Sergeant Fields and his men, but not one Indian was identified as being guilty. The soldiers examined the livestock of the tribe; not one mule was recognized as belonging to their wagon.

Livingston at least now had the grace to admit to General Connor that he had been wrong. "I am satisfied from the frank, open manner in which the chiefs met me, and their cheerful alacrity to carry out any suggestions of mine tending to discover the culprits I was in search of that the Pawnees are guiltless of any participation in the murder of the men on Little Blue River."[29]

The Pawnees, however, were a long time in forgiving this heavy-handed discredit to their loyalties. They wondered if they dared form an alliance with such soldiers against their traditional enemies, the Sioux and Cheyennes. How could they trust soldiers who knew so little they could not tell a friendly from a hostile, who were so lacking in faith they suspected friends of treachery until suspicions were disproved by degrading searches?

Before marching to the Pawnee reservation, Colonel Livingston should have taken a closer look at the sworn testimony of the unfortunate Private Twyman, who was so certain he had lost his scalp to a Pawnee. Twyman probably could not have distinguished a Pawnee from an Apache, but he had listened closely to the broken English of his assailants. "I think they did it in revenge for something," he said, "as they spoke of the whites breaking a treaty with them."

No treaty had been broken with the Pawnees. The cry of broken treaty came from the Cheyennes, who were burning for revenge because of Chivington's November massacre of their women and children at Sand Creek. As the summer wore on this fact would become clear to all who encountered them. From the Little Blue westward to Platte Bridge, from Fort Dodge northward to Tongue River and beyond, Sand Creek would be the war cry of the Cheyennes and all their allies.

During Captain Gillette's long pursuit march, he met a stagecoach on May 23 at Big Sandy Station carrying his commanding general, Patrick Connor, as well as several other very important persons, including Speaker of the House Schuyler Colfax, Albert D. Richardson of the *Boston Journal,* and the editor who was to describe the U.S. Volunteers as Galvanized Yankees, Samuel Bowles of the *Springfield Republican.*

A detail of Gillette's Nebraska cavalrymen escorted these travelers up the line until they reached stations guarded by Company B of the 3rd Regiment, so that U.S. Volunteers had the honor of bringing the coach into Fort Kearney. "We had, as all the stages now have," wrote Bowles, "a guard of two to four cavalrymen . . . that constantly galloped by our side from station to station, with pistols at holsters and rifles slung in the saddles." Connor evidently informed Bowles that these men were from the Rebel army. "They were all young but hardy looking men; and the colonel, who is of course from the federal army, testified heartily to their subordination and sympathy with their new service."

The Massachusetts editor remarked on the rapid speed maintained by the line: "an average of six miles an hour, including all stops, sometimes making full ten miles an hour on the road. . . . Every ten or twelve miles we come to a station, sometimes in a village of log and turf cabins, but often solitary and alone, where we change horses; and every two or three stations, we change drivers, but except for meals, for which half an hour is allowed, our stops do not exceed five minutes each."

This stagecoach escorted by successive details of Company B men was a Concord, as were all the other 109 in service that year on Ben Holladay's Overland Stage Line. Proud New Hampshire workmanship had gone into the strong white-oak bodies braced with iron bands and slung upon stout leather braces. Wheels were extra heavy with thick tires, and the wide brake stick was supplemented by a sand box so that 2,000 pounds of rocketing coach could be brought to a quick stop.

Concords cost about $1,500 new, were fitted with side lights and interior candle lamps. Leather curtains were supposed to keep out rain and dust, but on the Plains nothing could have kept out rain or dust. Mail sacks and ordinary baggage went into the boot at the rear; valuables were stored in a treasure box beneath the driver's seat. Each passenger was allowed 25 pounds of free baggage, paid $1.00 a pound for extra weight. The fare from Atchison to California was $450. Nine passengers could ride shoulder to shoulder on three inside seats, and if necessary seven additional passengers could ride behind the driver on top.

Holladay insisted that his drivers wear flamboyant dress—broad-brimmed sombreros, corduroys trimmed in velvet, high-heeled boots. He furnished them with nine-foot rawhide whips, elaborately decorated with silver. In cold weather they wore overcoats of Irish frieze, lined with blue shaker flannel, cut long with capes that reached to their hands.

The U.S. Volunteers soon learned that in the social ranking of road drivers, the coachmen were lords of the lash. Next in order came the horse and mule teamsters, and then the lowest class— the bullwhackers, who drove oxen. As time passed the escort troopers identified themselves with the stagecoach drivers, soon knew them well enough to call them by their nicknames—One-eyed Tom, Rattlesnake Pete, Happy Jack, Fiddler Jim, Cross-Eye Jack. On the Kearney-Plum Creek run, there was a William Cody, who later would be known as Buffalo Bill. The soldiers took as much pride in the flashy operation of the Overland Stage Line as did the drivers, and joined them in shouting scornful phrases mixed with colorful oaths at the lowly teamsters and bullwhackers: "Clear the road for the U.S. Mails! Git out of the way thar with your damned bull teams!"

It was the custom to bring the horses to full speed when a coach approached a station, making a dramatic entrance with manes flying, wheels spinning, harness metal jingling, and the drivers shouting or blowing a fanfare on a bugle. The military escorts added flair by galloping their mounts in alongside, the soldiers' blue uniforms contrasting with the brilliant red coach body, striped with black and labeled in bold letters: OVERLAND STAGE LINE.

The coach carrying General Connor and his charges ran into a fierce storm a few miles east of Kearney, a small tornado which overturned wagons on the road, tore baggage loose from the top of the coach, and frightened the team to a halt. Bullet-sized hail set the four horses to rearing, and Connor advised his passengers to join him in leaving the coach. Bowles later said the military escort proved themselves real heroes by preventing the coach from overturning and the team from running away. "The horses were quieted and restored to their places, and we got into a drowned coach, ourselves like drowned rats, and hastened to refuge over a prairie flooded with water."[30]

The refuge was Fort Kearney, headquarters for A and B Companies of the 3rd, and the western terminus of the first division of the line from Atchison. The stage station was a short distance west of the fort, with an office, tavern, stables, and blacksmith shop. By late May, the U.S. Volunteers had been at Fort Kearney long enough to know their way around, and only the most confirmed gamblers and the hardest drinkers of the two companies spent much time anymore in Kearney City, or Dobytown, a collection of sod buildings where "large quantities of the meanest whiskey on earth were consumed," and where professional gamblers secured their livings from gullible travelers in games of poker, old-sledge, and seven-up.[31]

General Connor's party remained at Fort Kearney long enough to dry out, and then a detail from Company A saddled up to escort the coach over the next 10 miles to Platte Station. In a dispatch to his newspaper, Albert Richardson noted that the escort consisted of rebel prisoners who had taken the oath of allegiance. "They styled themselves 'galvanized' Yankees; were faithful, prompt and well-disciplined." He also related an account of how one of the escort, "with a cavalry rifle at four hundred yards, brought down an antelope with great branching horns, which he flourished wickedly about our soldier, who boldly seized them and then cut his throat. Strapping the fallen chieftain to our coach, we contributed him to the larder of the next station-keeper."[32]

Both Richardson and Bowles were fascinated by the road ranches, where the food was plain but unexpectedly good, where news of the outside world flashed by on the telegraph wires to enliven the lonely lives of the telegraphers, station-keepers, and soldiers. "We met the California papers daily in the coaches coming east," said Richardson, "and were permitted to read the dispatches from the Associated Press at telegraph stations. The breakfast . . . was the more palatable, when the New York bulletins of the same morning were spread upon the board—literally the board—in the hurried handwriting of the operator, who caught and transfixed them flying on the lightning's wing to San Francisco."

The escort detail ate army fare—hardtack and bacon—but occasionally after payday a soldier might join the passengers and squander a dollar at one of the better ranche taverns and dine on hot biscuits, ham and eggs, and dried-apple pie.

Life was strenuous, life was dangerous, for these soldiers new to the West, but most of them would have agreed with Samuel Bowles's comment that the Plains country was an exciting place to be in late spring of 1865. With the coming of fine weather, it seemed that every adult male in the East was heading West. Recently discharged Civil War veterans were going to the mines or searching for homestead sites. Politicians, land speculators, theatrical companies, parties of Mormons, government contractors, railroad surveyors—everybody was on the road. And each day there were more and more freighting trains, sometimes stretching as far as one could see, lines of heavy wagons with their white canvas billowing over loads of corn, hardware, groceries, whiskey, clothing, kerosene, machinery. To the Galvanized Yankees, the Overland Route must have seemed the highway of the world, and they were the guardians for its surging stream of humanity.

To add zest was the ever present threat of Indians. Westward from Plum Creek (35 miles beyond Fort Kearney) vigilance was redoubled. "There seemed to be something in the very air at Plum Creek," a teamster recorded, "that was different from what we had left behind. A feeling of danger, invisible but present, was openly manifested when an escort of U.S. soldiers moved out ahead of us when the bull train started."[33]

All along this section of trail were signs of recent Indian raids—burned ranches, wrecked corrals, freshly mounded graves. But after a few escort marches, the Volunteers scarcely noticed these grim reminders. There were too many interesting things to see along the way, too much vitality in the continually changing traffic on the road.

Among the sights to see and be taken in by was a huge square stone beside the trail west of Plum Creek. "Daniel Boone" had been carved into its surface, and below that well-known name was a mysterious message advising passersby to turn the stone over and learn some very important information. Many westbound travelers paused here, hitched teams to the stone, and struggled desperately until they turned it over only to read the same words on the other side.

West of Julesburg, the men of Captain Thomas Kenny's Company H became well acquainted with a road ranche built like a medieval fort. The inner structure was of thick sod and adobe, surrounded by a moat and an outer wall of stone. It was impervious to bullets, arrows, or fire, and above the entrance a crudely lettered sign informed the world that this was

FORT WICKED

KEPT BY W. GODFREY

GROCERY STORE

When asked why he called his place Fort Wicked, Mr. Godfrey would usually reply: "Well, I guess the Sioux and Cheyenne know well enough." He had survived several strong attacks during the raids of 1864.[34]

Every day was new and different on that highway of the world. Some days the wind blew up great clouds of black stifling dust. Other days there would be sudden rain squalls, but after a rain the sky would turn sapphire and the air would be as bracing as a swig of brandy, so clear that distant landmarks seemed to move into the foreground of vision.

Almost every day brought a magnificent sunset against clouds or dust, the sun's rays flaming fire and gold, crimson, purple, pink and rose. Occasionally a great swarm of grasshoppers would sweep over the land like a snow shower, glittering in sunlight, filling the air in all directions, piling upon the ground. And everywhere along the way were prairie-dog villages, the inhabitants amusing to watch, their holes dangerous to horses' legs.

The rarest sight of all was a pretty girl. Most of the travelers on the road were men, but sometimes among a party of Mormon emigrants the U.S. Volunteers would catch brief glimpses of fair faces beneath sunbonnets. One day a party of Mormons, all females, passed Plum Creek heading west for Salt Lake City. Their effect upon the males they met along the way was recorded by Billy Dixon: "Not a man among them, and they could not speak a word of English; I was told that they were Danes. All the women wore wooden shoes. They drove ox wagons. . . . The sight of these women so excited our curiosity that the trainmaster called a halt until they passed us."[35]

The Plains country was rough on women in 1865. They had to contend with shortages of water, wood, food staples, clothing, and furnishings. Household duties occupied most of their waking hours. They bore their children without benefit of doctors. They endured insects, blizzards, and drouths. Dust and sun ruined their complexions. And always in their minds was the threat of captivity by Indians—a fate which they feared more than death itself.

The men of Companies E and F on escort and guard assignments west of Julesburg often passed a neat grave beside the ruins of a road ranche. The large headboard told them that it covered the remains of W. J. Morris, killed by Indians January 10, 1865. Missing and supposed captured by the Indians were his wife, Sarah Morris, and her two children, Charles and Joseph. All along the Platte Valley, soldiers were told to keep an alert watch for white women and children who might be traveling with bands of Indians during the summer hunts, for there were several others missing in addition to the Morrises.

One day in June, the routine of post construction and garrison duty at Julesburg was interrupted by the arrival of Mrs. Lucinda Eubanks, who had been a captive for almost a year. She had been recovered near Fort Laramie and brought down to General Connor's headquarters for interrogation. Mrs. Eubanks reported that she had seen Sarah Morris some weeks earlier with a band of Cheyennes moving north. (By an odd coincidence, on the very day Lucinda Eubanks was telling her story at Julesburg, Sarah Morris was being delivered to the commanding officer of the 1st

U.S. Volunteers 500 miles to the north, at Fort Rice, Dakota Territory. An account of her ordeal is told in Chapter IV.)

Lucinda Eubanks was only 24 years old, but the soldiers who saw her at Julesburg would have believed her to be twice that age. She had seen her home burned, her husband killed, and then she and her two children, a six-year-old nephew, and a 16-year-old girl, Laura Roper, had been taken prisoners by Cheyennes.

Soon after being captured, Lucinda Eubanks was claimed by an elderly chief. "He forced me, by the most terrible threats and menaces, to yield my person to him," she testified. After a few weeks, the Cheyenne sold her to a Sioux named Two Face. "He did not treat me as a wife, but forced me to do all menial labor done by squaws, and he beat me terribly. Two Face traded me to Black Foot (another Sioux) who treated me as his wife, and because I resisted him his squaws abused and ill-used me. Black Foot also beat me unmercifully, and the Indians generally treated me as though I was a dog." Lucinda Eubanks' three-year-old daughter and her nephew were taken from her and she never saw them again. (Both died later from harsh treatment.) She was nursing her infant son, and refused to wean him for fear he would also be taken from her. "During the winter the Cheyennes came to buy me and the child, for the purpose of burning us, but Two Face would not let them have me. . . . We were on the North Platte. . . . The Indians were killing the whites all the time and running off their stock. They would bring in the scalps of the whites and show them to me and laugh about it."[36]

In the same North Platte region (now east-central Wyoming) where Lucinda Eubanks spent her terrible winter, Companies I and K of the 3rd U.S. Volunteers were having their troubles with these same Indians during the summer of 1865. Captain A. S. Lybe of Company I reported in June and July that Indians "were very annoying" between the Sweetwater and South Pass stations. "The garrison consisting of two non-commissioned officers and twelve men at Sweetwater had several spirited fights with the Indians near that station, in one of which First-Sergeant William R. Moody took command and fought heroically, bringing off all his men except one killed and one wounded."[37]

One of Lybe's routine reports is indicative of the damage done by Indians to telegraph service. At 6:00 P.M. on July 12, Lybe started west from Sweetwater with a detachment to find and repair a break in the line. After a 12-mile march, he discovered almost a mile of wire had been ripped out and taken away. In the vicinity was a recently abandoned Indian camp. "I had not wire enough to fix it," Lybe reported. "July 13, 4 P.M. I telegraphed Platte Bridge for wire which arrived July 16, 8 A.M. by freight train. 5 P.M. July 16 wire up."[38]

Lybe's company was given favorable notice by Captain Stephen E. Jocelyn, an inspecting officer who passed through the district in July. "At South Pass," he said, "there is a detachment of fourteen infantry of the 3rd U.S. Volunteers . . . a portion of what is called the 'galvanized regiment' of which there are several on the plains, recruited from the 'Bull Pen' at Rock Island, Illinois. . . . Generally they are a fine looking lot of men, hailing from nearly every state in the South, generally however from Georgia and Alabama—quite a few belonging unmistakably to the class called 'poor whites' and very few can write their names, as we saw by an examination of their muster rolls. Yet they are intelligent and obedient, standing in the latter respect, as in efficiency, much above the 'jayhawkers.' "*[39]

Before Company I marched from Fort Laramie to man these stations, the section of telegraph line beyond Platte Bridge had been guarded by units of the 11th Ohio and 11th Kansas Cavalry. Lybe expected to take over rations and corn left by the cavalrymen, who were preparing to march East for mustering out, but these supplies were almost exhausted in July. As the long-overdue payroll for his men was being held in Laramie for an appropriate officer, Lybe arranged to go there himself with a platoon escort, and draw the pay as well as such rations, corn, and blankets as were obtainable.[40]

Early on the morning of July 25, a wagon train and detachment of 11th Kansas cavalrymen under Sergeant Amos Custard left Lybe's Sweetwater headquarters en route for Fort Laramie. A few hours later Lybe and his platoon, with Captain Henry Bretney and six 11th Ohio cavalrymen, saddled up and started for the same destination. At Willow Spring Creek, Lybe and Bretney overtook Sergeant Custard's wagon train as it was going into camp. The two officers informed Custard that they intended to make a night march to Platte Bridge, and suggested it might be advisable for the train

* A reference to the 11th Kansas Cavalry, units of which mutinied on more than one occasion.

to accompany them because of reported heavy concentrations of hostiles between Willow Spring and the bridge. The sergeant respectfully declined, saying that his teams were fatigued; he also expressed confidence in the ability of his men to resist any attacks by Indians.

Lybe and Bretney resumed march, and about two o'clock in the morning as they were coming down the river road near Platte Bridge, they caught a strong smell of horses and the unmistakable sound of many animals grazing off to their left. Certain that these must be Indian ponies, they urged their own mounts to a faster pace. A few minutes later the clatter of their horses' hoofs brought a loud challenge from a picket at the north end of the bridge. After they identified themselves, the picket opened the bridge gate; they crossed to the stockade, where to their surprise they found about half the station's 100 defenders doing duty as guards, molding bullets, and making cartridges.

The new arrivals soon learned that a large party of hostiles had raided Platte Bridge that afternoon, driving off several horses and putting up a sharp fight when soldiers went in pursuit. Major Martin Anderson, commanding post, had withdrawn his 11th Kansas cavalrymen from the field because of a shortage of ammunition, which explained the night bullet-molding detail. The general opinion inside the stockade was that a full-scale attack on the station was imminent.

Lybe and Bretney informed Anderson of Sergeant Custard's wagons, which would be approaching the bridge the next day, and suggested that a relief party be sent out under cover of darkness, but Anderson decided to wait until morning. The Laramie-bound horsemen dropped their saddles on the ground inside the stockade, unrolled their blankets, and stretched out to sleep during the remaining two or three hours before daylight.

When the 14 U.S. Volunteers awoke in the summer dawn of July 26, they found themselves inside a small but solidly built fort. The telegraph station was buttressed by warehouses, stables, squad rooms, officers' quarters, and a blacksmith shop, all protected by a 14-foot pine-log stockade with heavy gates. A howitzer commanded the bridge, the south end of which lay a few yards north of the post.

At the first show of light on the hills across the Platte, sentinels called a warning of Indians, and the Company I men went to the gate to have a look for themselves. Morning mists were rolling away from the thousand-foot span across the Platte—the most magnificent bridge west of the Missouri—heavy cottonwood logs resting on cribs of stone. Beyond the bridge was a screen of green willows, and above them a V-shaped ridge of hills. On the hilltops a hundred or so Indians were scattered, some on foot, some mounted—all watching the station. "They looked as if they were out of a job and did not know just where to find one."[41]

As yet the U.S. Volunteers felt no sense of alarm. In their two months of service west of Laramie they had grown accustomed to seeing Indians almost every day. They rolled their blankets, prepared their breakfasts, and waited for Captain Lybe to give the order to resume march to Fort Laramie.

Meanwhile Lybe and Bretney had discovered the presence of a fellow officer at the station—Lieutenant Caspar Collins of the 11th Ohio, who had arrived with a mail escort late the previous day from Fort Laramie and was en route to one of the Western stations to rejoin his company. Collins was only 20 years old, a dashing young officer, son of the colonel commanding the 11th Ohio.

By 7:00 A.M. the Indians were out in force, moving closer to the opposite end of the bridge. A few warriors forded the river east of the station, and began galloping back and forth just out of rifle range, whooping and calling insults. Major Anderson summoned Lieutenant Collins to his office, told him that his experienced officers were all on sick call, and ordered him to take 25 of the Kansas cavalrymen and ride to the relief of Sergeant Custard's wagon train.

Collins was surprised that he—an Ohio cavalryman and unattached to the post—should be called upon to lead out the Kansans. He said nothing to Major Anderson, but went directly to Captain Bretney, his superior officer, and informed him of the order. Bretney could not countermand the order, but he advised Collins not to obey. There were five Kansas officers including Major Anderson in the post, and it did not seem proper to Bretney that they should shift this dangerous assignment upon a boy lieutenant from another regiment. Collins, however, could not bring himself to refuse the order. He asked the loan of Bretney's pistols, thrust them into his boot tops, and strode off to seek a horse. For some reason he was given one of the regimental band's mounts, a spirited gray, fast-footed but difficult to manage under fire.

When Captain Bretney saw that Collins meant to carry out Major Anderson's orders, he demanded permission to support the relief party with the escort troop which had accompanied him and Lybe down from Sweetwater. Anderson granted permission, but cautioned that no shots be fired unless absolutely necessary because of the shortage of ammunition.

Thus it was by happenstance that Captain Lybe and his 14 men of Company I were drawn into the fiercest Indian engagement of the summer—the Platte Bridge fight.

Collins mounted the restless gray, and gave the forward command. He was wearing a new full-dress uniform which he had recently purchased at Fort Laramie. He and his 25 men crossed the bridge at a walk, and then started in a slow trot along the road. As soon as Collins was across the bridge, Lybe and Bretney mounted their small force and moved out to protect the lieutenant's rear.

The U.S. Volunteers had just reached the north bank of the river when they saw several hundred Cheyennes swarming out of hollows and sand hills between them and Collins' detachment. Lybe immediately ordered his men into a skirmish line and started forward to assist the trapped lieutenant.

Because of the rough terrain and the screen of willows, Collins was late in observing that he was outnumbered. When he did realize his predicament, he wheeled his men by fours and ordered a charge into the Cheyennes. At the same time, a force of about 500 Sioux came whooping out of a gulch toward the bridge. Later evidence indicated that this combined force of Sioux and Cheyennes meant to capture and burn the bridge, then cross the river at the ford below and lay siege to the station. The presence of the U.S. Volunteers and Bretney's Ohioans foiled the plan; these men stood their ground and poured volley after volley into the Sioux until they pulled back out of range.

Meanwhile 20 of Collins' party had broken through the Cheyennes and reached the end of the bridge. The missing six, which included Lieutenant Collins, were nowhere in sight. Some of the survivors reported that Collins had turned back to assist a wounded man; others said that his horse became unmanageable when the firing started and had taken him into the midst of the Indians.

For several minutes Lybe and Bretney held their position at the north end of the bridge. At least a thousand Indians were massed along the hills, and it was clear now that only a heavily armed force could hope to get through to the wagon train. All hope for Lieutenant Collins was abandoned when a mounted Indian appeared on a nearby ridge, leading the gray horse which the lieutenant had been riding.

Captain Bretney covered his grief with a blast of rage against Major Anderson. Bretney felt that he was personally accountable to the young lieutenant's father for permitting his son to obey the Kansas commander's order. Leaving a small detachment to guard the bridge, he and Lybe returned to the post.

In the bitter discussion which followed, Bretney accused Anderson and his officers of cowardice, and then demanded that he and Lybe be permitted to take a force of 100 men and the howitzer and go to the relief of the wagon train, which all of them knew must be approaching the vicinity of Platte Bridge. Anderson declared that if he sent out 100 men and the howitzer he could neither defend the bridge nor the station from the overpowering force of hostiles. Bretney then used such language that Anderson placed him under arrest.

Anderson now turned to Captain Lybe and informed him that he was to take charge of the post's defenses. Lybe immediately ordered details to start digging rifle pits and throwing up an earthen embankment around the howitzer.

The morning was well along when reports came in from the bridge guards that a number of Indians were fording the river about a mile to the east. A short time later the telegraph operator reported the line from the east was dead. As the wire to the west had been cut earlier in the day, the station was now isolated.

Convinced that the hostiles were preparing a massive attack against Platte Bridge, Major Anderson ordered his adjutant, Lieutenant George Walker, to take 20 mounted men and repair the telegraph line to the east. Too late, Anderson realized that he should have asked for reinforcements from one of the neighboring stations.

Because most of the post's horses were exhausted after the hard fighting of the morning, Lieutenant Walker could mount only 16 men. Captain Lybe—an experienced veteran who had fought through much of the Civil War with the 5th Minnesota Infantry—saw that Walker's small detachment needed a supporting force at the ford, which lay about half-way between the stockade and the break in the wire. He volunteered to take his platoon on foot to a sandy mound overlooking the river crossing. Major Anderson agreed to the plan, and added that he would fire the howitzer if large numbers of Indians were seen approaching the wire repair detail.

The horsemen moved out rapidly, Lybe's infantrymen following to the mound above the ford. From their elevation, the U.S. Volunteers could see that the break in the telegraph line ran about a thousand feet. The Kansas lieutenant ordered three pickets out, sent half his men to the far end of the break, and then started the remaining half stringing wire to meet them. "I went to the party on the east end," Lieutenant Walker said later, "and was just dismounting when we heard the report of the howitzer."[42]

Accounts of what happened next vary considerably. Lieutenant Walker afterwards accused Lybe of withdrawing from the mound before his horsemen reached that position. Walker himself was accused of riding for the stockade before his three pickets could join him. Lybe probably put his men in motion early because they were on foot, while Walker's were mounted.

Regardless of the manner of withdrawal, the telegraph wire was not repaired; one of Walker's men was dead, one severely wounded. As soon as the parties were all in, Lybe calmly put his men back to work digging rifle pits.

Shortly afterward, a sentinel called out: "There comes the train!" This was the moment everyone in the post had dreaded all day. What could Sergeant Custard, his 10 soldiers, and 14 teamsters do to save themselves from more than a thousand swarming hostiles? Would Major Anderson risk his whole command to rescue the train? Bretney, still under arrest, would have taken the risk. Lybe also, had he been in command, probably would have gone out. As the men inside the station watched anxiously, they soon knew that the Indians also had sighted the approaching wagons. "In a minute every one of them was on his pony and urging his animal at the fastest pace in that direction."[43] But Major Anderson gave no order to assemble a relief force; the only action he took was to fire the howitzer, hoping it might give some warning to the train.

"The Indians forced the wagon into a shallow ravine about five miles westerly from the station, and cut off Corporal Shrader and four men from the balance of the force. With field glasses we saw the men cut off and watched them ride toward the river, followed by nearly one hundred Indians, and could see enough of the wagon covers to show the position of the train. We saw the smoke from the men's carbines as the Indians charged into them, and after the volley the Indians scattered like a flock of birds shot into. This was continued for about four hours. The wagons were burned about three o'clock in the afternoon."[44]

Late that same day, Corporal Shrader and two men made their way into the station. They were the sole survivors of Sergeant Custard's wagon train. That night, Major Anderson paid two half-breed Shoshones $150 to carry a message 18 miles east to Deer Creek Station; the message urgently requested reinforcements.

Next afternoon the reinforcements arrived, and Anderson took a large force across the river to recover the dead. The U.S. Volunteers with that party witnessed the most appalling display of violent death they would ever see again during their service on the frontier. "Twenty-one of our dead soldiers were lying on the ground, stripped naked and mangled in every conceivable way." On the field where Lieutenant Collins had died, they found the same shocking mutilations. They also discovered near one of the bodies a scrap of paper torn from a pocket diary, with a message scrawled upon it. No exact transcription of the note appears to exist, but General Connor referred to it in his first report of the fight: "Note picked up on the field today, evidently written by a prisoner, who stated that he was captured on the Platte; states that the Indians say that they do not want peace and expect an increase of 1,000 to their force."[45]

The boys of the 11th Ohio believed that the writer was one of their comrades, a former Confederate who joined their regiment in 1864; he had recently disappeared at La Bonte Station, and they had assumed he had deserted. However, in the first telegraph dispatch sent from Platte Bridge after the fight, the operator described the note as being "written in a female hand, which described that the war party was composed of Arapahos, Cheyennes, Sioux and Blackfoot, and that they intended to besiege the post for four days and that the soldiers had killed one of the leading Cheyenne chiefs."[46]

In a later reconstruction of the message from memory, Lieutenant William Drew of the Kansas Cavalry recalled the contents as substantially the same as given by the telegrapher, but he could not remember the writer's name. Considering the customs of the Indians—seldom taking male prisoners, usually taking female prisoners—it seems likely the writer was a woman, but her identity remains one of those curious mysteries of the Western frontier.

The siege of Platte Bridge Station thus came to an end. Lieutenant Caspar Collins and 24 men were dead, nine men were severely wounded. Captain Lybe's 14 U.S. Volunteers considered themselves lucky indeed to be still among the living.[47]

When Lybe and his platoon resumed their interrupted march to Fort Laramie they met along the way their commanding general, Patrick Connor, hastening to the scene of the bloody encounter. Connor had been waiting impatiently for ammunition, stores, and fresh horses, so that he could strike hard against the enemy's bases in their Powder River stronghold. The fight at Platte Bridge convinced him that he could delay his summer campaign no longer.

Although some Galvanized Yankees would go with Connor on the Powder River expedition, the 3rd Regiment continued in its duties along the Overland Stage and Pacific Telegraph roads throughout the summer and into the autumn of 1865. Connor's expeditionary columns drew off much of the cavalry from the overland routes, and these mounted troops had scarcely departed before more raiding parties were striking at isolated stations and travelers along the roads.

Raids became so frequent that the Denver *News* kept a standing head: ANOTHER INDIAN ATTACK! The telegraph line was cut so often that Western newspapers went for days without news from Eastern states. Attacks on wagon trains increased in fury, the brutal details becoming so common they were seldom entered in the sparse language of official communications: "Indians attacked an emigrant train at Rock Creek . . . burned train, killed eight men, took stock, captured three women and killed one of them and horribly mutilated her. . . . Indians attacked train within forty miles of Julesburg, stampeded 400 head of cattle, horses and mules, burnt sixty wagons, killed and scalped twelve men. . . . Party attacked below Julesburg in five miles of a military post. Killed two, wounded ten of white party."[48]

Colonel McNally, who was responsible for the safety of all trains between Fort Kearney and Post Junction, tightened regulations and ordered Lieutenant Campbell, the adjutant at Kearney, to make certain that 100 armed men were included in every train moving west from there. This was the same Lieutenant Campbell who had marched the 3rd Regiment out on the plains in March, and the testimony of one of the travelers on the route indicates that Campbell took his job seriously. "We were compelled by U.S. army officers to halt and await the arrival of a train of fifty armed men before being allowed to proceed. In a few hours the required number came up. . . . No train was permitted to pass a government fort without one hundred well-armed men. A captain was appointed by the commander of the fort to take charge."[49]

In his recollection of the dangers of the Platte route during the late summer, General Dodge said the Indians became so aggressive that even with the teamsters armed and placed under an officer, "a great many of their people were killed and a great deal of stock run off."[50]

When the trains reached Julesburg, they were inspected again under Colonel McNally's watchful eye. Small parties were reorganized into larger parties before they could proceed to the next inspection point, Post Junction, or Camp Wardwell as it was renamed July 15.

Although Camp Wardwell was a peaceful island in a sea of violence, the men of Companies G and H seldom seeing any hostiles, they were kept busy supervising wagon trains which, if bound West for Oregon, Utah, or California, had to pass through the extremely dangerous North Platte country. Because most trains in the summer of 1865 bypassed Fort Laramie and followed the route of the Overland Mail, Camp Wardwell was made an official counting station for westbound traffic. Keeping these records was the responsibility of the post commander, Captain Thomas Kenny of H Company, and they show that an average of 140 wagons rolled through Camp Wardwell every day.

In addition to escort duties along the 600-mile line held by the 3rd Regiment, details were assigned to the onerous tasks which all soldiers must endure. Captain Byron Richmond of C Company noted in August that a detachment of his men from Cottonwood "has been on daily duty making hay and cutting wood for the use of troops garrisoning this post." Captain David Ellison reported that half of the men of Companies E and F were engaged most of the summer in building Fort Sedgwick at Julesburg. Lieutenant Will Whitlock recorded that a detail from Company A was "building government houses and stables between Fort Kearney and Big Sandy."[51]

With the approach of autumn, the men of the 3rd began looking forward to mustering out. They had signed up for one year, and

although they had spent four months awaiting orders at Rock
Island, they were told that this time would count on their term
of enlistment and they could expect to be mustered out in November. By October most of them probably had made up their minds
individually as to whether they would return to their homes in the
South or remain in the West to seek their fortunes.

In October, Colonel McNally was authorized to bring his scattered
companies—excepting A and B at Kearney—together at Julesburg
headquarters. When the regiment was assembled there, it would
receive further orders as to place and date of mustering out. As
the companies marched into Julesburg, Indian raids became so
frequent and severe in that vicinity that many of the U.S. Volunteers wondered if their orders might not be delayed. For a hundred
miles on either side of Julesburg, reports of attacks came in daily,
sometimes hourly.

On October 22, Indians drove the mail coach into Cottonwood
and attacked the garrison at Alkali. On that same day the 3rd
Regiment received orders to march east toward these scenes of
violence—but not for the purpose of pursuing the raiders. Companies of the 5th and 6th U.S. Volunteers had come up from
Kansas to relieve the 3rd, and the men of that regiment could now
proceed to Fort Leavenworth for mustering out.

Eight companies moved east from Julesburg on October 23,
reaching Butt's Ranche on the first day's march. "On the night of
the 23rd October 1865 experienced a severe snowstorm. The snow
remained on the ground for five days. Weather very cold. The men
and animals with the train suffered severely."[52] Toward the end
of the second day's march, near Alkali, the advance had a brush
with Indians, but the raiders shied away when they discovered
several hundred soldiers coming up.

At Fort Kearney on November 3 they were joined by Companies
A and B, and the full regiment moved on to Fort Leavenworth,
arriving there November 16. In summing up the record of his
regiment on November 29—the day the 3rd U.S. Volunteers became civilians again—Colonel McNally said: "Both officers and
men have behaved themselves well. Of the latter I desire to say
no better regiment of soldiers need be wished for."[53]

In comparison with some of the state volunteer regiments alongside which these men had soldiered, the record of McNally's 3rd
was better than average. G Company's high record of five desertions

was normal for that time and place, and E Company's record of no desertions was unusual.[54]

Perhaps the most important element of all was an intangible which would appear in no record, the psychological effect of frontier duty upon these former enemies of the army in which they had served. All their lives before the Civil War these men had conceived of the United States as being divided into North and South. Now they were reoriented so that they could view their country as a geographical entity running East and West. For many of them on that mustering-out day at Fort Leavenworth, the future must have held a great deal more promise than any of them had dared dream it ever would again during the dark days of Rock Island prison.

2

When the 3rd Regiment left Fort Riley in March 1865 en route for Fort Kearney, most companies of the 2nd Regiment were also on the march toward assigned stations along the Santa Fe Trail. Company I was to garrison a post at Salina, 50 miles west of Riley; Company C, Fort Ellsworth, which was still farther west; B and K, Fort Zarah; E, F, and H, Fort Larned.[55]

A, D, and G remained with regimental headquarters, established at Fort Riley late in March by Colonel Andrew Patrick Caraher. A considerable number of men in the 2nd believed they were lucky to have this Irish-born veteran of the 28th Massachusetts Infantry as their regimental commander. Caraher had been second in command at Rock Island prison, and had earned a reputation for fair and humane treatment of the captured Southerners. On occasions he had counseled with them and listened to their grievances. It was Caraher, they remembered, who had stopped the guards from firing without provocation into barracks when the prisoners were sleeping there.[56]

William Darnell, a civilian teamster for the army, was at Fort Riley in March, and he later recalled that the 2nd Regiment was encamped below the fort on the Republican River.

These men had been captured during the war, and had been paroled on condition they would go west and fight the plains Indians who at this period were most troublesome. These Confederates . . . were a miserable looking, decrepit lot, run down physically, and unable to make a long march. They were to accompany a train of twenty-five wagons loaded with supplies about to be sent out to Forts Ellsworth, Zarah, Larned and

Dodge. On account of their poor physical condition, orders had been given to limit the daily marches of these "galvanized soldiers" to eight miles a day, the teams also being limited to an eight-mile haul instead of the usual twenty-mile haul.[57]

With the coming of April weather on the Kansas plains, Colonel Caraher moved his headquarters out to Salina. Captain John Cowgill's Company I, already stationed there, was assigned full-time escort duty for mail stages and government trains running over the 35-mile stretch of road between Salina and Fort Ellsworth. Because there was no telegraph line adjacent to the Santa Fe Trail, regular courier duty was also necessary for all military units stationed along its length.

Other changes in orders during April sent two companies of the 2nd to the farthest and most dangerous post in southwestern Kansas, a new fort near which in a short time would develop the rip-roaring cattle trail town of Dodge City. In 1865, Fort Dodge was little more than a few sod dugouts overlooking a crossing of the Arkansas River; the country roundabout was inhabited by thousands of buffalo and hostile Kiowas and Comanches. On April 6, Captain William Hayward's Company F was transferred there from Fort Larned, and on April 16 Captain Thomas Molony's Company G began a 12-day march from Fort Riley. Molony and Hayward would have their troubles at Fort Dodge.

Another rugged post on the southwestern route was Fort Zarah,* 120 miles southwest of Fort Riley, and headquarters for Companies B and K. When the U.S. Volunteers arrived, efforts were being made to construct buildings from sandstone blocks taken from a nearby bluff, but most of the quarters were still dugouts and adobe. William Ryus, a stage driver on the Santa Fe line, said Fort Zarah's headquarters was a small dugout on the side of a hill along the bank of Walnut Creek. "They had a gunny sack for a door, and I went into the first room, which was used for a kitchen, and the cook told me to go to the next room, it had a gunny sack door, too, the First and Second Lieutenants were in there. They told me to go on to the next room that the Captain's headquarters was in the other room. I had my mittens and overcoat on, and the Captain said, 'you pull off your hat, you insolent puppy, and salute me.' "[58]

Life at Fort Zarah certainly was not polished or refined, but

---

* Fort Zarah was named for Major Henry Zarah Curtis, killed in action in 1863.

something exciting always seemed to be happening there. According to teamster William Darnell, the news of the ending of the Civil War was brought to Fort Zarah by the famed Wild Bill Hickok. Darnell, who was driving one of the supply wagons for the U.S. Volunteers, said that when they were within about half a mile of the fort, Hickok

came riding by on a run shouting as he rode by: "Lee's surrendered! Lee's surrendered!" He was a striking figure as I noticed him, a large broad-brimmed hat on his head, long drooping moustache, long flowing hair that fell about his shoulders, a brace of ivory-handled revolvers strapped to his waist, and an extra pair in holsters that fitted about the horn of his saddle where he could reach them instantly.

As our wagon train neared the fort the soldiers, having a few minutes before obtained word of the surrender of Lee, decided to celebrate the good news. Dragging out their small brass cannons, they loaded them with a good charge of powder and crammed them to the muzzle with wet gunny sacks. As soon as the lead wagons of our train came within shouting distance of the outpost the gunners pointed their cannons up into the air and fired. The firing alone probably would not have frightened our mules, but when those gunny sacks hurtled up into the air, were caught by the wind and opened up and then went floating off, they were enough to startle the dead.

The result was chaos; the lead wagon team stampeded across the prairie, followed by the others, the drivers leaping off their mounts to save themselves. "It took some time," Darnell commented, "to round up that train."[59]

After a few weeks, the men of the 2nd grew accustomed to the Kansas winds and dust and the harsh life at the widely separated posts. They became acquainted with cavalrymen of the 11th Kansas, 2nd Colorado, and 7th Iowa regiments, who shared duties and dangers along the Santa Fe Trail. By the end of May the U.S. Volunteers were so thoroughly merged into the military network of Colonel James Ford's District of the Upper Arkansas that General Dodge authorized Colonel Caraher to move his headquarters from primitive Salina back East to Fort Leavenworth. For the remainder of the 2nd's period of service, regimental orders would come to the scattered companies by way of the cut-off route to Little Arkansas Station and then westward to Zarah, Larned, and Dodge. To form a new link in this chain, Captain Carter Berkeley's Company K marched east from Fort Zarah to take up post at Little Arkansas.

Throughout the month of May the Volunteers were constantly

warned to be on guard against expected spring raids, but they saw few Indians, only occasional small hunting parties, which usually kept a considerable distance from the trail. Then one day in June, a train of 48 wagons bound for New Mexico rolled into Little Arkansas Station, and the following morning when they moved out, a platoon of mounted men from Company K rode alongside as escorts. On the morning of June 9, near Chavis Creek, a war party of 60 Indians struck the train in camp so suddenly and unexpectedly that the Company K men could fire only two or three rounds before the raiders stampeded a hundred mules and 75 cattle, leaving the wagons stranded.

More than a hundred miles to the west on the previous afternoon, the U.S. Volunteers at Fort Dodge also learned their first lessons about Indian fighting.

Because of Fort Dodge's importance and vulnerability in the westward chain of stations, Colonel Caraher had relieved Captain William F. Armstrong from command of Company C, promoted him to major, and transferred him from Ellsworth to Dodge. Armstrong's first objectives were to speed up construction of fortifications and strengthen escort protection over the long arid route to Fort Lyon, Colorado.

Armstrong's forces consisted of the two companies of the 2nd Regiment which had arrived there in April, a small detachment of Kansas cavalrymen, and about 70 horses and mules. Most of his men were quartered in badly worn tents, and he put them to work constructing more dugouts—10 by 12-foot cellars, five feet deep and roofed over with poles, brush, gunny sacks, and earth. Each unit had a narrow door, a hole for a window, a sod chimney, fireplace, and shelves cut out of the earthen walls for bunks— space enough to house four men.

Because he had no grain or forage, Major Armstrong organized daily herding details to drive the horses and mules out to graze, sometimes as far as a mile from camp. Soldiers detailed as herdsmen were warned to be always alert for Indians, but as day after day passed with no sign of hostile action, they became less vigilant. Armstrong himself became incautious, and began sending the entire herd out, keeping no mounts in camp for emergencies.

About three o'clock on the afternoon of June 8, the herders were drifting the stock back toward the dugouts, letting them graze as they moved. The sun was warm, the day lazy, everything peaceful. Off a mile or so, a line of blue-uniformed riders appeared out of a ravine. The herdsmen watched them angling toward the river, surmising that they must be an escort platoon scouting off the trail, probably looking for water for their mounts. Sure enough, the horsemen moved in a slow gallop toward the Arkansas, watered their horses leisurely, then in the same easy manner approached the Fort Dodge herd. The herdsmen supposed they were coming by to pass the time of day; perhaps they were some of the Company H boys from Fort Larned.

Suddenly the blue-coated riders darted into the horse herd and commenced yelling and shouting. Too late the herders realized they had been duped by one of the Plains Indians' favorite tricks— these were not U.S. soldiers but Kiowas dressed in army blues!

The herders ran forward to protect their stock, but succeeded in turning only 10 horses away from the raiders. With a thunder of hooves, the Kiowas swept away the other 60 animals.

The remaining 10 horses, Major Armstrong later reported, "were brought into camp and saddled and mounted by cavalry and infantry, who continued the chase until dark, and they finally succeeded in recapturing some 15 or 20 more horses and mules. Everything was done by me that could be done to save the stock. . . . I have sent Captain Molony (G Company) with a party on a scout to follow the trail."[60]

Taking a lesson from this costly Indian trick, Armstrong doubled his night pickets, but four days later out of an early morning fog several hundred Kiowas made a direct attack upon the camp, capturing almost all the remaining stock.

We had three men wounded and two captured or killed, whose bodies have not been found. There was a very heavy fog in the early part of the morning, under cover of which the Indians hid themselves in the ravines close to camp and waited there until the fog cleared up; and before the pickets could give the alarm the Indians were between them and camp. . . . They drove the herd of horses and mules some three miles up the river and crossed, then moved in the direction of Mulberry Creek. I would respectfully request that there be sent to this post two pieces of artillery. The force for duty is very small, and we are liable to be attacked by superior numbers any night. Having no mounted men or transportation at present here, and rations rather short, I think the post is in rather a dangerous situation.[61]

Among the defense weaknesses revealed by the Indian attack were the rifle pits, which had been made almost useless by soldiers carelessly walking over them. Armstrong issued a stern order: "The rifle pits are a thing that must be preserved. We shall need them in case of another attack and if they are trampled down by the men running over them they will be of little use. Any citizen or soldier found violating this order will be punished to the extent of the law."[62]

Fortunately for Major Armstrong and his U.S. Volunteers, the Indians shifted their attacks from insubstantial Fort Dodge and spent the rest of June raiding wagon trains and stampeding cattle herds near Cimarron Crossing, and annoying herders outside Fort Larned.

Fort Larned, between Dodge and Zarah, was a tempting target for horse raiders. Almost every week during the early summer more and more mounts were brought there and turned out to graze on the excellent grass between the adobe buildings of the post and the Arkansas River. More soldiers were also constantly arriving. The reason for this concentration of military strength was that Fort Larned had been chosen as the assembly point for General Dodge's planned campaign against the Southwestern hostiles, the second half of the striking force which included General Connor's expedition against the Northern hostiles.

In this general movement of troops, Captain William Hayward's Company F transferred from Dodge to Larned and began training with mounted howitzers for battery service in the forthcoming campaign. To replace F at Dodge, Captain John Cowgill's Company I marched west from Salina.[63]

Meanwhile at Fort Larned, as preparations continued for the late summer campaign against the Kiowas and Comanches, various companies of the 2nd U.S. Volunteers became actively involved. On July 29, a news dispatch from Fort Leavenworth reported that one of the regiments of "ex-rebels that were sworn into Government service some months ago . . . is at Fort Larned, Kansas, preparing for a campaign against the Indians."[64] While the 2nd U.S. Volunteer Infantry was by no means the only regiment based in and near Larned, the importance of its role is indicated by the selection of Colonel Caraher's top-ranking staff officer, Lieutenant-Colonel Josias King, as commander at the fort.

Before being commissioned to the 2nd Regiment, Lieutenant-Colonel King had gained considerable experience as an officer of the 1st Minnesota Infantry. A letter which he wrote late in July to a friend in Minnesota reveals something of life at Fort Larned and plans for the campaign. "We are about 1,000 miles from nowhere excepting it be the verges of hell, and I think we 'ain't no more nor' ten rods from that delightful spot. I am in command of 3rd Sub-district, Upper Arkansas. I have the 14th Missouri Cavalry, 15th Kansas Cavalry, three companies 2nd Colorado Cavalry, two companies 3rd Wisconsin, four companies U.S. Volunteer Infantry with a Battery of Mounted Howitzers [Company F]. I have been preparing for a raid after Indians—intend to take 1,000 Cavalry, three companies Infantry and the Battery. Expect to have some fun as well as hard knocks." Concerning lighter pursuits, King mentioned "buffalo hunts for amusement, chess and cribbage for recreation, and 'draw poker' for profit or loss."[65]

Another view of Fort Larned during this period is given in the rambling reminiscences of William H. Mackey, civilian blacksmith at the post.

About this time there was a company that came to the post, I don't know where from, we called the "galvanized company." One of the officers of this company was a Dutch lieutenant built like a beer keg and very pompous [probably Lieutenant Peter Schwartz]. He came to my place one day and, tapping me on the shoulder and pointing out his horse, ordered me to shoe the same, and left the shop. When he returned, he found his horse where he had left him, and not shod. He came into the shop snorting. I told him I had no time to shoe his horse, and he left. In the afternoon he came back and told me his horse was outside, and he must have it shod. I then told him to bring me an order from the quartermaster. He said, "No, I will get one from the commander of the post," which he did. As I was working for the quartermaster, I did not recognize his order. The next morning he came in and handed me a five-dollar gold piece and asked me to shoe his horse, which I did, and would have done on his first call if he had not commanded me to do it. So you see I always get some mirth besides pay for my work.[66]

At the height of the swirl of activity at Fort Larned, a sudden change of policy in Washington brought everything to a standstill. Four years of Civil War had wearied the country of bloodshed; the national mood was against a punitive Indian war, which might last for several years. "We believe it would be a war thrice the length of that lately waged against the Southern Confederacy," the New York *Times* declared, "and would entail great bloodshed on our side as well as the other, and also enormous expense."[67] In response to this general attitude, the government proposed a series of peace councils, which it hoped would lead to treaties with all the hostile tribes. Commissions were sent to parley with tribal leaders at Forts Sully and Rice, and other points along the Missouri. Patrick Connor's military offensive north of the Platte was already in motion, but he was recalled early in the autumn in favor of the new policy.

In the Southwest, military commanders who had been preparing for war were replaced by officers with experience in dealing peacefully with Indians. Colonel John B. Sanborn became the new commander of the district in which the 2nd U.S. Volunteers were serving, and on August 18 he announced that Colonel Jesse H. Leavenworth had secured an agreement with Lone Wolf, Satanta, Ten Bears, and other Southwestern chiefs "to cease all acts of violence or injury to the frontier settlements, and to the travelers on the Santa Fe road. . . ." The chiefs also agreed to meet and counsel on October 4, 1865, at Bluff Creek, about 40 miles south of the Little Arkansas "for a perpetual peace between the government of the United States and our various tribes."[68] Kit Carson, among other former Indian fighters, gave his indorsement to this agreement, and almost overnight there was a wave of optimism throughout the Southwest in expectation that Indian troubles would soon end along the Santa Fe route.

At Fort Larned all campaign preparations came to a halt, of course, and Lieutenant-Colonel King was relieved and sent back to 2nd Regiment headquarters at Leavenworth. On August 28, his successor, Colonel William F. Cloud, received orders from Sanborn to start the scattered companies of the 2nd moving toward Fort Riley. Their term of service, Sanborn pointed out, would expire in about 40 days.[69]

Before any companies of U.S. Volunteers departed from Larned, however, a gruesome incident occurred within a few miles of the post—a reminder that chiefs' signatures on treaty papers did not necessarily end Indian raids. Four soldiers on messenger detail to Fort Zarah were ambushed at Ash Creek. One man escaped back to Larned, and a pursuit party was ordered out. Accompanying the party was the post blacksmith, William Mackey, who said they discovered the first body three miles east of the fort.

About two miles further on, we found another body filled with arrows, the hands taken off at the wrists, the feet taken off at the ankles, the heart taken out, and the head scalped. The third body was found within about 500 yards of the crossing of Ash Creek, filled with arrows, hands and feet taken off, the head skinned and heart taken out and laid on the body. About a hundred yards off a wolf was scampering off with a hand. While we were gathering up the last body we spied the Indians making a dash for a team that was just passing Pawnee Rock. We made a dash for them. The train formed its corral at once, and the Indians, seeing us coming up on the opposite side of the corral, bore off to the Arkansas river and we after them. But they had too much advantage in the start, and were all on the opposite bank among the sandhills by the time we struck the river. We returned to the Rock and escorted the train into Larned. We had our dead with us, which were buried next day with military honors.[70]

Because of recurrent incidents of this sort, marching orders for companies of the 2nd U.S. Volunteers stationed at Larned, Zarah, and Little Arkansas were postponed until after Colonel Leavenworth's October peace council. Companies F and H formed part of a force assembled along the Little Arkansas to impress the chiefs of the Kiowas and Comanches with the power of the Great White Father's army.

On October 10, General Pope wrote an urgent appeal to General Grant requesting authority to consolidate the 2nd and 3rd Regiments and re-enlist the best men for one more year. "They are good soldiers, in good discipline," Pope wrote. Grant, however, denied the request, and in mid-October, after the peace council ended with a treaty signing, the eight companies stationed from Fort Riley westward began marching to Fort Leavenworth. There on November 7, 1865, all officers and enlisted men of the 2nd U.S. Volunteer Infantry were mustered out of service.[71]

Oaths and Allegiances  III

1

Most famous of all the Galvanized Yankees was Henry Morton Stanley, newspaper correspondent and African explorer, best known as the man who found David Livingstone on Lake Tanganyika and uttered the immortal words, "Dr. Livingstone, I presume."

Stanley did not serve in any of the six U.S. Volunteer Infantry regiments. He was among several captured Confederates who took the oath of allegiance and were inducted into a regular Union regiment—two years before the U.S. Volunteers were organized.

Stanley's real name was John Rowlands. Born illegitimately in northern Wales, he lived a precarious existence until the age of 15, when he sailed for New Orleans as a cabin boy. He jumped ship, and by chance met a wealthy Southern businessman whose name was Henry Morton Stanley. The elder Stanley gave John Rowlands employment and eventually adopted him, insisting that the boy take his name. Among other resolutions, young Stanley pledged himself never to drink intoxicating liquors, a promise which he was to break only once in his lifetime.

In 1860, the father placed his adopted son on an Arkansas River plantation to learn its management, and then sailed for Havana to attend to some urgent business matters. Young Stanley did not like plantation life, and he soon took a job as a clerk in a store at Cypress Bend, anxiously awaiting the return of his adopted father.

A few months later the Civil War began. At first, Stanley had no strong feelings about the war. He was then 20 years old and small for his age—he stood only five feet, five inches—and was shy and lonely. He considered himself an outsider, an Englishman; the war was an American affair and no concern of his. By early summer, however, he was caught up in the war fever, and in July 1861 he joined the Confederate Army.

He saw no major action until the spring of 1862, when his regiment moved to northern Mississippi. On April 6 he was in the midst of the carnage at Shiloh. The next day, when Union forces pushed the Confederates back, Stanley was captured. A few hours later he was on a steamboat with hundreds of other prisoners bound for St. Louis. From there he was sent to a new but already overcrowded military prison, Camp Douglas in Chicago.

"Our prison-pen," Stanley later wrote,

was a square and spacious enclosure, like a bleak cattle-yard, walled high with planking, on the top of which, at every sixty yards or so, were sentry-boxes. About fifty feet from its base, and running parallel with it was a line of lime-wash. This was the "deadline" and any prisoner who crossed it was liable to be shot. . . . To whatever it was due, the appearance of the prisoners startled me. The Southerners' uniforms were never pretty, but when rotten, and ragged, and swarming with vermin, they heightened the disreputability of their wearers; and if anything was needed to increase our dejection after taking sweeping glances at the arid mud-soil of the great yard, the butternut and gray clothes, the sight of ash-colored faces, and of the sickly and emaciated condition of our unhappy friends, were well calculated to do so.[1]

At one end of the prison enclosure was the office of the commandant, Colonel James A. Mulligan, a considerable hero at that time to the numerous Irishmen of Chicago. The long-haired, droopy-moustached Mulligan had earned a reputation as a wild fighter at Lexington, Missouri, even though he and most of his Irishmen had been captured there. After being exchanged for a Confederate colonel, Mulligan returned to Chicago as commander at Camp Douglas, but he was only marking time until he could organize another Irish regiment.

Among the Confederate prisoners captured at Fort Donelson in February 1862, Mulligan had discovered a number of Irish-born prospects who seemed willing to fight for the Union in exchange for their freedom. Before Stanley's arrival, Mulligan had sent a message to General H. W. Halleck asking if it were permissible to enlist prisoners of war into the Union Army. Halleck did not know. On March 4 he informed Mulligan that he was passing the query on to General McClellan. A week later Halleck wrote again to Mulligan: "As the War Department does not answer my letter in relation to your enlisting prisoners of war I shall take the responsibility of authorizing you to immediately fill up your regiment in that way. Great caution, however, must be used as to the character of the persons so enlisted. You should make yourself personally acquainted with the history of each recruit received and exercise a sound discretion in the matter."[2]

Mulligan of course was delighted. He virtually converted Camp Douglas from a prison camp into a recruiting station and began mustering in Irishmen and other foreign-born recruits. A few days later, however, he received another message from Halleck, dated March 15: "I have just received instructions from the War Department not to permit the enlistment of prisoners of war. You will be governed by these instructions."[3]

Evidence indicates that Mulligan conveniently "lost" that second message, and because of poor communications between various divisions of the burgeoning and far-flung U.S. War Department, several months passed before Washington authorities discovered that the fiery Irishman had gone blithely ahead with his enlistment of prisoners. Not until October did the Commissary General of Prisoners discover a roll of 228 Confederate prisoners "who while in charge of Colonel Mulligan at Camp Douglas, Ill., were permitted to enlist. . . . All this was done without authority and in violation of Colonel Mulligan's special duty."[4]

Sometime in April, at least a month after Mulligan was ordered to discontinue recruiting, a Camp Douglas official informed Prisoner Henry M. Stanley that he could be released "by enrolling as a Unionist, that is becoming a Union soldier." Although Stanley debated the matter for six weeks, he finally volunteered as a recruit on June 4.

Harsh as were conditions in the prison, it was no easy decision for young Stanley to make. In his autobiography he described his feelings with his customary vivid style:

> We found it to be a dreary task to endure the unchanging variety of misery surrounding us. I was often tempted with an impulse to challenge a malignant sentry's bullet by crossing that ghastly "deadline" which I saw every day I came out.
>
> In our treatment I think there was a purpose. If so, it may have been from a belief that we should the sooner recover our senses by experiencing

as much misery, pain, privation, and sorrow as could be contained within a prison; and, therefore, the authorities rigidly excluded every medical, pious, musical or literary charity that might have alleviated our sufferings. . . .

Left to ourselves, with absolutely nothing to do but to brood over our positions, bewail our lots, catch the taint of disease from each other, and passively abide in our prison-pen, we were soon in a fair state of rotting, while yet alive. . . . Everything we saw and touched added to its pernicious influence—the melancholy faces of those who were already wearied with their confinement, the number of the sick, the premature agedness of the emaciated, the distressing degeneration of manhood, the plaints of suffering wretches, the increasing bodily discomfort from ever-multiplying vermin, which infested every square inch. . . . The men began to suffer from bilious disorders; dysentery and typhus began to rage. Day after day my company steadily diminished; and every morning I had to see them carried in their blankets to the hospital. . . . Those not yet delirious, or too weak to move unaided, we kept with us; but the dysentery . . . was a peculiarly epidemical character, and its victims were perpetually passing us, trembling with weakness, or writhing with pain, exasperating our senses to such a degree that only the strong-minded could forego some expression of their disgust.

The latrines were all at the rear of our plank barracks, and each time imperious nature compelled us to resort to them, we lost a little of that respect and consideration we owed our fellow-creatures. For, on the way thither, we saw crowds of sick men, who had fallen, prostrate from weakness, and given themselves wholly to despair; and, while they crawled or wallowed in their filth, they cursed and blasphemed as often as they groaned. In the edge of the gaping ditches, which provoked the gorge to look at, there were many of the sick people, who, unable to leave, rested there for hours, and made their condition hopeless by breathing the stenchful atmosphere. Exhumed corpses could not have presented anything more hideous than dozens of these dead-and-alive men, who oblivious to the weather, hung over the latrines, or lay extended along the open sewer, with only a few gasps intervening between them and death. Such as were not too far gone prayed for death, saying, "Good God, let me die! Let me go, O Lord!" and one insanely damned his vitals and his constitution, because his agonies were so protracted. No self-respecting being could return from their vicinity without feeling bewildered by the infinite suffering, his existence degraded, and religion and sentiment blasted.

Yet, indoors, what did we see? Over two hundred unwashed, unkempt, uncombed men, in the dismalest attitudes, occupied in relieving themselves from hosts of vermin, or sunk in gloomy introspection, staring blankly, with heads between their knees, at nothing; weighted down by a surfeit of misery, internal pains furrowing their faces, breathing in a fine cloud of human scurf, and dust of offensive hay, dead to everything but the flitting fancies of the hopeless![5]

When Stanley was first presented with the possibility of escaping this desolation by taking an oath of allegiance and enlisting in the Union Army, he refused. "Every American friend of mine was a Southerner, my adopted father was a Southerner."

Perhaps it was his bunk mate, W. H. Wilkes of Mississippi, who unintentionally helped the young English-born prisoner to make his decision. Wilkes was a nephew of the Union admiral, Charles Wilkes, who had forcefully taken Confederate commissioners James Mason and John Slidell off a British vessel. The young Confederate Wilkes did not seem to think it strange that his family should be divided by the war, and Stanley may have reasoned that changing allegiances could not be so reprehensible after all.

Six more weeks of prison horrors, the useless flight of time, the fear of being incarcerated for years, led Stanley to the belief that he was going mad. "Finally I was persuaded to accept with several other prisoners the terms of release, and enrolled myself in the U.S. Artillery service, and on the 4th June was once more free to inhale the fresh air."

Two or three days later he fell ill from dysentery, but sought no medical aid for fear he might be returned to prison. On the day he arrived at Harper's Ferry, he collapsed, was taken to a hospital, and on June 22 was mustered out of service, a physical wreck.

Stanley's career in the Union Army was brief, but he was not yet finished with the American Civil War. He left Harper's Ferry on foot, and spent almost a week walking 24 miles to a farm near Hagerstown. There a kindly farmer took care of him until he regained his health. He worked in the Maryland harvests, went to Baltimore and took a job on an oyster schooner, eventually found a berth on a sea-going ship. He was determined to make his way to Havana and rejoin his father, but when he reached Cuba he learned that the elder Henry M. Stanley was dead.

Once again he was alone in the world. Returning to New York, Stanley enlisted in the U.S. Navy, and thus probably became the only man ever to serve in the Confederate Army, the Union Army, and the Union Navy. By now a fair sailor, he soon earned a rating on the *Minnesota* as ship's writer, his duties being to transcribe the log and other ship records.

While the *Minnesota* was off Fort Fisher, North Carolina, Stanley witnessed at close hand several sea and land battles, and while writing these up for the ship's records, an idea came to him to compose some narratives of the exciting events and send them to newspapers. Thus began Stanley's career as a journalist and writer.

He became so interested in writing that he wanted to do nothing else. After the *Minnesota* docked in Portsmouth, New Hampshire, Stanley became so bored that he decided he had had enough of the U.S. Navy. On February 10, 1865, in company with another young sailor, Stanley deserted.

Stanley's three failures as an American soldier and sailor seem a strange beginning for a man who in a few years was to become one of the great figures of the nineteenth century.

There was one final piece of irony in his American adventures. After he deserted the navy, Stanley felt a compulsion to see the West. He reached the frontier in the spring of 1865, just as the organized regiments of Galvanized Yankees were marching out from Fort Leavenworth to help hold together the breaking lines of communication between East and West. He visited many of the same places where these men soldiered—stations along the Platte, Salt Lake City, Denver. In Colorado he built a flat-bottomed boat and floated down the Platte, stopping occasionally at camps and forts manned by the 5th and 6th U.S. Volunteers. When he reached Omaha, for some inexplicable reason this sober young man got gloriously drunk. He roamed the streets all night, singing and yelling, and next morning swore he would never become intoxicated again.

Stanley was a Galvanized Yankee before that epithet was even invented—and then only for a brief time—but he surely met and talked with some of the men who had made the same hard choice he had made back in 1862 in Camp Douglas prison. One can but wonder what his emotions were toward these erstwhile brothers-in-arms. Sympathy, pity, envy? Or was it remorse? Why, when he reached Omaha, did he feel compelled to break a pledge he had made to himself as a youth never to touch intoxicating liquors, a pledge he did not break again as long as he lived?

2

In the first year of the Civil War, military leaders were too much occupied with other matters to give any deep thought to conversion of allegiances. No large-scale battles were fought in that preparatory year and comparatively few prisoners were taken. In 1862, however, events moved on a grander scale. Many thousands of soldiers were engaged across half a continent; captives began to crowd each other in dreadful prison pens.

Because the Union did not recognize the Confederacy as a sovereign nation, the business of exchanging prisoners presented a tricky problem, but eventually a cartel was devised for the parole and exchange of captured soldiers. The system never was very satisfactory to either contender; one side or the other would suddenly change the rules or suspend exchanges altogether.

Not long after this exchange system was put in operation, Northern prison commandants—such as Colonel James Mulligan—discovered that some of their prisoners had no desire to be exchanged. In the spring of 1862 these defectors were few, and most of them were foreign-born, with no strong sense of allegiance to any country. Yet they were there and something had to be done with them.

After Colonel Mulligan audaciously arranged to enlist Henry M. Stanley and 227 other Confederate prisoners into the Union Army, leaders in the upper echelons of the War Department began to ponder the problem of loyalties. Americans had inherited the English ideal of natural allegiance to one's country, yet they had also endured a long period of travail from the Revolutionary War through the War of 1812 during which they had rejected that doctrine. By the 1860's, however, loyalty to the Union was a sacred thing to millions of Americans, and there was something repellent in the idea of lightly transferred fealties.

The fact that the Confederacy was not recognized as a legitimate government, but only as an erring group of states, made it possible for Union leaders to reason that *nemo potest exuere patriam,* the doctrine that no one can cast off his country, was not applicable to captured Confederate soldiers. If there was no Confederate States of America, then a captured Confederate soldier was not committing an act of treason if he took an oath of allegiance to the United States. In the spring of 1862 the policy makers could reason that far but no farther; the idea of *enlisting* former enemies was still too uncomfortable to accept. Prisoners were permitted to take the oath on condition that they would remain north of the Confederate lines, and they were required to give a bond of $1,000 as security for this condition.[6] For the next two years, the War Department would approach and retreat from the idea of enlistments with great caution and suspicion—until at last in 1864 President Lincoln gave it his endorsement.

The most powerful man in the cabinet, Secretary Edwin M. Stanton, was one of those who seemed unable to make up his mind on the question. As early as July 10, 1862, Stanton authorized United States Marshal Robert Murray to interview prisoners of war in New York "for the purpose of ascertaining whether any and how many are willing to enter into the military service of the U.S."[7] About the same time, the commissary general of prisoners, William Hoffman, informed Adjutant-General Lorenzo Thomas that some prisoners had expressed a wish "to remain at the North and enter our service." On August 5, the governor of Indiana wrote General Halleck that a number of rebel prisoners in Camp Morton "desire to volunteer into our Army instead of being exchanged. I am in favor of accepting them, believing they can be trusted and it will have a good effect."[8]

Stanton could not bring himself to take definitive action on any of these openings, and the final steps toward enlisting prisoners might never have been taken had not the Sioux Indians started their war along the Minnesota frontier in late summer of 1862.

Under the fierce generalship of Little Crow, the Sioux attacked the Minnesotans at a time when most of their soldiers were away fighting Confederates, and in a few days slew more than 1,500 settlers. Governor Alexander Ramsey of Minnesota bombarded the War Department with pleas for help at a time when one Confederate Army was thrusting north into Kentucky and another was driving General John Pope back upon the defenses of Washington. No troops could be spared for fighting Indians. After Pope was dismissed from command, Stanton transferred him out to Minnesota to redeem himself, and then gave consideration to a suggestion made by Governor Ramsey: "The 3rd Regiment of Minnesota Volunteers is on parole at Benton Barracks, St. Louis. We need a well-drilled force of which we are now utterly destitute to resist the overwhelming force of Indians now attacking our frontier settlements. Cannot you order the 3rd Regiment to report at once to me, with arms and ammunition, of which we are in great need? This service would not be in violation of their parole. The exigency is pressing. Reply immediately."[9]

Stanton was inclined to agree with the governor of Minnesota. The parole system as originally arranged between the Union and Confederacy provided that when one side had an excess of prisoners they were to be paroled and sent home, not to engage in further military activities until exchanged. In 1862 both sides stopped the practice of permitting parolees to go to their homes, and established parolee camps so that men awaiting exchange could be drilled and kept under military discipline. Such was the condition of the 3rd Minnesota, and after studying the parole agreement, Stanton convinced himself that it would not be in violation of the cartel to send these men back to Minnesota to fight Indians. Orders to that effect were issued, but a test of whether or not this was in violation of the parole agreement was avoided because the regiment was declared exchanged on August 27.

On September 9, Governor David Tod of Ohio telegraphed Stanton: "If the Indian troubles in Minnesota are serious and the paroled Union prisoners are not soon to be exchanged would it not be well to send them to Minnesota? It is with great difficulty we can preserve order among them at Camp Chase." Stanton immediately replied that this was an excellent suggestion, and a week later he sent General Lew Wallace to Camp Chase, near Columbus, to organize the paroled Union soldiers into regiments "for service against the Northern Indians." He also arranged for several thousand other parolees in camps at Annapolis and Harper's Ferry to be transferred to Camp Chase for ultimate service against Indians.[10]

By the end of September, so many parolees were pouring into Camp Chase that Wallace could not handle them. "Do not send any more paroled prisoners here," he wired Stanton. "It is impossible to do anything with those now at Camp Chase. They generally refuse to be organized or do any duty whatever. Every detachment that arrives only swells a mob already dangerous. The Eastern troops are particularly disinclined to the Indian service."

In a lengthy report to Adjutant-General Thomas, September 28, Wallace explained that almost every man in camp was "possessed with an idea that because he was paroled he was until exchanged exempt from duty of any kind. . . . A large number in fact hold paroles which they have sworn to, obligating them not to go into camp or take arms for any purpose in behalf of the United States. . . . When I announced my purpose in camp that I was to organize them for service against the Northwestern Indians a very few received it with favor. Nearly the whole body protested. Especially was this the case with the Eastern troops. Every objector intrenched himself behind his parole."[11]

To further complicate Lew Wallace's difficulties, the Confederate Army got wind of the scheme to use parolees against Indians, and immediately attempted to block it by adding a no–Indian-fighting clause in their paroles. This came to President Lincoln's notice on October 3, and he asked the War Department to rule on its validity "based upon the general law and its cartel. I wish to avoid violations of law and bad faith." After deliberating for 24 hours, Stanton and Halleck telegraphed Lincoln "that the parole under the cartel does not prohibit doing service against the Indians."[12]

But this was not the end of the matter. The very next day, October 5, the Confederate government through its prisoner exchange agent dispatched a message to the Union exchange agent, protesting the sending of

officers and men of the U.S. forces who have been paroled and not exchanged . . . to your frontiers to fight the Indians now in arms against you. This is in direct conflict with the terms of the cartel. Its language is very plain. It says: "The surplus prisoners not exchanged shall not be permitted to take up arms again, nor to serve as military police or constabulary force in any fort, garrison, or field work held by either of the respective parties, nor as guards of prisons, depots or stores, nor to discharge any duty usually performed by soldiers, until exchanged under the provisions of this cartel."[13]

In Minnesota by this time, General Pope had scraped together enough volunteer soldiers and militia to put down Little Crow's Sioux. Two years later when a more widespread Indian war broke out across the Plains, the War Department had reached a position where it could accept without too many qualms the principle of enlisting former enemies into its armies.

The steps by which it arrived at this rationalization were gradual, and make an interesting study of the pragmatics and absurdities of civil wars. The question of foreign-born prisoners, for example, was forever arising. In February 1863, the commandant at Camp Butler, Illinois, reported the presence of a large number of Irish, German, and Polish prisoners of war, some of whom had gone from Illinois to the South for employment before the war, and who claimed they had been conscripted by force. "They are willing to take the oath of allegiance and fight for the Union, and but for the misfortune of locality would ere this be found in the ranks of loyal regiments."[14]   Colonel Christian Thieleman, who was organizing a German cavalry regiment, the 16th Illinois, became interested in enlisting these men and brought pressure to bear on the War Department.

At this time Stanton was firmly against such action, and forbade enlistment of former Confederates, even though foreign-born. A month later, however, after receiving notices from other camps of many more such prisoners who were about to be exchanged and returned to the South, he softened his attitude: "The rule is not to permit Confederate prisoners to join our Army. But in any case in which you are satisfied a prisoner is sincerely desirous of renouncing all connection with the rebels, you may on his taking the oath of allegiance send him to Fort Delaware, to be released there after further investigation as to his sincerity and sent North to reside."[15]

Meanwhile commanders at various camps were occasionally taking matters into their own hands and permitting small groups of prisoners to swear allegiance and enlist in Union regiments. (Prison commanders changed frequently, and some had no knowledge of War Department policy in the matter.) At Camp Douglas in March 1863 a few former Confederates were inducted into Illinois regiments. At Camp Morton in June, 50 Tennesseans enlisted in the 71st Indiana, 155 in the 5th Tennessee Union Cavalry. "Quite a parade was made of the departure of this last group for Lexington [Kentucky] on June 13. With an escort from the 71st Indiana they marched down Pennsylvania Street to Market and through the heart of the town [Indianapolis] to Union Station where they entrained with rousing cheers."[16]

Oddly enough this latter incident occurred on the very day that Confederate General John Morgan was starting his columns North for his great raid through Indiana and Ohio, a raid which would result in the capture of a number of his cavalrymen, some of whom later became Galvanized Yankees and served with the 11th Ohio Cavalry in the West.

In that same month events had moved far enough for Stanton and the War Department to take one more official step toward enlistment of Confederates. Union armies were sweeping up so many prisoners that there was not room for all of them in Northern camps, and commanders in the field began requesting permission to enlist those who expressed a desire to transfer their allegiances to the Union. Reacting to these demands, Stanton directed on June 20 that "when it can be reliably shown that the applicant was *impressed* into the rebel service and that he now wishes in good faith to join our army, he may be permitted to do so on his taking the oath of allegiance."[17]

This ruling was so loosely administered, however, and so many of the freed and enlisted Confederates deserted at the first opportunity, that Stanton reversed himself on August 26: "The Secretary of War directs that hereafter no prisoners of war be enlisted in our Army without his special sanction in each case."[18] The order of course virtually halted enlistments in the field. Stanton gave General William Rosecrans special permission to enlist a few foreign-born Confederate conscripts, and in September he authorized Governor Morton of Indiana to muster more than 100 Irish Catholic prisoners into an Indiana Irish regiment.

About this time someone—probably General Gilman Marston at Point Lookout prison—conceived the idea of enlisting captured Confederates into the U.S. Navy. Stanton turned this proposal over in his mind for several weeks, consulted with the Secretary of the Navy, and at last on December 21, 1863, issued instructions to prison camp commanders to make arrangements to enlist into the Navy prisoners willing to take the oath of allegiance.

There was no great rush of prisoners desiring Navy service. Not many of them had any sea experience, and in at least one camp, Rock Island, loyal Confederates organized themselves to block the efforts of the camp commandant to so enlist them. The leaders of this movement secretly enlisted 1,300 fellow prisoners into a paper cavalry regiment of 10 companies, which held steadfast until the autumn of 1864, when a few were beguiled into the Galvanized Yankees with the offer of freedom for going West to fight the Indians. The majority of this group remained loyal to the Confederacy until freed by exchange or the end of the war.

Near the end of 1863, one of the most controversial figures of the Union Army, General Benjamin Butler, entered the listings of those in high command who were interested in converting Rebels into Yankees. Butler was a shrewd politician, a poor military leader, a good hater with a genius for creating enemies as well as whipping his followers into line, ruthless and possessed of such abounding energy that few could ignore him. As Commander of the Department of Virginia and North Carolina, he was responsible for the operation of one of the largest of all prison camps, Point Lookout, a Maryland sandspit thrusting into Chesapeake Bay.

Late in December, Butler began an earnest correspondence with Stanton, in which he expressed the opinion that many more prisoners could be enlisted into the army than into the navy. As Butler was a political power in Massachusetts, the Secretary of War decided to bring the matter to President Lincoln's attention. On January 2, 1864, Lincoln addressed himself directly to the general, informing him that enlistments of prisoners of war into either the army or navy would be permissible under certain conditions. These conditions, the President added, would be explained by his secretary, John Hay, who was to deliver the letter in person. That same day Stanton sent a telegram to Butler stating that the President was sending Hay "to Point Lookout with a letter to you. . . . You will please meet him there, if convenient, and come to Washington for the purpose of explanations and further instructions."[19] Evidently no effort was to be spared by the administration in gaining Butler's good will. 1864 was a Presidential election year.

John Hay met Butler on January 9, presenting him with a questionnaire which Lincoln had composed, four questions which were to be asked in privacy to every prisoner at Point Lookout. In addition to the questionnaire, the President had sent a large blank book in which each prisoner was to sign his name and his replies to the interrogation:

1. Do you desire to be sent South as a prisoner of war for exchange?
2. Do you desire to take the oath of allegiance and parole, and enlist in the Army or Navy of the U.S., and if so which?
3. Do you desire to take the oath and parole and be sent North to work on public works, under penalty of death if found in the South before the end of the war?
4. Do you desire to take the oath of allegiance and go to your home within the lines of the U.S. Army, under like penalty if found South beyond those lines during the war?[20]

With characteristic dispatch, Butler appointed one of his protégés, Lieutenant F. M. Norcross, a lamed war veteran of the 30th Massachusetts, to direct the questioning of prisoners and recruit those who answered the second question in the affirmative.

On March 1, Private Bartlett Malone, a Point Lookout prisoner from North Carolina, noted in his diary: "Our Company was examined on the Oath question evry man was taken in the House one at a time and examioned; the questions asked me was this: Do you wish to take the Oath and join the U.S. Armey or Navey; or work at government work or on Brestworks or Do you wish to take a Parole and go to your home if it be insied of our lines or do you wish to go South. I told him I wished to go South."[21] This answer kept Malone in prison until a few days before the end of the war.

The interrogation of some 8,000 prisoners individually was a slow process, and it was late in March before Butler informed Stanton that he had "more than a minimum regiment of repentant rebels, whom a friend of mine calls *transfugees,* recruited at Point Lookout. They behave exceedingly well, are very quiet, and most of them I am certain are truly loyal, and I believe will make as efficient a regiment as there is in the service. I should like to organize and arm it at once."

Fours days later Butler received his final authorization "to recruit and organize a regiment at Point Lookout, Maryland, to serve for three years or during the war." On March 28, the regiment was officially designated as the 1st U.S. Volunteer Infantry.[22] This was the culmination of the War Department's two years of circling the sensitive question of allegiances—a complete acceptance of all erring brothers who were willing to repent.

In the early months of 1864, about one in eight of the prisoners at Point Lookout took the oath and became Galvanized Yankees. Many of them had been there on that flat stretch of sand, which was bare of trees, shrubs, or vegetation of any kind, for two years or more. They had endured scorching summers "whose severity during the day is as great on the sandbarren as anywhere in the Union north of the Gulf," and hard winters "more severe at that point than anywhere in the country south of Boston." Surrounded by a 15-foot board enclosure, they were "confined in open tents, on the naked ground, without a plant or a handful of straw between them and the heat or frost of the earth."[23]

Private Malone recorded the deaths of five men from freezing, hunger so acute "that they caught a Rat and cooked him and eat it." He also made three entries in April and May 1864, referring to guards shooting into prisoners' tents, killing and wounding several, and then on June 14 noted briefly that "500 rebels taken the Oath and went outside."[24]

To remain loyal to the Confederacy, they had to resist not only their physical discomforts, the brutality of guards, rumors of a collapsing South, but also pleading letters from home. Evans Atwood, captured in Virginia, wrote his wife of the opportunity to take the oath, and she urged him to do so—anything to escape the debilitating prison life.

"Since the receipt of your letter," he replied,

ten thousand thoughts have wearied my mind, my soul, my very life. . . . After calm, sober and serious meditation, I have weighed, wondered and re-examined your request and excuse me for so saying—I must follow the path of duty to my country, for which I am now a prisoner. I have gone through many dangers, have passed often by the gates of death . . . but amid all this I ever thought that your prayers, your sympathy, and your love followed me; but now what must I say? What must I do? I must not disgrace friends, character and more than all, kindred—wife, child! No . . . I do not think you desire this. Let me stay in prison until released honorably; let me discharge my duty.[25]

Lieutenant Atwood did not become a Galvanized Yankee. We have no record of his emotions as he watched 1,000 of his former comrades board the convoy ship *George Henry* late in April 1864 to sail to their first duty assignment at Norfolk, Virginia. "We arrived at Norfolk," Captain Robert Benson of the *George Henry* noted in his diary of April 24, "with our load of soldiers, all Confederates—soldiers who have been as prisoners but are now Federal soldiers, having gotten tired of the Rebel side are disposed to try Uncle Abraham a short time."[26]

Thus far in the War Department's game of oaths and allegiances, nothing had been said about sending the 1st Regiment to the frontier to fight Indians. The regiment was assigned to routine police duties at Norfolk, but under the hard driving of young Colonel Charles Dimon and his eager New England officers, the 1st U.S. Volunteers quickly became a first-class body of soldiers. It was inevitable that Butler and Dimon would want to test them in the field, and on July 27 the regiment was marched down to Elizabeth City, North Carolina. The mission was of no military consequence; they seized a few horses and some bales of cotton, fired a few shots at some fleeing guerrillas, and returned to Norfolk.

When General Grant heard of the incident, however, he was disturbed. He had no enthusiasm for trifling with loyalties. Very likely he viewed the experiment as an extremely unmilitary business conceived by three civilians—Lincoln, Stanton, and Butler—who were too much inclined to meddle in military matters which none of them properly understood.

On August 9, Grant as general in chief of the armies, informed the War Department that he was ordering the 1st Regiment U.S.

Volunteers to the Northwestern frontier. "It is not right," he explained, "to expose them where, to be taken prisoners, they must surely suffer as deserters." From that date to the end of the war, Grant was firmly opposed to using former Confederates against Confederates; in fact, he was opposed to enlisting prisoners for any kind of military service.* On August 28 he issued an order forbidding assignment of military duty to Confederate deserters in the field, but permitting them to be employed as civilians in the quartermaster department provided they took the oath of allegiance.[27]

As late as January 1865, Grant's opposition to permitting former Confederates to fight Confederates undoubtedly led the War Department to forbid enlistments of North Carolina prisoners by a Union officer from that state. A considerable number of North Carolinians, the would-be recruiter claimed, "have written from time to time to me to come and get them out of prison" for enlistment in the 2nd North Carolina Union Mounted Infantry. The War Department's ruling was brief: "It is not believed to be expedient to adopt the policy here urged."[28]

Again on February 19, after it was apparent that Galvanized Yankees were the only troops immediately available for service against Indians and that several regiments would probably be organized, Grant wrote Stanton to protest the payment of bounties to these enlisted prisoners. "The most determined men against us," he said, "would be the first to enlist for the sake of the money and would return with it to their friends. I would make no special objection to trying the experiment of one or two regiments raised without bounty, but even this would be risky. The men who want to enlist are those whom really it is most desirable to exchange first."[29]

Although the organization of the Galvanized Yankee regiments was not a military secret, those responsible for the operation apparently never made any announcements to the press. The fact that recruiting was carried on in prisons served as a cover until the regiments appeared on public view. The first notice of their existence appeared in a few newspapers at the end of August 1864 when "the 1st U.S. Volunteers, one thousand strong, passed over the New York Central Railroad *en route* for the West. . . . The train which carried the regiment numbered 29 cars."[30] The report was

* See Chapter II, pp. 12-13.

erroneous in that it stated they were to be employed against hostile Indians on the Overland Stage route. The 1st Regiment was bound for Minnesota and the Missouri River forts.

This brief item apparently attracted little attention, and not until six months later when the 2nd and 3rd Regiments moved out upon the Plains did the Congress of the United States take notice of this unusual military activity. On February 25, 1865, the actions of the War Department were questioned in the House of Representatives, which passed a resolution directing the Secretary of War "to inform this House whether rebel prisoners have been enlisted into our service, have received bounties, and have been credited to quotas of one or more States; and if so how many have been enlisted and credited, and when and to what States."[31]

Stanton made a hasty attempt to satisfy the House's demands, but his listing was far from complete. He included the men of the 1st and 4th Regiments at Point Lookout, and the 2nd and 3rd at Rock Island, which had been paid Pennsylvania bounties, but he made no mention of preparations then under way to recruit the 5th and 6th, nor of the numerous "special permissions" his department had given to various governors, commanders in the field, and organizers of regiments to induct prisoners here and there for service in Union organizations. Perhaps he had forgotten most of the latter; certainly the records were scattered and far from complete.

No doubt Congress eventually would have launched an investigation and become engaged in a series of debates on the difficult subject of oaths and allegiances, but the war was rushing to its end. After Lee surrendered on April 9, nobody of authority in Washington, except Ulysses Grant, gave any more thought to the origins of the 6,000 Galvanized Yankees soldiering on the faraway Western frontier.

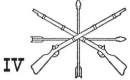

IV Soldiering on the Wide Missouri

1

General Grant's order transferring the 1st U.S. Volunteer Infantry Regiment from Virginia to the Western frontier specified Milwaukee, Wisconsin, as point of destination. "They will proceed *via* New York . . . reporting on their arrival to Major General John Pope, commanding Department of the North West."[1]

Most officers and men received the news with enthusiasm, and on Monday afternoon, August 15, 1864, the regiment, 1,000 strong, boarded the transport ship, *Continental*. This vessel was destined to play a romantic role in the history of the West; less than two years later the *Continental* would carry more than 100 unmarried women, known as Asa Mercer's belles, around Cape Horn to Seattle as prospective brides for lonely male settlers.

Only one woman was aboard with the 1st Regiment—Elizabeth Cardwell, 21-year-old wife of Private Patrick Cardwell, Company E. Patrick was a year younger than Elizabeth; he had married her before he shouldered a musket and marched away from his Virginia farm to be captured and sent to Point Lookout. After he took the oath and went with the regiment to Norfolk, Elizabeth had come down the James River from their home place near Charles City so that she might see him occasionally when he was off duty. Patrick and Elizabeth evidently were a winsome pair; when they asked Captain Alfred Fay if she might go West with the regiment, the captain recommended to his colonel that permission be granted. The regimental colonel, Charles Dimon, was a strict disciplinarian, but he was only 23 himself and filled with romantic notions. He granted permission, and so began a journey of youthful lovers; the Cardwells became the darlings of the regiment.

The *Continental* docked at New York Wednesday morning, August 17, and for the next 24 hours regimental and company officers had their difficulties with the usual military confusion which prevails in large cities during wartime. Because of a misunderstanding by the local quartermaster, they marched to the wrong railroad station. Then after another march through August heat across the city, they learned that no train would be ready for them until the next day.

"When at the wharf and en route to the stations," said Captain Richard Musgrove, "the men were not allowed to leave the ranks, yet a swarm of pocket peddlers sold whisky in bottles to the men in spite of all that could be done to prevent it. While waiting in line before entering the station, I captured one of these men. He made no resistance as I worked two bottles from his pockets and then he turned to run. I threw one at his head, which struck him in the back and then broke on the pavement causing a round of applause from the mass of spectators gathered on the sidewalks."

It was no wonder that under these conditions about 20 men vanished from the ranks, but Musgrove considered them good riddance. In describing the composition of the 1st Regiment, the captain said that "many were Unionists from North Carolina, who had been forced into the Confederate service, and now were glad to transfer their allegiance and fight under the old flag. Others from the south were men of no principle and were as much at home under one flag as the other. This class was augmented by foreigners, who found themselves by force of circumstances in the rebel army and then prisoners of war. These took the oath of allegiance and enlisted in the Union Army to better their condition, and, as soon as opportunity offered, some deserted."[2]

Musgrove naturally was prejudiced. The company descriptive books indicate that North Carolinians made up about 40 per cent of the regiment; Virginians 15 per cent; foreigners 10 per cent, with Germans and Irishmen predominating. The remaining 35 per cent were composed mainly of Georgians, Louisianians, South Carolinians, and Tennesseans, with a scattering of Alabamians, Kentuckians, Mississippians, Floridians, and Marylanders.

At last, around noon of August 18 the regiment moved out

aboard a 29-car New York Central train bound for Chicago. But even then the troubles of Musgrove and his fellow officers with liquor peddlers were not ended.

At every station in New York State, whisky was sold very freely. At one point where the train stopped there were but four houses in the hamlet, and I thought it probable that no liquor was sold there, but I soon found that in three of these buildings there was a licensed saloon. Boiling with indignation, as I saw the whisky traveling in bottles to the train, I told one of the proprietors if he sold any more whisky to my men I would tear his shanty down over his head. If the fellow did not go "into the air," he fairly foamed with rage, and stepping to his desk placed a gun in his pocket, saying he paid for a license and had a right to sell. Just then the engine bell rang and hostilities were averted.[3]

In New York, Colonel Dimon had received a change of orders. Six companies were to proceed to St. Louis, four to Milwaukee. Arriving in Chicago on August 21, the regiment was divided, Lieutenant-Colonel William Tamblyn taking companies A, F, G, and I to Milwaukee, Colonel Dimon continuing to St. Louis with the remaining six.

On August 22, Dimon and his reduced regiment reached St. Louis, where further orders from General Pope awaited him. "Immediately take boat up Missouri River, destination Fort Rice, Dakota Territory. On arrival at Fort Rice, Colonel C. A. R. Dimon will report himself and command to Brigadier-General A. Sully, commanding Northwestern Indian Expedition." Pope meanwhile had notified Sully that the 1st U.S. Volunteers were not to be considered as additional troops but replacements for the 30th Wisconsin, which was badly needed in the South. "The six companies I send," Pope added, "consist of refugees and rebel deserters, and whilst many of the men are excellent, I do not doubt there are also many who will require strict discipline."[4]

About a dozen of those whom Pope lacked faith in deserted while the regiment was quartered in St. Louis, and on the journey upriver several more would go over the boat's railing. On August 27, the six companies boarded the *Effie Deans,* captained by the famous riverman, Joseph La Barge. Thus in little more than a fortnight after General Grant decided to send them West, they were well on their way into the heart of the hostile Indian country of Dakota.

"The *Effie Deans,*" Colonel Dimon wrote on August 29, "has a large stern wheel 25 feet high and makes just 45 miles a day . . .

is a regular Indian trading boat. . . . All the crew wear moccasins. The captain and pilot are Frenchmen and the steward is an Indian."[5]

Within a week after the *Effie Deans* splashed away from its landing at St. Louis, the 600 soldiers aboard grew restless from close confinement and lack of activity. One night near Independence, Missouri, several men left the boat for good, and from that time Dimon began to worry about possible wholesale mutiny and desertion. He knew that for days at a time as they moved farther up the river the *Effie Deans* would be as isolated as a ship at sea, with only the boat's crew and a handful of officers against 600 former enemies.

Dimon ordered his officers to be doubly alert, to keep their eyes and ears open for any sign or rumors of sedition. On the evening of September 5, Captain Alfred Fay of E Company was informed by one of his corporals that Private William C. Dowdy had threatened to desert.

Two days later Dowdy was brought to trial on two charges before a general court-martial on board the *Effie Deans*. The first charge was violation of the 7th Article of War: *Any officer or soldier who shall begin, excite, cause or join in, any mutiny, or sedition, in any troop or company in the service of the United States, or in any party, post, detachment or guard, shall suffer death, or such other punishment as by a court-martial shall be inflicted.*

The specification was: "In this that he the said William C. Dowdy, Company E, 1st U.S. Volunteers, did make use of the following seditious language 'that he would be damned if he would not take the first opportunity to desert the Regiment' and also cursing his Superior Officer and this on board the Steamer *Effie Deans,* Missouri River, on or about the 3rd day of September 1864."

The second charge was violation of the 21st Article of War, or absenting himself from his company without leave.

William Dowdy was a fair-skinned, blue-eyed, red-haired young man who had been a blacksmith in Bedford County, Tennessee. He was big and muscular and carried a hot temper. He was 22 years old, one year younger than his colonel. On the advice of counsel he plead not guilty to the first charge, guilty to the second.

After spending two days hearing testimony, the court found the accused guilty of all charges and specifications "and does therefore sentence him, Private William C. Dowdy . . . that considering the best interests of the service and Regiment he be shot to death by musketry in the presence of his Regiment at such time as the Commanding Officer may direct."

Within an hour after the trial ended, September 8, Colonel Dimon received the written proceedings, and without even a day's delay to review the testimony he approved the court's sentence: "He will be shot to death by musketry in the presence of his Regiment on the 9th Instant at 3 P.M. Officer of the Day is charged with the execution of this order. Private Dowdy has had full warning and after betraying the confidence of his officers and inciting his comrades to unlawful acts can expect no sympathy of officers or men."[6]

Shortly after noon of September 9, the *Effie Deans* passed Omaha, and at the first convenient landing point on the Iowa bank of the river, the boat was moored, planks run ashore, and a grave-digging detail ordered off. Not long afterward the six companies marched off the boat into the hazy September afternoon and formed three sides of a hollow square, with the fresh grave in the open side. To the doleful beat of drums and in a slow measured tread, the officer of the day with his firing squad, four men bearing a board coffin, and the manacled prisoner marched to their positions. Promptly at 3:00 P.M. Private William Dowdy died from musketry fire.

To say that Colonel Dimon exceeded his authority is an understatement. The entire affair was in violation of the Articles of War, for even in wartime, regimental commanders had no authority to try or punish capital offenses.* And on the basis of recorded testimony in the case of William Dowdy, no responsible reviewing board would ever have approved the death sentence. Only the slightest evidence was brought forward to show that Dowdy had begun or joined in any mutiny.

Captain Fay's original informant was a 19-year-old, Danish-born corporal, Alexander Hardy, whose English was not of the best. Under questioning, the most damaging remark Hardy could recall Dowdy saying was that "if anybody wanted to desert he did not

---

* Although the wartime Congress had given field commanders more authority in courts-martial proceedings, the law concerning death sentences was clear and specific: "No sentence of death shall be carried into execution until the same shall have been approved by the President." (U.S. Statutes, 37th Congress, Session II, July 17, 1862, p. 598.) As is well known, President Lincoln commuted most death sentences when they reached his office.

care when they went, he had as lief they would go one time as another." Dowdy's sergeant, Alvin C. Harrold of Hinds County, Mississippi, testified that he had heard Dowdy say that "he would be damned if he didn't leave the first opportunity that he got." Captain Fay told the court that Dowdy was "a poor soldier . . . a very hard man to get along with," but that he had never heard him make any remarks about desertion. It was largely from the testimony of these three witnesses that the court found Dowdy guilty of violating the 7th Article of War, that is, engaging in mutiny or sedition.

As for the second charge, absenting himself from his company without leave, the court relied entirely upon Captain Fay's testimony. Like everyone else in this affair, Alfred Fay was young and inexperienced; he was a slender 21 year old, sprouting a downy moustache and chin whiskers, a special friend of Dimon, who liked to listen to him sing. Fay said that Corporal Hardy came to him on the night of September 5 and reported hearing that Private Dowdy "was going to leave to desert." Instead of assigning a noncommissioned officer to observe Dowdy's movements, Fay decided to watch the man himself. "About eleven o'clock [P.M.] I went out to his quarters and found him lying down. I should judge he was asleep. His eyes were closed. The next place I saw him to recognize him was about 3 o'clock A.M. down by the gun on the starboard side."

When defense counsel asked Fay if Dowdy might not have changed his position on the boat to find better shelter from a heavy rain which was falling that night, Fay replied in the negative. "During the night," he concluded, "Dowdy was seen by me in several different places on the boat, evidently with the intention of deserting." Although he never left the *Effie Deans* and was scarcely out of sight of his hovering commanding officer all night, Dowdy was found guilty of "absenting himself from his company without leave."[7]

On a river boat filled with several hundred soldiers whose loyalties were yet untried, and with the power of life and death in the hands of a man as young and inexperienced as Colonel Dimon, Private Dowdy was, of course, doomed. At least a week before the events of September 5, Colonel Dimon had marked him for death. In a letter to his sweetheart dated August 29, Dimon noted casually: "Shall shoot one of my men for desertion next week. It's hard but an example must be set."[8] One can not help but be reminded of Herman Melville's young sailor, Billy Budd, who was goaded into committing an act of violence that ended in tragedy.

Charles Augustus Ropes Dimon of Salem, Massachusetts, was a romantic young man. He was also equipped with the egotism of youth, at times overconfident, at times badly frightened. Yet most of his men respected him. He had come up through the ranks, serving as a private in the 7th Massachusetts from the first months of the war. Before the end of 1861 he was a first lieutenant of the 30th Massachusetts. He won the favor of Ben Butler, who promoted him to major in 1862, to lieutenant-colonel in April 1864, and then to full colonel in August, just before the regiment left for the West. After taking command of the 1st Regiment, Dimon operated in the approved Butler manner, issuing a constant stream of special orders relating to saluting and drilling. He forbade profanity, consumption of alcohol, card playing on Sundays. He insisted that blankets be aired daily and that every man in the regiment take a bath each Tuesday and Saturday afternoon.

On the day Butler sent Dimon a colonel's commission, the general enclosed a letter, which may partly explain Dimon's later behavior:

I have sent you a commission in order to show that I appreciate your soldierly qualities, and that I am kindly disposed. There are and have been grave charges against your *personal habits*. If I did not believe that you both could and would alter them, I should not have sent the commission. Pray do not attempt to deny the habit of drinking to excess, and absence from Quarters to late hours of the night. These are not recommendations, and must now cease. A Colonel can not afford to do so. Officers should not suppose that they are out from under my eye when I happen to be away. It is not so. Now, your officers are getting into bad habits—one was arrested in a drinking-house asleep, and it was reported to me. Three others, for one of whom you have asked promotion, have been arrested for drunkenness. Many are getting so that their Colonel will be ashamed of them, and he cannot control them, and why, they may accuse him of the same offence. I have written this letter as the kind friend. Be sure and not give further occasion either for caution or action. The last will come if it is needed. I reward good service and punish for bad, with equal facility. Remember the words of a friend.

Truly yours,
Benj. F. Butler.[9]

Even after he was transferred from Butler's command, the impressionable Dimon may have felt that he was still not out from under the watchful eye of his ubiquitous protector. Perhaps in that brief hour when Dimon held in his hands the power of life and death over Private William Dowdy, he asked counsel not from God but from the all-knowing Benjamin Butler.

There is evidence that some of Dimon's officers—including one who served on the court-martial and did not vote for the death sentence—were shocked by the hurried execution and expressed themselves openly against the action. Less than a week after Dowdy was taken ashore and shot, Dimon issued an order calling attention to an army regulation which prohibited military discussions, whether of a political or a military nature. "Hereafter, any officer," he decreed, "who may in violation of said order engage in any discussion either to the praise or censure of any officer will be immediately reported to the Secretary of War for immediate dismissal from the service." It was an edict worthy of Dimon's military mentor.

Meanwhile many miles up the Missouri, Dimon's new commanding general was returning from a summer expedition into hostile Indian territory. General Alfred Sully was by temperament the exact opposite of Ben Butler. He was a professional soldier who could smell a pretender a mile off; Dimon would soon have to adjust to West Point ways modified by frontier conditions. On September 16, Sully wrote Pope from Fort Rice, notifying him that he did not expect the 1st U.S. Volunteers to arrive until some time in October because of low water in the Missouri. "No boat can get up here now. . . . They will have to march up."[10]

The regiment knew nothing of this until September 27 when the *Effie Deans* settled into a sand bar five miles below the mouth of White Earth River. After scouting upstream, the boat's captain announced that farther progress was impossible for an indefinite period. Fort Rice was 272 miles to the north, but Crow Creek Agency was only 40 miles upriver, and Dimon hoped he might obtain transport wagons there. He ordered his officers to load their men with all the ammunition and rations they could carry, disembarked, and "in heavy marching order" started for the agency. Dimon, and those of his junior officers who had brought their own horses with them on the boat, rode in the advance.

They marched 13 miles the first day, young Elizabeth Cardwell, the only woman in the column, walking cheerfully beside her heavily laden husband. "The country," one of the officers recorded, "was barren and desolate, monotonous hills and prairies, nearly destitute of vegetation, all dreary, all a blank, the marching regiment the only living objects about, birds few, wild animals seldom seen, but many grasshoppers. The wind swept with unchecked fury over the forestless waste, great clouds of dust hung like a mist over the empty space."[11]

On the second day rain and hail pelted the marchers. "I was so much overcome," Dimon wrote, "that when I got off from my horse I reeled and went down like a log—the first time I ever fainted in my life. A good fire and constant rubbing brought me to. . . . I had before that put one of my men on my horse to ride, he had given out, and walked several miles." In this same letter, the colonel mentioned that they had "no tents and nothing to cover us." Rations were two hard crackers and two tablespoonsful of coffee grounds and sugar mixed together per day, and three-fourths pound of pork every four days.[12]

At noon of the third day, September 30, they reached Crow Creek Agency, "a little fort surrounded by its village of tipis and their wild inhabitants." The fortified area was 300 feet square with a stockade of 12-foot cedar pickets. "We were glad to see any human form, motley though they were, with robes, feathers, beads and fringes, and not a slight admixture of grease and dirt." Elizabeth Cardwell had the pleasure of meeting a member of her sex, "a pretty black-eyed schoolma'am. . . . Her husband was the Principal, but with her sparkling glances and ceaseless activity she seemed the presiding genius of the institution. . . . Instruction was given in the Sioux language. . . . We met Lieutenant Marshall and lady and soldiers of his company."[13]

After a three-day delay, Lieutenant S. B. Noyes, regimental quartermaster, managed to collect a few ox-drawn wagons, and on October 3 the column moved north for Fort Sully, a 60-mile land journey. "The vegetation beneath our feet was crisped and parched with drought. Prickly pears covered larges spaces of ground. . . . In the low bottoms the tall wiry grass rustled like shattered glass in deserted houses. Soon gone from sight were the tipis, gone the fort . . . hid by the everlasting, barren bell-shaped hills. The first night after we left the Agency we camped at Soldier's Creek."

The night of October 6 they were on Medicine Creek. "Here was a beautiful lovely sheet of water, but nauseous to the taste. . . . The night was cold and the crackling fires burning briskly made the scene one of unique beauty. What so fine a subject for a painter, as soldiers round a camp fire at night, in an uninhabited country. . . . The various expressions of countenance brought out in relief by the glowing firelight, showing brighter from the clouds of smoke that whirl up and roll off through the empty void of the heavens."[14]

Elizabeth Cardwell could have traveled in one of the wagons, but most of the time she chose to walk with her husband. She was a symbolic heroine, an inspiration for the long column of foot-sore soldiers. "We shall never forget how she endured the fatigue of the march," one of her admirers recorded.[15]

On October 7 they arrived at Fort Sully, a crude post consisting of a pair of earth-roofed barracks running parallel, the ends connected by picket stockades. To their surprise they found General Sully and his returning expedition camped nearby. "There we first saw the old warrior, General Sully. No pomp or parade—but practical, energetic, and simply great he appeared. His face betokened a man of action, and theories—the right man in the right place."[16]

Sully expressed sympathy with Dimon for his lack of supplies, and transferred a few of his wagons and shelter tents to the regiment for the 170-mile march they had to make to reach Fort Rice. "I was much pleased with the appearance of the officers and men," he reported later to General Pope.[17]

One of Sully's sergeants, J. H. Drips of the 6th Iowa Cavalry, was less impressed. "At Fort Sully we met six companies of the 1st U.S. Volunteer Refugees from Alabama who were on the march to Fort Rice where they were to relieve the 30th Wisconsin who were ordered south. The Alabama fellows looked rather seedy. Their marching and the difficult climate account for that."[18] Sergeant Drips evidently conversed with some of the few Alabamians in this predominantly North Carolina regiment.

The sergeant was not mistaken about the poor condition of the men, many of whom were suffering from acute dysentery brought on from drinking stagnant water along the route, and after march was resumed for Fort Rice their condition was aggravated. "The country from Fort Sully to Fort Rice," Colonel Dimon noted, "is ill adapted to moving large bodies of troops owing to the scarcity of wood and water, the latter mostly in stagnant pools and that at an average distance of twenty miles."[19] On October 13, the first death occurred on the march—Private John Blackburn, 21 years old, of Pike County, Kentucky, from chronic diarrhea. His company commander wrote in the record book: "A good and faithful soldier." Three others would die of the same ailment before the column reached Fort Rice.

They sighted their first Indians October 14 at Wood Lake, and Dimon prepared for action. "We were nicely in line and expected a fight."[20] After a few nervous minutes, he was relieved to learn they were friendlies, a band of 60 Yanktonai Sioux under Two Bears, who had waged war with Sully for two years and then had signed a peace treaty. "This was our first acquaintance with this good Indian and true friend. In simple majesty, he stood, this king of the uncultured waste. Gay as an eastern king in his fancy trappings, a combination of simplicity and style, which no being exhibits so much in the wide world as an Indian."[21]

Colonel Dimon held a long parley with Two Bears, and at its conclusion convinced himself that he was already an authority on Indians. He prepared a report for Sully, informing the general that he had arranged with the Yanktonais to bring a number of hostile chiefs to Fort Rice for peace overtures. "I think . . . that there is an opportunity by proper management to conclude an honorable and lasting peace. . . . The commanding general is so well acquainted with the question that I will not propose how this may be brought about until I am informed of my power to act in the matter."[22] Dimon would learn soon enough that one friendly Indian chief could not make a peace, and Sully would learn than an earnest but inexperienced young colonel seeking peace could stir up more Indian trouble than an armed expedition.

After leaving Two Bears's camp on Wood Lake, the column moved on to Beaver Creek. "The woods looked like old deserted orchards on a worn-out farm," one of the officers from New England recorded. "In the ravine we found skulls of men, whether Indians or whites we could not tell. The shrubbery was full of wild fowl, and our men put in practice their early lessons in the art of hunting with good effect."

Early in the morning of October 17 they sighted Fort Rice, on the west bank of the river, and began crossing on the post ferry. "What a cry of joy burst out, as we saw its unfinished battlements! As joyous were we as the relics of Xenophon's ten thousand, when they beheld the sea whose waters laved their homes."[23] They had marched 272 miles since leaving the *Effie Deans*.

Fort Rice, which was to be the regiment's headquarters for the next year, was then only about four months old, having been established by General Sully in July and named for the late General James C. Rice. It lay on a five-acre stretch of table land a hundred feet above the river, the earth-roofed, cottonwood-log buildings forming a square 400 by 500 feet. The 30th Wisconsin, which had been building the fort during the summer, had departed for the South a few days before arrival of the Volunteers, and only a small detachment of the 6th Iowa Cavalry was present to receive the new arrivals. The Iowans left the next day, using the ox-wagons Dimon's soldiers had brought up from Fort Sully.

As many of the post buildings were incomplete—there were roofed quarters for only four companies—Dimon's first orders assigned details to cutting timber, operating the two small sawmills, and constructing buildings. Reveille was posted for 6:00 a.m., surgeon's call 6:15; breakfast 6:45; guard mountings 7:30; dinner 12 noon; recall from fatigue 4:30 p.m.; retreat at sundown; tattoo 7:45; taps 8 p.m. He announced there would be no drill until necessary buildings were completed, ordered officers in charge of fatigue parties to report in person each evening at retreat the results of that day's work, and set 10:30 a.m. Sundays for weekly inspections.

Before the end of the month, four more men died from diarrhea contracted on the march, and 19-year-old Thomas Hobbs of North Carolina, who had been detailed as a ferryman because of his experience as a sailor, fell in the river and drowned.

Construction work continued through November, the increasingly colder weather spurring the men to extra efforts. Dimon kept a close watch on all building details, insisting that elaborate shelving and gun racks be added to the bare interiors. He made a point of living in a tent himself until all his men were in barracks, and to relieve them of time-consuming cooking duties he ordered the standard army mess system abandoned. Instead of four men rotating duties of preparing food for each other, regular cooks were assigned to company cookhouses.[24]

By mid-November it was obvious that food supplies would have to be rationed carefully during the coming winter. No boats could be expected before spring, and the regiment had only the limited stocks hauled overland from Fort Sully, supplemented by what had been left behind by the 30th Wisconsin. To build up a meat larder, Dimon occasionally released a few men from work details to go out as hunting parties, never less than six privates with a noncommissioned officer in charge. These hunting parties were instructed "to be always on the alert for Indians but never to molest them unless attacked by them."[25]

Before the end of the month Dimon learned that not all the Indians around Fort Rice were as friendly as Two Bears's Yanktonais. On November 21, a band of supposedly peaceful Indians attacked a group of soldiers outside the fort, wounding Private Edwin Durham. Six days later Lieutenant Noyes's hunting party had to beat off a similar attack. Private George Townsend was killed, Lieutenant Noyes and his quartermaster sergeant, C. D. Thompson, were wounded.

"I have been in the saddle 20 miles in pursuit," Dimon wrote that evening.[26] He immediately discarded his ideas of peace, and issued a new general order concerning Indians: "On and after Tuesday November 29, 1864, all armed Indians except those dressed in soldier uniforms and on the west side of the Missouri River will be regarded as enemies and be immediately fired upon and if possible killed."[27] This order, and precautions adopted by officers and men whenever duties took them outside the fort, ended for a time the casualties inflicted by Indians, but disease continued to take its toll of life in the post hospital. At the month's end Surgeon George H. W. Herrick reported seven deaths from chronic diarrhea, typhoid fever, dropsy, and consumption.

On Thanksgiving Day, Dimon wrote his parents that the barracks had been completed and he was in his new quarters. "I have four rooms, an office, sitting room, sleeping room and dining room . . . a good stove and plenty of wood. . . . All is ice and winter about us." He also proudly reported: "My men among themselves have raised $1,000, *one thousand dollars,* to buy me a gift sword, as a token of their esteem."[28]

Early in December a few horses were brought up from Fort Sully, and Dimon organized a mounted infantry force for use in patroling the area and for carrying mail to Forts Berthold and Sully. Severe winter storms came now with increasing frequency, and during a howling night blizzard Sergeant Aquilla Williams, believing that no Indians would be on the prowl in such weather, took pity on his guards and sent them to their quarters. For this he was reduced to the ranks for "exposing the garrison to danger from attack and from fire."[29]

To keep officers and noncoms busy during days of inclement

weather, Dimon organized regular classes in tactics and army regulations. He also issued a series of orders to enforce cleanliness. Barracks floors were to be washed spotless twice a month. "Sinks for washing will be built in company quarters and in future any soldier appearing on duty with face or hands dirty will be punished the same as if clothing or accoutrements were dirty. . . . Bastion in southwest corner to be outfitted as bathroom. Companies to rotate using it daily except Sundays. Company commanders will be held responsible that every man of their company washes himself thoroughly once a week."[30]

In mid-December, Dimon put himself in the role of a knight-errant by taking his mounted patrol on a 40-mile circuit in search of Fanny Kelly, a captive of hostile Sioux reported to be in the vicinity. He did not find Mrs. Kelly, but some Indians he met presented him with three fine horses. The temperature dropped to 34° below zero, and several of his men suffered frozen feet, faces, and fingers.

During December he also ordered a flagstaff mounted in front of his headquarters at the west end of the parade ground. On Christmas Day the regiment was assembled, and the first United States flag was raised over Fort Rice. "The cheering was long and loud when the flag fell open and swept out upon the breeze." Colonel Dimon dedicated the banner to General Sully and made a stirring speech: "Let Fort Rice stand as a monument of what soldiers once Rebel, now Union, can do for the cause they have espoused. In this inhospitable region, this desert sea of land, they have reared a light house whose beams shall conduct in safety the Ship of State across these vast shoals into the broad and deep bays of the Pacific."

Two Bears had brought his band of friendlies in to draw rations, and after the ceremonies, Dimon ordered a Christmas feast spread for the Indians. Through the fort's resident interpreter, Frank La Framboise, he explained that his mission in their country was to keep peace. The occasion was later described by Captain Enoch Adams of D Company: "Bears' claws, bears' teeth, feathers, fringes, beads and porcupine quills, and an abundant supply of red and yellow paints. . . . The way they stowed away the groceries in their human bread-baskets was a caution to beholders. As the camels drink water, so the Indian eats, laying in at once in his stomach enough to last him for a week."[31]

The regiment closed out the year of 1864 by mustering for pay. It was an empty ceremony, for there was no paymaster, and probably none would appear until the boats arrived in the spring. The new sutler, W. L. Marsh, who had come out from New Hampshire to prosper from the soldiers, would continue through the winter selling his tobacco and candy and ale for credit. He ran no risk of loss; the army's benevolence guaranteed him first claim at the pay table.

The first three weeks of the new year were without incident, except for a march which Colonel Dimon and his mounted patrol made to Fort Sully. The detachment was on the trail for nine days, going and returning. "Nearly perished in a blizzard," Dimon noted laconically. He obtained a small supply of medicines and rations, and had the pleasure of meeting Fanny Kelly, who had recently been given her freedom and brought into the fort by the Indians.*

Meanwhile at Fort Rice, the weather was the coldest the Southerners had ever experienced. It was an ordeal to go to the outdoor sanitary trenches in below zero temperatures, and an order had to be issued authorizing the sergeant of the guard to arrest all persons found committing any nuisances in places other than the sinks provided. "Said nuisances includes urinating in the immediate vicinity of the Fort."[32]

Late on January 19 some excitement was created by a band of 30 hostiles swooping down on Two Bears's camp and stampeding 60 Indian ponies. Two Bears's warriors pursued; a short fight occurred in view of the fort, and most of the ponies were recovered.

On January 24 Colonel Dimon held a conference with Two Bears and some young Yanktonais who had come down from Fort Berthold with disturbing reports. Half-breed traders flying the British flag, they said, had come into the winter camps near Berthold to stir up the Indians for a big war against American forts along the Missouri. The Yanktonais quoted the Canadian invaders as saying: "This flag will not be put down for anybody, only for God Almighty. Those who join us will not get hurt. We will return

* In her book, *My Captivity Among the Sioux,* 1871, Fanny Kelly gave the men at Fort Rice some of the credit for effecting her rescue, stating that Colonel Dimon "came to visit me ere I left Fort Sully. . . . He told me of his efforts to obtain my release, and that he, with his men, had searched the Indian village for me, but found no warriors there, as they had already taken me to the fort."

the last of the month with more powder, ball, and arms, and some Santees and will take Fort Berthold and Fort Rice."

In reporting this information to General Sully, Dimon requested permission "to break up these trading parties from the British possessions and execute summary justice on the principals engaged this winter. I have do doubt but what there is a Confederate element at work."[33]

In this same report Dimon noted that the health of his command was poor. As a result of scanty and unbalanced rations, scurvy had broken out among the men. "My supply of anti-scorbutics is limited, but I trust will be sufficient to soon check its progress." He was overly optimistic. One man had already died of the disease, and before spring many more would be fatally stricken, to be buried in "this waste, howling wilderness, far from home and the place that saw their birth and the sports of their childhood."

Monotonous and unpalatable as the food was, some of the men began complaining that their company cooks were not serving sufficient quantities to fill a soldier's belly. Surprise inspections showed shortages in two kitchens, and although the indefatigable Dimon was unable to obtain proof, he suspected the cooks of "trading rations for their own benefit to Indian squaws." He returned the two cooks to the ranks and ordered that "any cook or cooks giving, selling, or disposing in any way of any rations, will be subject to immediate confinement and trial. . . . Any cook or cooks allowing any Indians to enter their cook house will be severely punished."[34]

Early in February an overland mail brought the gift sword and other accoutrements for which Dimon's men had raised $1,000, and the presentation was made on Lincoln's birthday. In a letter to his sweetheart, the young colonel described his emotions: "The regiment was formed in a hollow square by Captain Upton and I was sent for. A sergeant stepped out . . . and presented me with a sword, silk sash, embroidered belt, silver mounted pistol and field glass. I felt so completely worked up I could not hardly speak."[35]

Dimon, however, did not allow the gifts to soften his strict disciplinary program. Later in the month when the weather turned surprisingly warm, he ordered company commanders to resume drill on the parade, from 2:00 to 3:00 P.M. daily. Snow having melted off the grassy bottomlands, Dimon also ordered a herding detail to drive the remaining beef cattle 10 miles south to the

FIGURE 1. One of the principal duties of the Galvanized Yankees was guarding wagon trains across the plains, as shown in this drawing by Frederic Remington.

Illinois State Historical Society

FIGURE 2. Some of these Confederate prisoners of war at Rock Island, Illinois, in 1864, no doubt enlisted in the 2nd and 3rd U.S. Volunteers for service against hostile Indians on the Western frontier.

Minnesota State Historical Society

FIGURE 3. Fort Rice, North Dakota, as it looked in 1864. Here the 1st and 4th U.S. Volunteers were attacked by heavy forces of Sioux Indians on July 28, 1865.

FIGURE 4. Confederate prisoners of war at Camp Douglas, Illinois, where several companies of the 5th and 6th U.S. Volunteers were recruited in 1865. The man seated second from the left in the front row is believed to be John T. Shanks, later commissioned captain of Company I, 6th U.S. Volunteers.

Western History Collection, Denver Public Library

FIGURE 6. General Alfred Sully, commander of Galvanized Yankees in the Northwest.

University of Illinois Library

FIGURE 5. Henry Morton Stanley in 1861, as he began his career as soldier in the Confederate Army, soldier in the Union Army, and sailor in the Union Navy.

FIGURE 7. A contemporary drawing of U.S. Volunteers escorting General Grenville Dodge's supply train past Scotts Bluff en route from Julesburg to Fort Laramie, August 1865. A Pacific Telegraph line runs along the left side of the trail.

FIGURE 8. Fort Kearney, with passing wagon train, as sketched by William H. Jackson at the time Galvanized Yankees were stationed there.

FIGURE 9. The guardhouse at Camp Douglas, Utah.

FIGURE 10. The crude dugouts and stockades of Fort Berthold as they appeared in 1865-66 when companies of the 1st and 4th U.S. Volunteers were stationed at the Missouri River post.

FIGURE 11. Camp Douglas, Utah, which was built by California and Nevada Volunteers. It was the luxury garrison of the West when the Galvanized Yankees served here in 1865-66.

FIGURE 12. Platte Bridge Station as it appeared in a drawing by Bugler C. Moellman, 11th Ohio Cavalry, when Captain A. S. Lybe's Galvanized Yankees participated in the famed Indian fight of July 1865.

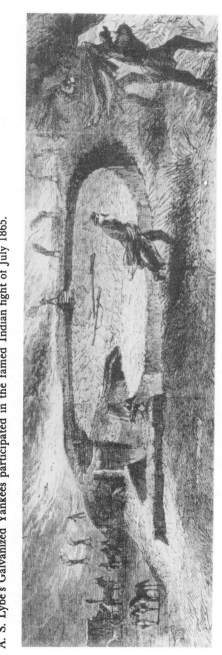

FIGURE 13. An Indian attack upon dugouts defended by a battalion of 1st U.S. Volunteers near Monument Station, Kansas, as depicted by one of the participants, Theodore Davis, artist-correspondent for *Harper's Weekly* (April 21, 1866).

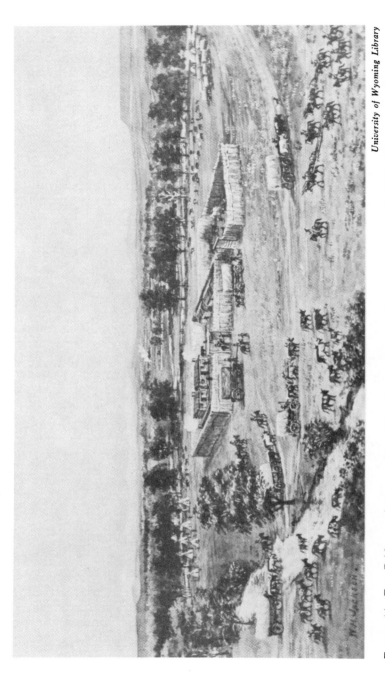

FIGURE 14. Fort Bridger as it appeared in 1866, the same year that companies of the 6th U.S. Volunteers were in service there. From a painting by William H. Jackson.

Colorado State Historical Society

FIGURE 16. George Bent, who led Cheyenne warriors against Captain Williford's Galvanized Yankees in the Powder River Country, with his wife Magpie.

W. H. Over Museum, State University of South Dakota

FIGURE 15. Spotted Tail, his wife, and his daughter, the legendary Fleet Foot. Photograph by S. J. Morrow.

FRONTIER SCOUT.

Capt. E. G. Adams, Editor.   LIBERTY AND UNION.   Lieut. C. H. Champney, Publisher.

Vol. 1.   FORT RICE, D. T., JULY 6, 1865.   No. 4.

JULY 4th, 1865, AT FORT RICE, D. T.

A meeting of the officers at the Fort was held on the evening preceding and a purse was made up for the amusement of the soldiers. At an informal dress parade, after the square was formed, the Adjutant read the following order:

HD. QRS., POST COMDT.,
FORT RICE, D. T.,
July 3d, 1865.

GENL. ORDER No. 25.

To-morrow, the 4th inst., will be regarded as a holiday at this Post, and all business will be suspended for the day. A salute of thirteen guns will be fired at sunrise and sunset. The Troops will be reviewed at 9½ o'clock, A. M. Amusements of all descriptions will be encouraged from the men, and prizes will be awarded.   By order of

Col. C. A. R. DIMON, Comdg.

W. H. BACKERMAN,
Adjt. & Act. Post Adjutant.

Promulgated in General Order N. 38 through Regimental Hd. Qrs., by Capt. E. etc. G. ADAMS, Comdg.

The night preceding the 4th there was a shower which laid the dust, and truly ushered in a day remarkably cool. The heavens were full of clouds, and now and then would come a slight sprinkle of rain attended with winds that blew in puffs, and betokened an uncertainty of weather. Capt. Mishio, Co. H, superintended the adornment of the Fort, his company being the principal workers in this particular field of operations. The main entrance had above it an arch of green leaves. The motto painted on the curve was "4th July;" on the left side as you enter, "1776," on the right, "1865," with scrolls of yellow and miniature flags pointed. On the top of the entrance. "Peace," with stars of red, white, blue and yellow on each side, on the left pillar, "Founded," on the right "Sustained." The American colors crowned the apex of the arch. Festoons adorned the entrance, and two large wreaths, one bearing the motto "G. W.," the other "A. L." the the storm doors of the officers' qrs. both Field and Line, were wreaths with the alternate mottoes "1865" and "1776." The wreaths were principally manufactured by 1st Sergt. Edwards, and the lettering and ornamental painting by Carl Muller.

At 9½ A. M., the troops, commanded by Capt. E. G. Adams, were reviewed by Col. Dimon, the Commandant of the Post, on the beautiful plateau in front of

the Fort. They consisted of Companies C, D, E and H., 1st U. S. V. Inf., and Co. G., 6th Iowa Cavalry, commanded by Capt. A. B. Moreland.

The whole appearance of the troops was martial, their equipments and musket's glittered in the light, and they march ed as only the soldiers can. A square was formed and after a few congratulatory words from Col. Dimon, Capt. Adams addressed the troops. It was a burst of thankfulness that he and they had lived to behold the dawn of the 4th of July 1865, the most glorious epoch in all the world's history.

He likened the American people to old Noah and his family escaping the horrors of the Deluge. That as they so we as a nation, had been delivered, the ark of our liberties resting on a mountain forever immovable, the dove gone forth with the olive branch in her mouth through all the length and breadth of the land, and the rainbow of peace extending its arch from the Atlantic to the Pacific sea. He congratulated his Regiment on the course they had taken, and bade them liberated as they had been from their prison-house by the Good Angel of our institutions, go forth like Paul and Silas, apostles through their native climes, preaching Liberty and Union.

The Review being ended, the sports of the day commenced.

The first was a Foot Race three times round the Fort, or a mile.

6 ENTRIES.

1st Prize $5.00, won by Corpl. W. H. Green, Co. B, Time 3 5-4

3d Prize $3.00, won by Private M. W. Winfrey, Co. C, Time 4.

Immediately followed the Wheelbarrow Race Blindfolded. By the way all the sports took place on the West side of the Fort. This same wheelbarrow race was very amusing. Some of the competitors groping about, their bearings entirely lost, provoked the loudest laughter from the spectators.

A group of ladies consisting of Mrs. Larned, Mrs. Galpin, the Misses Galpin and Miss Picot, with officers and civilians, stood on the parapet of the Fort watching the sport; below were the soldiers and frontier's-men with slouched hat, moccasins and Canadian sashes, and lounging and leaning against the Fort's sides were the Indians in their grotesque costume, young boys with nothing but a breech-clout on, and squaws bearing their offspring—A LA pig-back—their faces painted with vermilion and a streak of red showing the parting place of their hair—Fringes, beads, feathers, paints, buffalo robes, tassels and a conglomeration of everything that hangs, shines and

flatters, they exhibited like a Punchinello.

In this race there were 6 Entries.

Prize $3.00; won by Private J. R. Howell, Co. E. Distance 60 yards. Time 3 minutes.

The crowd then adjourned for dinner. Dinner was succeeded by Target Practice. The Target was two feet by three. There were two rings and a bull's eye. The bull's eye was six inches in diameter, and the rings six inches apart. Distance 200 yards.

1st Prize $4.00, won by 1st Sergt. L. T. Southall, Co. C, 2 inches from center.

2d Prize $2.00, won by Private James Benoist Co. E, 4½ inches from center.

3d Prize $1.00 won by Private Henderson Davis, Co. H.

There was a bet of $5.00 on Benoist and McBride of Co. E. Benoist winner.

The sudden gusts of wind made it impossible to shoot with success.

Next came the Sack Race with five Entries. The competitors tied up in sacks looked like mermaids, and produced much merriment, they went on the leap-frog principle, at the last second falling down and rolling over. Two lost their balance before they reached the goal, upsetting their own gravity as well as that of the beholders.

Time five minutes.

1st Prize $5.00, won by Corpl. W. H. Green, Co. B.

2d. Prize $3.00, won by Private Franklin Pardon, Co. C.

3d. Prize $2.00, won by Private James Fous, Co. D.

HORSE RACE.

1st Race, Wager $25.00.

Col. Dimon, R. M. Indian pony, Wes Washte.

Lieut. Champney R. S. Indian pony Tomahawk.

Half mile heat. Time 1.24

Wes Washte (Beautiful Lady) winning the race by half a neck.

2D RACE.

Capt. Moreland. L. B. S., American horse, Selim.

Lieut. Noyes, B. S. American horse, Charley.

Half mile heat. Time 1.22.

Charley winning by a length.

3D RACE.

Capt. Moreland, L. B. S. American horse Selim.

Lieut. Champney, R. S. Indian pony, Tomahawk.

Half mile heat. Time 1.22. A Dead Heat.

FIGURE 17. The *Frontier Scout* was published at Fort Rice by the members of the 1st U.S. Volunteers. It was one of the first newspapers to appear in the Dakota Territory.

Cannon Ball River, where forage of sorts was obtainable. On February 20, Private Francis Connor, one of the herders, carelessly left camp alone to go for water. A hostile Indian lurking in the brush put three arrows into him; he died two weeks later in the post hospital.

Dimon's assumption that the worst of the winter was over proved erroneous. On Washington's birthday a blizzard roared down from the north, dropping temperatures to 40° below; the herders and their cattle on the Cannon Ball barely managed to survive.

Inside the fort, officers and men huddled in their crowded quarters, and "cabin fever" was inevitable. One of Dimon's severest critics, Captain Enoch Adams, evidently went too far, and on March 3 Dimon felt compelled to issue a reprimand in the form of a general order: "Captain E. G. Adams, Company D, 1st U.S. Volunteers, having used complaining and mutinous language without the least cause (and such complaining being in the Commanding Officer's opinion the result of a diseased imagination) after having been repeatedly censured for so doing, it is ordered that he be, and he is hereby reprimanded. Any repetition of the offense will be met by immediate arrest."[36]

In an effort to reduce tensions, Dimon converted one of the commissary buildings into a post theater, where representatives from different companies competed with one another in the presentation of comical skits and musical performances. "The officers got so blue yesterday," he wrote, "that they got our string band and had a dance in their quarters. Of course I could not join them on account of my rank."[37] It was a desperate sort of cheerfulness, however, for death was ever present, the number of scurvy cases mounting, and burials occurring every few days in the post graveyard.

On March 5, the debilitating disease claimed the regiment's most highly respected member, Hospital Steward William H. Merriman. The post flag was lowered to half mast, and every officer and soldier of the regiment marched to his funeral. Surgeon Herrick delivered a eulogy in which he said he felt as if he had lost "a faithful friend and brother." Merriman was 28, a farmer from Rogersville, Tennessee. In the fall of 1862 he had bid his wife and child farewell and marched to Mississippi with the 60th Tennessee. After being captured in the fighting around Vicksburg, he was sent to Point Lookout, and a year later took the oath and became a Galvanized

Yankee. "He began reading books on drugs," Surgeon Herrick said, "and having an active mind and retentive memory became a trained apothecary. He was quiet and modest in his deportment. He always conducted himself in a gentlemanly manner towards his superiors and with kindness to his inferiors."[38]

The need for medicines and additional food supplies became so acute that Colonel Dimon sent a wagon train down to Fort Sully, but medicines and food were also in short supply there. At the same time he dispatched an urgent message to General Sully in Iowa, reporting the situation and requesting two companies of cavalry to protect the fort from Santee raiders, who were appearing more frequently in the vicinity.

Sully could offer no help in the form of supplies until the boats started running again, nor could he send any cavalry. He did make a strong effort to reclaim Dimon's four companies which had been sent to Milwaukee and then reassigned to Minnesota forts. But General Pope, who had originally been doubtful of the value of Galvanized Yankees, replied that he could not spare them.

On March 19 a mail arrived from Fort Sully, bringing news of the almost forgotten war in the States. The U.S. Volunteers learned that one month earlier Sherman's army had captured Charleston, South Carolina, and was invading North Carolina. Dimon and his officers were jubilant. A 13-gun salute was fired at noon and sunset, but the numerous Carolinians in the ranks must have viewed the celebration with mixed feelings.

The following week Dimon called in the cattle-herding detail from the Cannon Ball bottoms, and as the long winter appeared to be ending he turned his attention to sharpening up his soldiers. He decreed that guards should begin walking their beats in quick time, that hand salutes must be given with more exactness and celerity, that each man must "have his hair neatly trimmed, clothing clean and properly adjusted, hat properly looped up and trimmed, accoutrements blacked and put on in a soldier-like manner."[39]

Moderating weather brought out more prowling bands of Indians, and when a war party approached the fort on March 30, a platoon of mounted infantry dashed out to scatter them. Lieutenant Jeremiah Cronan, Company H, captured two warriors—hostile Santees from the north. The fact that they were armed with British rifles revived Dimon's suspicions of a Canadian-Confederate plot against the Missouri River forts. Had he been more experienced in Northwestern affairs, he would have recognized this constant manipulation of frontier tribes as being only a continuation of an ancient war between rival fur interests. For Colonel Dimon, however, there was only one war that mattered, and if there were any Confederate influences at work in Dakota he was determined to be the first man to find them.

The coming of April did not prove up to the sanguine expectations of the winter-weary regiment; in fact, it was the cruelest month of all, with 15 men dying of scurvy and two from Indian attacks. Scores were ill with the disease, and those who were able to go out on herding or logging details never knew when an arrow or bullet would strike them down. When Surgeon Herrick, whom they depended upon to relieve their illnesses and heal their wounds, suddenly fell ill himself, a spirit of gloom enveloped the post. Many of the men wondered if they had exchanged the uncertainty of life at Point Lookout for the certainty of death at Fort Rice.

The first major Indian skirmish occurred on April 12, when 200 mounted hostiles suddenly swept down from the hills behind the fort and attacked herders just outside the stockade. Privates William Hughes and John Odum were killed in the first onrush.

In his memorandum book, Colonel Dimon noted time of attack as 1:00 P.M.; he recorded the casualties, and losses of 36 cattle, 19 mules, and 13 horses. At 5:00 P.M. he made another entry: "Two Indians (Santees) captured by Lieutenant Cronan March 30 were shot to death."[40] This act of reprisal was not only ruthless but foolish. The raiders had been Cheyenne and Sioux from the Platte River country, and the deaths of two Minnesota Santees meant nothing to them. But when news of the executions leaked out, it would make General Sully's efforts to pacify the belligerent Santees exceedingly difficult.

Nor did the executions restrain the hostiles from further attacks. A few days later, 300 Indians surrounded the horse herd less than a mile from the fort. Only seven herders were on duty, but this time soldiers beat off the raiders without the loss of a single animal. Private Hiram Watson, 19 years old, of Harris, Georgia, took an arrow in the chest, an ugly wound from which he would recover. After the Indians suffered several casualties, they turned down toward the river bottoms, made an ineffectual attack upon the loggers, and then late in the day showed themselves on hill tops to the west. A few howitzer shells fired in their direction soon scattered them. Colonel Dimon was proud of the behavior of his Galvanized Yankees under fire, and praised them in a report to General Sully. "They appeared cool, calm and collected, determined not to give an inch of ground."

During a respite following these two Indian fights, Dimon appointed a courts-martial to deal with a growing number of prisoners in the guardhouse. Sentences were considerably more lenient than the one given William Dowdy on board the *Effie Deans*. Private S. H. Adams received four months at hard labor for leaving his guard post. Private J. R. Lucky was given two months for telling Drum-Major Conrad Badenhop "that he would not beat his drum if compelled to go on details for fatigue duty." A charge of mutiny against Private Francis McCarthy of Cork, Ireland, for declaring "he would whip any man who thought an Irishman could not fight" and then striking a corporal, was charged to "conduct prejudicial to good order and military discipline"; he received two months hard labor. Charges of desertion against Peter Johnson, Charles Snead, Newton Roach, and John Thompson were changed to absent-without-leave, and they were given two to three months sentences. The most serious charge was against Private John P. Allen, 16 years old, from Kershaw, South Carolina. Allen had been found sleeping on guard post, and was sentenced to 18 months hard labor and forfeiture of pay.

With the coming of May showers, the dreary Dakota landscape began showing traces of green. "The prairies and treeless hills are covered with a beautiful garment of verdure," one of the men noted gratefully.[41] But scurvy and the long winter had left two of every five men physically unable to perform normal duties. At the first signs of wild onions thrusting from the earth, Surgeon Herrick asked for a platoon detail, which he assigned to "digging onions for the benefit of the sick." This ancient antiscorbutic proved effective; Herrick reported a short time later that "the sanitary condition of the post is very much improved, the number on the sick list having decreased rapidly since the appearance of wild onions and the arrival of a few potatoes." The surgeon also had other medical information which he did not report; he was attending a new patient, Elizabeth Cardwell, who was pregnant.

Life at Fort Rice had been fairly pleasant for the Cardwells. They lived in private quarters and Elizabeth had the companionship of five others of her sex—wives and daughters of licensed traders. One of them, Mrs. Charles Galpin, was a full-blooded Teton Sioux. She could speak only a few words of French and English, but was so friendly and attractive that she was well liked by everyone, and did not bear the stigma of "brevet-wife," as did many Indian women married to white men on the frontier. Captain Adams described her as "one of the finest women in the world," and her own people called her The-Eagle-Woman-That-All-Look-At. She was especially kind to Elizabeth Cardwell.

The potatoes mentioned by Surgeon Herrick in his report had come up on the first boat from St. Louis, the *Yellowstone,* which lay at the Fort Rice landing for two days (May 9-10) while officers and men of Companies B and K packed their equipment and went aboard. In obedience to orders from General Sully, they were bound respectively for Forts Union and Berthold to relieve companies of Wisconsin and Iowa troops.

On May 12, an additional detachment under Lieutenant Cyrus Hutchins, Company H, embarked on the *Deer Lodge* for Fort Benton, Montana, "to control the trade with Indians between that point and Fort Union."[42] This group of 10 men had the honor of serving at the farthest point north of all posts and stations occupied by Galvanized Yankees.

Departure of these units left Fort Rice garrisoned by slightly less than 300 men at a time when hostile Indian demonstrations were becoming more frequent. On May 19, a fatigue party was attacked near the blockhouse, and Private John Cumbey of Campbell, Virginia, was wounded. One week later, 25 Sioux ambushed Lieutenant Benjamin Wilson as he was leaving the post with a logging detail. Wilson, who was riding ahead of his men, was cut off when the Indians dashed upon him from a ravine. Three speeding arrows knocked him from his horse—one in the shoulder, one in the thigh, another in the back.

From the trader's house at the edge of the fort, Mrs. Galpin witnessed the attack. Without considering her own safety, the Teton woman rushed to Wilson's assistance, reaching him as the hostiles galloped up to scalp and mutilate their victim. Recognizing them as Sioux, she cried out in their own language: "This man belongs to me now! You cannot mutilate or touch him!" The Sioux swirled around her for a minute, then darted away in pursuit of the men who had been separated from Wilson. But already the long roll was sounding inside the fort, and soldiers came rushing out of the gates. The attackers galloped away.

Crazed with pain, Wilson had broken off two arrow shafts in attempts to withdraw them. Mrs. Galpin held his head in her lap until stretcher bearers arrived to carry him in to the post hospital. His condition was pronounced to be serious by Surgeon Herrick; the arrow in the back had penetrated to the young New Englander's lung. Once again a pall of gloom fell over Fort Rice. Lieutenant Wilson's cheerful nature had won him the friendship of the entire garrison.

About this time General Sully was reporting to his headquarters on conditions at the fort. "The great amount of sickness and death at Fort Rice is terrible," he said. "Eleven per cent of the command have died this winter. . . . The soldiers of that garrison are composed of rebel prisoners; men who have been a long time confined as prisoners of war, and of course they are now predisposed to such sickness as scurvy and diarrhea. As soon as possible I will have a more thorough investigation of the causes. I have been obliged to order two of the companies to garrison Forts Union and Berthold. This with the great amount of sickness will weaken that garrison too much. . . ."[43]

The survivors at Fort Rice like most men of their time had come to terms with death, and could even find consolation in the appearance of their enlarging cemetery. "There is a look of civilization about it," one of them wrote, "that reminds one of a cemetery in the States. Its fences as well as whole arrangement is neat, and shows the gallant dead are not forgotten."[44]

One more grave was added to the cemetery on June 2 when Lieutenant Wilson died. His last request was to look upon the Indian face of Mrs. Galpin; he thanked her for saving him from the scalping knife, and died holding her hand. Colonel Dimon declared a day of mourning, and the full regiment formed to march out to the burying ground.

June 2 was also a day of Indian demonstrations and some errors of judgment on the part of Dimon. Ever since the young colonel's October council with the Yanktonai chief, Two Bears, he had fancied himself as a shrewd diplomat in dealing with Indians. Throughout the winter, Dimon had cultivated Two Bears's friendship, occasionally distributing rations to his band; later the colonel had added a Hunkpapa Sioux, Bear Rib, to his list of favorites.

The two Sioux leaders set up semi-permanent camps just outside the fort, and became a sort of unofficial team of advisers on Indian matters to Charles Dimon. They flattered him by calling him "the Great Captain," and whether he was aware of it or not, Dimon had come to accept the enemies of Two Bears and Bear Rib as his enemies—a situation which could lead only to trouble for Fort Rice.

Early on the morning of June 2, when bands of Indians appeared simultaneously at five different points circling the fort, Dimon accepted the advice of his Sioux friends that these were hostiles bent upon attacking the fort. Actually, as events proved later, the demonstrators were only curious passersby, but when Dimon sent out his mounted infantry, a howitzer, and 60 warriors of Two Bears's and Bear Rib's bands, the wandering hunters accepted the challenge and offered fight. A few shells from the howitzer scattered them, however, and they fled so precipitately that they left numerous robes and blankets behind them.

It was a victory for Fort Rice, but was not the sort of action likely to win friends among all the tribes and subtribes frequenting the upper Missouri Valley. When cautious old Alf Sully, who was still down at Sioux City laying plans for a summer peace parley, received Dimon's glowing report of the affair, he was considerably disturbed. Sully had excused Dimon's execution of the two Santee prisoners in April as the foolish act of an inexperienced officer, but this time he decided he had better prepare General Pope for a possible change of command at Fort Rice:

General: There is a matter I wish to write to you unofficially, just as I would talk to you if I could see you, that is in regard to Col. Dimon, commanding 1st U.S. Volunteers and the post at Fort Rice. I admire his energy and pluck, the determination with which he carries out orders; but he is too young—too rash—for his position, and it would be well if he could be removed. He is making a good deal of trouble for me, and eventually for you, in his overzealous desire to do his duty. Toward yourself and myself he is very friendly and anxious to carry out his instructions, and he is one of the best disciplinarians and most energetic men I have met with. Perhaps when I see him and talk to him I can change matters and curb him; but if I cannot do this, and I feel it necessary to act, I should like to have the authority to do so, and I think the best way would be an order making his headquarters in Minnesota, with his other battalion, or any way you may think best. I do not wish to hurt his feelings, but I think the interest of the government would be advanced by having an older and cooler head at Fort Rice. This regiment was raised and organ-

ized by Ben Butler and he is too much like him in his actions for an
Indian country, but he is just the sort of a man I would like to have under
me in the field.

ALF. SULLY.[45]

Pope's immediate reply was: "In relation to Colonel Dimon you
can act as you think best."[46]

Sully meanwhile had ordered Company G of the 6th Iowa
Cavalry transferred from Fort Berthold to Rice. The company was
commanded by a veteran Indian campaigner, Captain A. B. Moreland, who Sully hoped would serve to counteract the influence of
Two Bears and Bear Rib. Moreland and his Iowans were well received by the U.S. Volunteers—"a genial, quiet gentleman and
officer, and his men well-behaved and willing to do their duty."[47]

2

Among various supplies left at Fort Rice by the 30th Wisconsin
was a small printing press and a few reams of paper. This press
had been used to publish a newspaper at Fort Union in the summer of 1864. When it was found in storage by Quartermaster S. B.
Noyes of the 1st U.S. Volunteers, he and some of the other officers
proposed publishing a newspaper at Fort Rice.

After securing Dimon's approval, Captain Enoch Adams and
Lieutenant Charles Champney set the press up in a workshop at
the northeast end of the fort. Champney agreed to be publisher,
and Adams volunteered as editor. In the ranks they found a type-
setter, Corporal William Johnson. Among the regular contributors
were Lance-Sergeant Pinkney A. Morgan, an amateur poet from
Greenville, South Carolina, and Surgeon George Herrick, who
composed essays on subjects ranging from the Empress Josephine
to memories of Mt. Auburn Cemetery in Cambridge, Massachusetts.
(Herrick had been a student at Harvard.)

Volume 1, Number 1 of the *Frontier Scout* appeared on June
15. "The *Frontier Scout*," editor Adams announced:

is published weekly by the 1st U.S. Volunteers for the edification of the
people of Dacotah, both civilized and savage; and as "green" spots and
"green" backs are so few, we will not mention terms, but bid it, like the
grace of God, go free! . . . You must support us with your contributions,
material and mental. We can make a paper lively, social, agreeable,
entertaining and refreshing, but all must contribute a mite. Put every
smart thought into writing. Jot down every little adventure. Fashion into
rhyme every practical idea. When this is done our paper is formed, a
living, speaking embodiment of the society in which we dwell. Let it be

a picture of the sunny side of Dacotah; something we shall keep or cherish like the lock of hair of a lost loved one, or a flower picked and pressed by a dead sister in far-away years.

In addition to reports of Indian activities, military matters, and deaths, the paper carried lighter sketches on such subjects as the post's numerous pets. A tame wolf Dicky had carried a ration of salt pork to a basin of water to freshen it. "He don't calculate to die with scurvy—not he." A bear named Grizzly was begging the post out of sugar. Two sheep arrived on the steamboat, *Silver Lake,* astonishing the Indians who had never seen such animals and believed them to be a strange species of deer.

Jokes appeared on the same pages with obituaries:

Q: Why is cottonwood like Ayer's Cherry Pectoral?
A: Because it is used for your (cough'n) coffin.
Q: In what military position is a soldier with a hole in the seat of his pants?
A: To the rear, open order.

An advertisement announced that D. W. Marsh, sutler, was "prepared to furnish you with all the necessities of frontier life." A spoofing notice declared that Quartermaster Noyes was accepting "sealed proposals for destruction of the numerous army of infernal grasshoppers that have had the audacity to destroy our fine garden . . . needed to fight our old enemy and conspirator against the life of this garrison, Scurvy."

Steamboat arrivals and departures were listed in almost every issue, the *Yellowstone, Deer Lodge, Lillie Martin, Twilight, Roanoke, Fanny Ogden, Hattie May, General Grant,* and their old friend, the *Effie Deans.*

Verse occupied an unusual amount of the limited space. A solemn dirge, "In Memory of Abraham Lincoln," appeared in the first issue. Doggerel, however, was more likely to be used, for example, "What the American Eagle Thinks of Dacotah":

> If this is the land of Dacotah, she cries
> I pity the 1st U.S.V. at Fort Rice
> Then plumes her gay wings, and soars far from the scene
> To lands more delightful and skies more serene.

Or in this excerpt from "Life at Fort Rice":

> Butter, cheese and woman's eyes
> Would make this a paradise . . .
> In this post we are like Adam
> Ere he had obtained his madam.

Practically all the humorous rhyme reflected the new and strange life, including the natives of Dakota Territory, as in "The Dying Indian's Request":

> O bury me not in obscurity,
> But bury me up in the top of a tree,
> When my spirit goes to the land of souls
> Set me up on two bean poles
> Where I cannot be eaten by wolves and foxes
> That eat "them" fellows they put in boxes.
> Fix round my head a feathery wreath
> Round my throat bear's claws like harrow teeth
> Bring me a bow and bring me an arrow
> And plenty of "toro" that's made of marrow.
> Set me a feast and light me my pipe,
> Each is a sign, and emblem and type
> Of something I never was able to tell,
> But do it all, and it will be well.
> Farewell squaw! farewell papoose,
> From life my spirit is cutting loose,
> My eyes grow dim, I cannot see,
> I have left this world, and climbed a tree.

Captain Adams signed his name to some of the metered compositions; others were anonymous. The more romantic efforts were probably the work of the love-smitten poet, Sergeant Pinkney Morgan. Morgan was a tall, gray-eyed, sandy-haired lad of 20, who pined for a girl name Jinnie somewhere back in South Carolina. For her he composed 14 quatrains which he called "Ballad of Love's Independence," and then must have decided this work was too personal to publish in *Frontier Scout*. Morgan set it into type, however, and published it privately, the first separate poem to be printed in Dakota. The closing verse is indicative of its nature:

> If I die far from thee, my love
> Oh bury me between a turtle-dove
> To show to your dearest love,
> In years to come I died for love.[48]

Editor Adams and his assistants saw that copies of the newspaper were distributed aboard every passing steamboat, and these in turn were passed on to other boats along the river so that the *Frontier Scout* became an unofficial news organ for the upper Missouri Valley. The editor also urged readers to "send our *Scout* down to our friends in the States, showing we are still living, moving, stirring, acting beings, that the great American heart still beats in our bosoms, that the genius, effort, and perseverance that settled the States, is taking deep root in Dacotah, on the banks of Missouri, the great highway of a broader, deeper civilization."*

3

In mid-June rumors of a captive white woman drifted into Fort Rice, causing much excitement. Everyone in the fort knew the story of Fanny Kelly, who had been miraculously rescued during the winter down at Fort Sully; already she was on the way to becoming a national celebrity. When Colonel Dimon was told by his Indian friends that a band of Cheyennes in the vicinity were in possession of another white woman, he was determined to rescue her.

His first move was to send a mounted force out on a pretended buffalo hunt; actually the hunters were searching for the Cheyenne camp. The party returned empty-handed, finding neither buffaloes nor Indians. Then on June 17, a small band of Tetons arrived at the fort; they were known as Blackfoot Sioux because they wore black moccasins. Their chief, Grass, was friendly toward the white men.

Through the assistance of the post interpreter, Frank La Framboise, Dimon arranged for Grass to act as intermediary with the Cheyennes. Within 24 hours, Dimon learned that a Minneconjou named White White who was traveling with the Cheyennes had purchased the woman captive from them for two horses; he would be willing to sell her to the soldier chief for two good American horses.

Dimon immediately agreed to trade, and Grass and one of his warriors, Red Horse, rode out to the Cheyenne camp, leading two of the fort's best mounts. On June 21, they returned with Sarah Morris, who had been captured January 10 during a raid along the Platte River in Colorado.

Sarah Morris was an attractive, small-featured young woman, her skin deeply tanned after six months of living in the open, her hair a lustrous black. She and her husband, who was killed in the raid, had moved to Colorado from Delaware County, Indiana. Her story, sometimes incoherent, sometimes graphic in its details, was taken down by one of Colonel Dimon's clerks:

* In the issue of September 7, 1865, is noted receipt of a letter from W. F. Poole, who promised to preserve copies of *Frontier Scout* in the Boston Athenaeum.

I was living at American Ranche on the Platte River in Colorado at the time of my capture by the Cheyennes. My family consisted of my husband, William Morris, one child, my own, and an adopted one. My child's name was Charley. The adopted one we called Joseph. It was the 10th of January 1865 the Indians attacked the house where we lived. The party consisted of about one hundred. It was near 10 A.M. We kept a hotel. They set the house and stables afire, and drove us into the pilgrim room. At last the doors of the pilgrim room got in flames, and we had to leave. We ran out towards the river, through the corral, hoping to make our escape. My husband said perhaps we could escape that way. When we got to the corral we found we could not. He told me to stop, that they would probably take me prisoner, and he possibly might get away. They surrounded him, and killed him and another man as they were running to the river. The Indians stood so thickly about me, I could not see him when he was killed. He had no arms of any kind with him. My baby, 15 months old, died about a month ago. The Sioux took Joseph and have him yet. They put me on a pony, and went south about fifty miles. They have been traveling, and I with them most of the time since. At their first camping ground they stayed three or four days, holding their scalp dances. Since they have been moving north. About four days ago they told me they were going to bring me in to the whites, pointing this way, saying "Sioux, sugar, coffee, heap." My joy knew no bounds. I certainly know they killed my husband, for they told me there were four men killed at the Ranche and they were all there were there. At the time of my capture I received five wounds from arrows and six stabs from knives. They also struck me across the head with their whips. My wounds are not entirely healed. An Indian, who could talk English, told me after I arrived in camp that if I showed them the wounds in my shoulders, they would not kill me as it was their intention to do. The old chief who took me doctored me with his medicine, and my wounds partially healed up. He treated me very well, making me do scarcely anything except pack on my back a few kegs of water, and saddle my pony. He gave me plenty of meat, which was all he had. He however did not like my little boy. My baby was afraid of him and would cry. One day he took him by the neck and threw him down, and stamped on him. The child then took sick, and died in about three weeks. They wanted to bury him before he was fairly dead. I had hard work to keep them from doing it. He sunk away, and I knew he was not entirely dead. After his death they put him in a coffee sack, and laid him in a hole in the ravine, hardly covering him over. I wanted them to dig the grave deeper, but they would not. The chief's name is White White. He is the one that brought me in. I think the Indians are getting frightened. I saw while a captive one white woman and baby, she was taken by the Sioux but traded off to the Cheyennes. They let her stay with me about two hours. They promised to let her visit me the next day, but did not. She stated that she was captured on the Little Blue. The circumstances of her capture were these. A young woman came to pay her a visit, and she and her husband went to see her home. They killed her husband, and the two women were taken captive. [They were Lucinda Eubanks and Laura Roper, whose stories are told in Chapter II.] She said that while with the Sioux she was used meanly, but better after sold to the Cheyennes. She knew of still another woman captured on the Little Blue."⁰

The six women in the fort took Sarah Morris under their care until passage could be arranged for her on one of the southbound boats. Life resumed its normal course. Summer was coming on; dust flew in clouds, and the *Frontier Scout* observed that the landscape was "like a Lybian desert when a simoon is raging." But the health of the garrison was much improved, Surgeon Herrick reporting that his scurvy cases had dropped from 50 seriously ill to 11 convalescents.

More and more Indians appeared outside Fort Rice, assembling for a grand parley which General Sully had arranged for mid-July. Most of them were friendly Yanktonais and Tetons. They brought many rumors concerning plans to attack Fort Rice.

Already the hostiles upriver had started a war against the white man's steamboats. On June 29, the *Cutter* docked at Fort Rice and reported one of the crew killed in a fierce attack. Later that same day the *St. Johns* arrived with a similar story; just below Fort Berthold the first mate had been shot to death from a river-bank ambush. A deck hand was badly wounded; a shot had grazed the forehead of the pilot.

The officers and men at Fort Rice accepted these events as warnings of things to come. They looked to their arms, kept an alert guard, drilled regularly, and on the last day of June assembled for a rigid inspection. For the tenth month they were mustered for pay without a paymaster. Personal finances, according to the *Frontier Scout,* were "embarrassing to officers as well as men."

July came in with blasts of hot wind, followed by booming thunderstorms which turned the earthen roofs of Fort Rice to dripping mud. Over in the small quarters occupied by Patrick and Elizabeth Cardwell, Surgeon Herrick spent a busy night. Next morning he announced to the post that the first white child had been born in the fort. "May she prove a perfect trump," declared the *Frontier Scout,* and the 1st U.S. Volunteers began a joyous celebration which lasted through the Fourth of July holiday.

All day of July 3, details worked diligently at decorating the stockade and gates. They twined garlands of green willow fronds over rails and posts. The regimental artist, Carl Muller, lettered the words "4th of July" and "Peace" above the entrance arch, and decorated it with huge red, white, and blue stars.

The Fourth dawned cloudy and cool, a 12-pounder howitzer booming 13 salutes. At 9:30 A.M. the regiment with Company G of the 6th Iowa Cavalry formed for review on the plateau in front of the fort. For a few minutes the sun broke through dark racing clouds, glittering on metalwork and muskets. After a short speech by Colonel Dimon, the sports of the day began—winners to receive money prizes. There were foot races, blindfold wheelbarrow races, sack races, horse races. The ladies of the fort, excepting Elizabeth Cardwell, who was still confined, stood with the officers on the parapet watching the events.

"Below were the soldiers and frontiersmen with slouched hats, moccasins, and Canadian sashes, and lounging and leaning against the fort's sides were the Indians in their grotesque costumes, young boys with nothing but a breechclout on, and squaws bearing their offspring . . . their faces painted with vermillion and a streak of red showing the parting place of their hair—fringes, beads, feathers, paints, buffalo robes, tassels . . . all shining and fluttering."[50]

In the afternoon the celebration ended with a mock dress parade, organized by Drum-Major Conrad Badenhop. The men had vied with one another in devising ridiculous uniforms. One wore a three-foot-high buffalo cap, another a pair of flannel drawers. Some carried crutches, others crossbows; all were streaked with Indian war paint. "The lines were formed as straight as a Virginia rail fence," the *Frontier Scout* reported. "The parade terminated by a march on the commissary, and every man taking a drink . . . the 13 guns of evening shook the dirt roofs of Fort Rice . . . and the sun set on the happiest Fourth of all time."

Five days later the joyous exuberation of the holiday was transformed to pity and sorrow. Elizabeth Cardwell was dead, followed a few hours later by her child. "Thus has passed away the young mother and her infant like a dream of morning," wrote editor Adams. "Green be the grass above them. . . . Carl Muller has painted a beautiful headstone for the mother and child. It is really tasteful and does his head and heart great credit."

Her chief mourners were the grief-stricken husband, Mrs. Galpin the Teton woman, and the four white women, Mrs. Yarbrough, Mrs. Kruger, Mrs. Larned, and a Miss James. Officers and men honored Elizabeth Cardwell in solemn procession as though she had been a member of the regiment.

For several days the mood of the fort was subdued, with none of the usual raillery among the men as they went about their routine tasks. When speech was necessary they talked in quiet tones. The death of the mother and child had affected them more deeply than any of the previous losses of their comrades.

But events were moving too swiftly at Fort Rice in July to devote many days to mourning. During the week of July 10, numerous bands of Indians gathered on both sides of the river, awaiting the expected council with General Sully. Three hundred lodges were encamped by July 13, when Sully and his column arrived and pitched tents on the plain east of the river. To the great delight of the 1st U.S. Volunteers, Sully had brought up two companies of a new regiment of Galvanized Yankees, the 4th U.S. Volunteers. Rumors spread that the 4th would soon replace the 1st, which might be mustered out before the end of summer.

Sully held his first all-day council on July 16, inviting Colonel Dimon to attend. The proceedings began with the usual smokes to the Great Spirit, and after Sully took three puffs from the pipe he passed it to Dimon, who followed the general's example. "All my friends are my brothers," Sully said. He was pleased to see several Hunkpapas among the Indians seeking peace.

In his dealings with the Hunkpapas—the most suspicious and warlike of the Sioux—Sully used special care; he was eager to win over the few representatives who had come to Fort Rice. The Hunkpapas told him that 130 more lodges of their people were waiting west of the river, waiting to see if Sully was setting a trap for them. Sully declared that he wanted only peace.

Late in the afternoon the council ended for the day, and by previous arrangement Sully and his staff crossed the river with Dimon to have dinner in the fort. Once again the inexperienced Dimon displayed his talent for doing the wrong thing at the wrong time; he had arranged for a howitzer salute to be fired as soon as the ferry boat reached the landing.

The result was disastrous insofar as Sully's negotiations with the Hunkpapas were concerned. "At the time," Sully wrote Pope the next day, "130 more lodges [of Hunkpapas] were on their way. When I landed the fort fired a salute. The advance, seeing this, thought they were firing on them, gave the alarm, and the whole party scattered. . . . The red man is a hard animal to deal with, and very uncertain."[51]

Sully knew he had lost a chance to make peace with the powerful Hunkpapas, but he did not learn until two weeks later just how far-reaching was the effect of Colonel Dimon's booming gun. The frightened Hunkpapas hurried back to their camp, spreading tales that General Sully had massacred all the Indians who had gathered at Fort Rice to smoke with him. This story soon reached the ears of a tribal leader who had been advocating war to the death against the white invaders of the Sioux country. His name, known then to few white men, was Sitting Bull. Using the rumors from Fort Rice to stir up his warriors, Sitting Bull organized a great war party and started for Fort Rice. On July 28, he and The-Man-That-Has-His-Head-Shaved would lead more than a thousand hostile Sioux in a mighty assault upon the hated fort on the Missouri.

In the meantime, Sully was the man of the hour at Fort Rice. The incident of the gun salute had convinced him that Dimon must be replaced, yet he did not conceal his admiration for the excellent appearance of the post, and issued a general order praising the regiment for its splendid behavior during the hard winter.

Alfred Sully was old enough to be the father of Charles Dimon and the other officers of the 1st Regiment, and their manner toward him was sometimes more filial than military. They soon discovered that his gruff frontier manner was only a cover concealing a gentle man, the son of Thomas Sully, who had painted portraits of many of the nation's greatest leaders. Alfred Sully was an excellent watercolorist himself, but he was primarily a soldier who had earned a considerable reputation in the West before the Civil War, and in Virginia during the war until Indian troubles brought him back to Dakota in 1863.

There were many stories of his eccentricities, true and half true. It was said that he sometimes cut off the heads of his enemies and paraded them on poles, but no one seems to have actually seen this. At one time when his quartermaster records showed a shortage of horses and a surplus of mules, he balanced his accounts by ordering a number of mules raised in rank to "brevet-horses." And he was so fond of fresh eggs that he always carried coops of hens on his expeditions. "He imagined that he was in appearance and ability only a very little, if any, behind Napoleon himself," wrote one of his Dakota sergeants. "General Sully was not a dude, by any means, while he was up in Dakota and was rigged out with corduroy pants, which he wore without suspenders, white shirt, white slouch hat and pants stuffed inside of long-legged boots. In hot weather this was his costume, when cooler an army blouse was added."[52]

One of the often told stories among the Galvanized Yankees concerned a young lieutenant just arrived, who was taken to the general's tent by a major. The lieutenant was wearing a brand-new uniform, equipped with red sash and saber belt, and was heavily perfumed with musk. Sully was in an undershirt, seated on a camp stool, sipping whiskey. The two visitors saluted, the major announcing: "General Sully, allow me to present Lieutenant ———."

The general looked the new arrival over sharply, sniffing suspiciously at the perfume. "Well, lieutenant, how long have you been in the service?"

"About six months, sir."

"Six months!" Sully roared. "Why, my God damned, man, I've been in the regular service twenty years and don't smell half as bad as you do." With that he waved to the major that the interview was ended.

While these and other stories were being told about him in the barracks of Fort Rice, Sully was preparing to dispose of the inexperienced Colonel Dimon. "Colonel Dimon is certainly an excellent officer," he noted. "A few more years of experience to curb his impetuosity would make him one of the best officers in the volunteer service."[53] Exactly what Sully said to Dimon is not on record, but a few days before the general departed on his summer expedition, he announced that Colonel Charles Dimon was going back to the States on an important mission and a well-deserved furlough. In a letter to his parents, Dimon explained that he was going to Washington to see the Secretary of War on Indian business, and would come home to Massachusetts on furlough later.[54]

Dimon left on July 22, and that same day Lieutenant-Colonel John Pattee of the 7th Iowa Cavalry replaced him as commander of Fort Rice. Pattee was Canadian-born and had known Indians all his life. He dressed like an Indian himself, preferring buckskins and moccasins to the regular uniform. He cared nothing for military ceremony, and the U.S. Volunteers would find him radically different from the spit-and-polish young man who had commanded them for the past year.

Next day Sully led his expedition off to the Northwest toward hostile Indian country. A last-minute transfer of surgeons left S. P. Yeomans at the fort in exchange for Dr. Herrick, who was eager for the adventure of a march.

During this eventful week another detachment of the 4th Regiment arrived on the *Belle Peoria,* reviving rumors of an early muster-out for the 1st. The long-expected paymaster also arrived, and for the first time since the U.S. Volunteers had left Virginia the men lined up at pay tables. To celebrate this happy occurrence, Captains Adams and Moreland organized a hunting party from among the more deserving men of the post. "They had a gay ride to the Cannon Ball. Jolly hunt. Chasing antelope over the Plain, elk, prairie chickens so plentiful men killed with clubs. Mosquitoes, misery with a big M. We were skinned if not scalped."[55]

The hunters stayed out for three days, and if they had not returned to the fort on July 27, they might well have been scalped. For swarming eastward between the Cannon Ball and the Heart were more than a thousand Sioux warriors led by Sitting Bull, determined to avenge the mythical massacre of their kinsmen. The man who gave the order to fire the salute gun which started the wild rumors was safely aboard a steamboat bound for St. Louis; the fanatical force which his mistake had put in motion would have to be dealt with by John Pattee, a few Iowa cavalrymen, and the Galvanized Yankees.

Early on the morning of July 28, they had their first look at the enemy. At dawn there had been no sign of them. About 7:00 A.M. a civilian employee of the sutler stepped outside the store at the northwest corner of the fort and saw several mounted warriors, naked and painted for battle, in pursuit of one of the post's Yanktonai police. Almost at the same moment, near the sawmill south of the fort, Private Andrew Burch was startled to see a red-painted Indian galloping in pursuit of Private James Hufstudler. Burch, Hufstudler, and a third private named Brown were guarding the horse herd. Each man was mounted and separated by considerable distance from the others.

Burch immediately spurred his horse forward, but the Sioux warrior had already shot Hufstudler with an arrow and was beating him over the head with a bow. Burch fired his revolver, and the warrior dashed away up a slope toward the post cemetery, joining three other hostiles.

"I ran them up a hill some 400 yards," Burch said later, "and shot at him five times with my revolver, but did not hit him. I should if my horse had not been frightened by his war rigging. His pony was hung with red tassels; he himself had a red blanket around his waist, his shoulders were naked and painted red, his hair was hanging loose, two feathers fluttering in it. He had a rifle or shotgun in a fringed covering hanging on his back and in one hand his bow and arrow. His horse was streaked off with red paint over his haunches. When he ran behind the hill, I pursued him to the top and saw over the hill 25 or 30 Indians—they kept pretty well concealed, as I could see only their heads."[56]

Meanwhile the fort was in full alarm, companies of both the 1st and 4th Volunteers pouring out the north gate, Captain Moreland with a platoon of Iowa cavalrymen dashing out the south gate to aid the horse herders. Moreland was too late to save the horses; when Private Brown went to assist Burch, more Sioux sprang from concealment and swept away the herd.

Moreland and his troopers galloped in pursuit, swinging around the hill where Burch and Brown were cautiously observing the 25 or more hidden enemies. As soon as these Sioux saw the cavalry pursuing their friends, they leaped on their ponies and rushed to lend assistance. "They went yelling like barking dogs," Burch said. "As they whipped across the creek they struck their ponies with their leather whips fastened around their wrists. Their horses went with the swiftest kind of a run into the fight. I saw three unhorsed, and I thought Captain Moreland shot them himself, as he was fifty feet in advance of his men and firing."

About this time, Burch and Brown heard a crackle of musketry on the west side of the fort. As the action had flowed beyond them, they had a moment to observe the horizon, now fully lit by summer morning sunlight. In an arc sweeping from north to west to south, every hill was covered with mounted Sioux, horses and riders painted for battle.

Lieutenant-Colonel Pattee also had discovered that Fort Rice was surrounded. He rode out a few yards on the plain west of the stockade, observed the situation, and began calmly deploying his forces. He dispatched a messenger to Captain Moreland with orders to pull back and fight nearer the fort, and then sent Company D of the 4th Regiment to reinforce the cavalry and form a left wing. He sent Company A of the 4th marching northward on the double-quick to form a right wing. Into the center went the four veteran companies of the 1st. Up in the bastions, the swiveled howitzers were manned and ready. The two 12-pounders on the parade were rolled outside and unlimbered. Pattee's orders were brief. Hold positions, don't pursue. He knew that if he could keep his outnumbered soldiers from panicking, the hostiles had no chance against the superior fire power of rifles and howitzers.

Along a line that at times stretched for two miles, the Battle of Fort Rice raged for three hours. Expenditure of arrows and ammunition was heavy, so many volleys being fired by the Galvanized Yankees that Captain Adams had to press the reserve cavalry into service as bearers, filling the nose bags of the horses with cartridges for each dash out to the lines.

It was a fight between superb horsemen inspired by Sitting Bull, and dismounted soldiers, who followed Lieutenant-Colonel Pattee's example of calm courage and refused to yield an inch of ground. "When the Indian ponies ran," one soldier said afterward, "they went so fast, they seemed to lie out entirely straight." In the early stages of the fighting, the Sioux rushed at full speed up to the line of battle, some of them standing on the backs of their ponies, firing arrows promiscuously, stabbing and slashing with lances and tomahawks.

As soon as the howitzers began firing, however, these acts of daring became less frequent, and gradually the attackers withdrew, seeking cover behind the hills. As Pattee had known it would, firepower made all the difference. Not even the strong medicine of Sitting Bull could prevail against living demons which flew shrieking from the big guns.

By late morning the Sioux had withdrawn from musket range, and shortly after noon every hostile vanished completely from view of the fort. Pattee ordered roll calls, and casualties were reported. Miraculously only one man was dead, Private James Hoffman, slain by arrow and gunshot wounds in one of the early charges. Private Hufstudler, struck by an arrow in the first fighting, was not expected to live. There were three other serious arrow casualties, and numerous cuts and bruises, which kept Surgeon Yeomans busy until late in the day.

No one could say how severe were the Indian casualties, but undoubtedly they were much heavier than those suffered by the fort's defenders. While the fighting was still in progress, the Sioux had removed all their dead and wounded from the field.

Nor could any one say how many hostiles there were—1,000, 1,500, 2,000—nor when they would come again. Pattee inspected the condition of his howitzers, ordered out a strong guard, and waited.

Around midnight nervous sentinels reported strange sounds outside the stockade, and the officer of the guard ordered a general alarm. Drums rattled, bugles blared, officers shouted commands. In 10 minutes every company was formed, arms at ready. With his usual calmness, Pattee went up to one of the bastion howitzers and told the gunners to throw some fireballs high over the prairie.* In a few moments the plain was illuminated several hundred yards out from the stockade. There was no sign of movement, no sound except the occasional chug of the howitzers and the explosion of shells. Pattee kept the men up until 2:00 A.M., then sent them back to their bunks.

Until the last day of July small bands of hostiles remained in the vicinity of the fort, showing themselves on distant hills, occasionally making half-hearted forays, usually well out of howitzer range. But there was no more fighting. Sitting Bull's medicine undoubtedly had told him that the time was not right for rubbing the white soldiers out of Dakota.

One can but conjecture, however, what the effects of the Hunkpapa chief's medicine would have been on July 28 had Charles Dimon been in command at Fort Rice. With his usual impetuosity, Dimon very likely would have pursued the Sioux as he had been trained to pursue Confederates. In that case, Sitting Bull would not have had to wait for George Armstrong Custer. He would have won his reputation a decade earlier with a massacre of Galvanized Yankees in 1865.

4

Fort Rice in August was hot and dry with blowing dust, and the men of the 1st U.S. Volunteers were talking more and more of their chances of being mustered out before autumn. Captain Adams grew homesick enough to write a poem to his wife:

> In this region, magificent, chilly and gloomy
> I sit all alone like discrowned Montezuma.

. . . .

* A fireball was an oval-shaped canvas sack filled with saltpeter, sulphur, antimony, and a powder-charged shell.

O roll round ye months with a swift revolution
That brings from celibacy glad absolution
The habits of anchorites, others may choose them,
But give me my wife to repose in my bosom![57]

Reflecting the mood of its readers, the *Frontier Scout* asked: "When will deliverance come for the 1st U.S. Volunteer Infantry? How long, O Lord, how long?" An editorial compared Fort Rice to Siberian exile, then grew rhapsodical about Home. "How the heart dilates at the thought of Home. War is over. The soldier grows restless. . . . He feels as if he was in an empty theater after the play is over."

An anonymous contributor from the ranks, a former member of the 18th Mississippi, began a series of reminiscent sketches of his career as a Confederate soldier. He remembered more about the girls than the battles, "the amaranths, water-lilies, and magnolias thrown in beautiful profusion among us." The girls along his route of march were so pretty, he declared, "that to be smacked to death by their tiny hands would alone be the quintessence of human happiness."

He recalled being in Winchester, Virginia, in June 1861, just before the Battle of Manassas. "O never shall I forget the sweet and winning smiles of Winchester's fair daughters. . . . O sweet were the hours we whiled away while basking in the sunshine of their merry and enchanting smiles as their fingers played on the piano-forte, accompanied by their melodious voices, some spirited and martial air. So sweet were they, that now even here amidst the wild, barren, bell-shaped hills of fruitless Dakota . . . I think with unmeasured delight of the fair damsels of Winchester, of the Old Dominion."[58]

Meanwhile hay was ripening in the river bottoms, and extra details marched out to mow and stack it; they harvested 300 tons. After the hay was in, they organized antelope and buffalo hunts, and fresh meat became plentiful. They enjoyed vegetables from the post gardens—green corn, turnips, and radishes. They invented wager games to kill rats, which were overflowing from storerooms to the barracks. They buried Private Hufstudler, who died a lingering death from the arrow wound in his lung. Each night packs of wolves gathered on the hills and howled until dawn, a sign the Indians said of cold moons ahead. But there was no news of mustering out.

On August 25, Sully returned from the North with his expedition; the general had encountered no hostiles, had sought none. He had planned this summer's march as a show of force meant only to maintain the uneasy peace along the Missouri. Surgeon Herrick was welcomed back, and he entertained his old friends of the 1st Regiment with tales of Canadian half-breeds the expedition encountered near Fort Berthold.

"They are half civilized, a mixture of Scotch, English, French, Irish, and Indian blood. . . . They carry their priest with them, families and fiddles, hunting and curing meats and hides by day, dancing and singing at night." Herrick had been surprised to meet a French nobleman among the Canadians, Viscount M. Hyacinthe de Balazic, who gave his address as 10 Cité Antin, Paris. The surgeon was fascinated by the Red River carts used by these hunters— vehicles made entirely of wood with wrappings of rawhide. "The hub is cut from a small tree with an auger hole through it, in which the axle is thrust without grease or other lubricating material, and as they go screeching, squeaking, squalling, and making most unheard of noises over these broad, desolate prairies . . . it does not require very great stretch of imagination to believe that we are listening to the weepings and wailings of the spirits of the damned."[59]

The next day a mail arrived from Fort Sully, and in a matter of minutes after it was opened, the 1st U.S. Volunteers were celebrating the good news they had been hoping for all summer. A Wisconsin regiment was en route from St. Louis to relieve them. As soon as the relief arrived, the 1st would start for Fort Leavenworth to be mustered out of service.

In anticipation of this order, Companies B and K had already been ordered down to Rice from Forts Union and Berthold where they had been stationed since spring. On the last day of August the two companies arrived on the *Big Horn,* and there was a second celebration in honor of their rejoining the regiment.

From now on officers and men of the 1st Regiment awoke to each new day at Fort Rice with happy expectations. They had the word of General Sully that they would not have to endure another winter of death in Dakota. "The men," Sully commented in a letter of September 14, "have such a perfect fear of staying up here another winter I verily believe many of them would die of fear alone should sickness break out among them as it did last winter."[60]

The Fort Rice officers gave the general a farewell dinner, and he departed with his expedition for Iowa winter quarters. A few days later news was received that the 50th Wisconsin had passed Fort Randall en route to Rice.

This cheering news was dampened somewhat by a rumor that Colonel Dimon was aboard the same boat. Why was Dimon returning? Had orders been changed? The soldiers grew apprehensive, and during the tedious days of waiting, 11 men deserted, the first to do so in many months. It was assumed they preferred to seek their chances in the gold fields of Montana, and little effort was made to apprehend them.

Not until October 6 were definite orders received from department headquarters authorizing the 1st U.S. Volunteers to leave Fort Rice. The regiment was to board the same boat bringing the 50th Wisconsin; it was expected to arrive in three or four days.

During this interval Captain Adams and his printers prepared a final issue of the *Frontier Scout*. They filled it with the usual post gossip, news of river traffic, Indian arrivals. "Just at retreat roll call the hills on the west of the fort were covered with Indians. They appeared against the amber of the sky like some caravan of Arabia, crossing the desert. They halted some time, and Major Galpin went out to meet them. They came riding in chanting a wild melody, fifty abreast, and marched like well-disciplined cavalry. Their gay robes and fancy saddles gave them a very unique appearance, and one that we shall not soon forget."

A short story by an unsigned author filled one page, "The Southern Mother's Pride, or the Loyalized Rebel; a Tale of the 1st U.S. Volunteer Infantry." The hero's name was Reginald Ravensworth, and the story was concerned not only with his adventures in the regiment but also his return to the old plantation—a look into the future of any Galvanized Yankee who might have a plantation to which he could return. There was also a poem, "Song of the 1st U.S. Volunteer Infantry":

> We are going home, o'er Missouri's foam
> While the ruddy sunlight flashes
> To the sunny South, from the land of drouth
> For Rebellion's burned to ashes.
>
> From the barren plain, where there is no rain
> From Dakota's Territory
> We are sailing down to village and town
> Of the Union in its glory.

In a final editorial salute to his "boys," Captain Adams wrote: "Our sojourn in the wilderness is nearly over. . . . We have a country redeemed from anarchy, redeemed from disunion, which we can call our own. We have served that country honorably, let us preserve our good name. We are the first fruits of a re-united people. We are a link between the North and the South—let us prove that it is a golden link, and of no baser metal."

Adams dated this last issue ahead to October 12, estimating that would be the day of departure. However, on October 9, Colonel Dimon arrived unexpectedly from Fort Sully, announcing that the 50th Wisconsin would reach Fort Rice the next day. Dimon quickly dispelled all false rumors that orders had been changed. His furlough had ended, and instead of waiting for the regiment at Fort Leavenworth, he had come up to join his men on their happy voyage downriver for mustering out.

A month later the six companies of the 1st arrived at Fort Leavenworth, where they expected to meet again their old comrades of Companies A, F, G, and K, who had spent the past year as garrison troops in Minnesota forts. The latter companies, however, had reached Fort Leavenworth some days earlier, and instead of being mustered out had been reassigned and were already en route to western Kansas to guard a new stage line to Denver (see Chapter X).

For several days, the veterans of Fort Rice waited in the Leavenworth barracks, expecting a similar assignment, but it never came. They were mustered out November 27, 1865.

"Give It Back to the Indians"

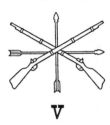

V

The 4th U.S. Volunteer Infantry Regiment was slow in getting started, never achieved its full strength, and from the time it left St. Louis until it reached the upper Missouri was exposed to so many exaggerated rumors of horrors endured by the 1st Regiment that practically every officer and man viewed his prospective service in Dakota with forebodings.

Although the 4th did not reach the West until May 1865, its history began eight months earlier in October 1864 when General Benjamin Butler was authorized to recruit a second regiment at Point Lookout. To command this new regiment, Butler selected another of his protégés, a former officer of the 12th Maine, Lieutenant-Colonel Charles C. G. Thornton, and instructed him to recruit prisoners for "service in the North West."[1]

After several weeks of effort, Thornton was able to organize only six companies, and the quality of these men was not as high as those of the 1st Regiment. In hopes that more prisoners would soon be available for recruiting, Butler transferred the six companies to Norfolk, and there they remained with very little increase in numbers until the war ended. Urgent calls for troops in the West in April 1865 finally led the War Department to issue orders transferring the 4th to General Sully's command in Dakota.

On April 30, Thornton and his six companies traveled by sea to New York, by rail to St. Louis, and on May 10 were aboard the steamboat *Mars*, en route for Sioux City to report to Sully.

Partly because of the quality of the men, partly because of the stories they were hearing of the 1st Regiment's ordeal at Fort Rice, more than one-tenth of the command deserted before the *Mars* reached Sioux City May 28.[2]

Sully reported the situation in a message to Pope that same day. "My cavalry are after them. I wish permission to execute if caught and sentenced. They have but one officer to a company, most of them boys. If officers are not on their way to join them I wish permission to appoint suitable officers. I can then enforce discipline."[3]

With little trouble, Sully's cavalry rounded up large numbers of deserters. The general confined them to the guardhouse, where he allowed them to repent for a few weeks until he had the regiment settled in the upper forts; then he released them to their company commanders.

As Sully planned to start his summer expedition northward in June, he ordered the 4th Regiment to precede him on a slow overland march, which he hoped would put the former Confederates in condition for frontier soldiering. On June 19 the 4th arrived at Fort Sully, which was then garrisoned by companies of the 6th Iowa Cavalry. When General Sully arrived he added the Iowans and three companies of the 4th to his column, and placed Lieutenant-Colonel Thornton in command of Fort Sully, leaving him the remaining three companies of the regiment.

It was probably a mistake on Sully's part to take Companies A, C, and D of the 4th to Fort Rice, where these newcomers to Dakota could hear firsthand reports from the hardbitten soldiers of the 1st. The general, however, had little choice in the matter; he had been instructed to relieve the 1st for mustering out when suitable placements became available, and the only replacements he had at that time were these companies of the 4th. Veterans are always inclined to exaggerate to recruits, and whatever apprehensions the 4th had about military life in Dakota must have been reinforced many times over by what they heard from survivors of the 1st. And then of course came the Battle of Fort Rice on July 28, which was enough to convince the 4th that the Dakota Indians were in earnest about fighting for their land.

Thus it was that early in their period of service on the Missouri, the Galvanized Yankees of the 4th Regiment developed a rather jaundiced view toward their mission. Their philosophy was that "they hadn't lost any Indians." If the Indians wanted to live in such a grim place as Dakota, then why not give it back to them? The 4th had none of the *esprit de corps* of the 1st, and after the regiment was divided among three forts, it soon lost what little sense of cohesion Lieutenant-Colonel Thornton had tried to impart among his men.

Sully sent C Company up to Berthold, an old fur-trading fort built upon a high bluff on the north bank of the river. Formerly the property of Charles Chouteau's American Fur Company, it had been taken over by the U.S. Government after Chouteau was accused of being a Confederate sympathizer. The Northwestern Fur Company, which acquired Chouteau's interests, claimed ownership, but Sully insisted upon keeping troops there to protect the friendly Rees, Gros Ventres, and Mandans from hostiles. The Berthold Indians maintained vegetable gardens around their villages, and soldiers stationed at the fort were able to obtain corn, beans, squash, pumpkins, and potatoes from the squaws who performed most of the work in the fields.

After disembarking from their boat, the men of Company C discovered that their new home was surrounded by numerous dead Indians mounted on scaffolds, the bodies fastened in wooden boxes stamped "U.S. Army Subs. Dept.," "Hospital Dept.," "Q.M. Dept.," "Ordnance Dept.," and "American Fur Company." The fort was as gloomy as its surroundings—ancient log houses squared off inside a stockade. Living quarters consisted of long, low, poorly ventilated barracks. There was no mess room. For each meal the men lined up, entered the dingy kitchen, and carried the rations to their barracks, eating on their bunks.[4]

Fortunately the company was commanded by one of the regiment's best captains, Adams Bassett, who proudly recorded on arrival that Company C was stationed at Fort Berthold "on the Missouri River some 2000 miles from its mouth."[5] The company also had a first-rate surgeon, 22-year-old Washington Matthews. Matthews had been sent out to Dakota from Rock Island Prison, where he had attended many of the Confederates who joined the 2nd and 3rd U.S. Volunteers. He knew all the strengths and weaknesses of Galvanized Yankees. In spite of his cramped quarters, Dr. Matthews maintained one of the best hospitals on the Missouri. While at Berthold he mastered the languages of the Mandans and Rees, and in later years of service became an outstanding military surgeon and a famed anthropologist.

Bassett and Matthews kept their men busy and in fair health through a year of dreary routines. After cold weather came, drill and target practice were abandoned and never resumed. The men were occupied mostly with cutting and hauling wood across the river in order to keep from freezing in their dank quarters. They had no Indians to fight, but kept up a continuous and unsuccessful war against bedbugs and fleas.

When General Delos B. Sacket arrived to inspect the post in the spring of 1866, he reported Company C as "the best I have inspected belonging to the 4th U.S. Volunteers."[6]

Less fortunate were the other companies. Late in the autumn, Lieutenant-Colonel Thornton and A, B, and D Companies were sent down to Fort Randall, with Thornton as post commander. E and F remained at Fort Sully, and after the 50th Wisconsin arrived at Fort Rice, Lieutenant-Colonel Pattee transferred to Sully as post commander.

As both companies at Fort Sully were understrength, they were commanded by lieutenants—Leopold Parker and William Vose. Before the winter ended, the contrast in appearance and attitudes of the soldiers of E and F were striking, reflecting sharp differences in leadership abilities.

Lieutenant Parker gave his men rigid inspections, insisting that uniforms be tidy and that arms and accoutrements be kept in good order. He permitted no slackness of discipline, and dealt out immediate punishments for infractions of regulations. Because of his coal-black hair and beard, his piercing black eyes, and the black pipe which he smoked almost constantly, his men called him "Black" Parker. Some may have feared him; all respected him. (Leopold Parker was to serve the army for more than 30 years, much of the time with Mackenzie's Raiders.)

Lieutenant Vose, on the other hand, was an indifferent officer, allowing his men to appear in dirty, ragged uniforms, their hair unkempt. Part of his command was mounted, but these men gave little attention to the care of their horses, allowed their carbines to become rusty, and performed their duties in an unmilitary manner.

Although the post commander, Pattee, was an excellent frontier Indian fighter, he disliked garrison duty, and his own casual dress and disregard for military ceremony set a poor example for soldiers who had no fighting to do.

Fort Sully was a depressing place to be, located almost a mile from the river, with not a stick of wood, a bush, or a blade of grass within two miles. The well water was so alkaline that no one could drink it, and river water had to be hauled laboriously up the slope from the Missouri. The only available wood was on an island, and details were always busy cutting and hauling. Winter rains dripped mud into the quarters; the rotting rafters were beginning to collapse. Blizzards whistled through cracks in warped cotton-wood-slab walls, and snow drifted in upon the bunks. Bedbugs and fleas invaded barracks, defying all efforts to keep them out. Then the rats came, so many that uniforms had to be locked into sheet-iron boxes to keep them from being gnawed to bits.

By midwinter grain and hay for horses and cattle became so scarce that Pattee ordered the cattle driven across the frozen river to an island where they could forage on brush and trees. An unexpected early thaw swept away the fort's only flatboat, and there was no way to obtain wood until a replacement could be nailed together from scraps. Meanwhile the flooding river inundated the island, almost drowning the cattle before they could be taken off on the flimsy boat.

In March 1866 a smallpox outbreak brought more misery to Fort Sully, but Surgeon L. F. Russell quickly isolated his patients in one building. He forbade any one to go near it, or any of the hospital attendants to leave it, and soon had the epidemic under control.[7]

During the last weeks of winter the men lived on a diet of wormy bacon and weevily beans, and then at last came May and the first supply boat. In that same month, General Sacket arrived on his inspection tour. "The only structure I saw in and around Fort Sully of the least value," he reported, "was the flagstaff, and it was only a tolerable one." Sacket approved of only one officer, Lieutenant Parker. He was shocked when John Pattee asked to be excused from accompanying him on the inspection tour. Pattee said he had no uniform to wear. "His dress while about the garrison is shirt-sleeves," Sacket wrote, "a citizen's pants and moccasins. Pattee may be a most excellent man, but he certainly has not the first element of a soldier in his composition."[8]

More than 100 miles farther south at Randall, conditions were not much better. In addition to his three infantry companies, Lieutenant-Colonel Thornton had a detachment of 7th Iowa Cavalry. The cavalrymen were supposed to carry mail and perform other mounted duties, but they had only two or three serviceable horses.

A few weeks after Thornton assumed command at Fort Randall, he wrote a rather obsequious letter to General Butler in which he stated that Randall was the "largest and pleasantest post in the district." While this may have been true, relatively, Thornton failed to mention that winds were constantly blowing alkali dust into eyes, ears, and noses, that the water was unpotable, that the rotting cottonwood quarters were almost uninhabitable and so infested with biting insects and rodents that the soldiers preferred to sleep out-of-doors, except in the bitterest weather. Thornton of course was trying to impress Butler, the purpose of the letter being to gain the general's support in securing another command after the 4th was mustered out.[9]

For lack of stimulus, Thornton gradually lost all enthusiasm for his assignment, and but for the cheerful efficiency of Surgeon S. P. Yeomans—who had served at Fort Rice during the previous summer—conditions at Randall probably would have degenerated more rapidly than they did.

As it was, by the time General Sacket reached Randall on his 1866 inspection tour, regular drill had been suspended and the men were allowed to report for duty in shaggy hair and beards and dirty uniforms. "Unsoldierly in the extreme," Sacket noted, and then related an account of a visit to Lieutenant-Colonel Thornton's quarters. "Two bugs dropped from the ceiling upon me. The bedbug is, without doubt, indigenous to the cottonwood tree." The general surely must have voiced the collective opinion of the garrison when he declared emphatically that "Fort Randall should be abandoned."

And the entire regiment no doubt would have endorsed Sacket's summary recommendation: "This Territory of Dakota, north of the Vermilion River, never will be settled by the white man, and it will make a very good and cheap donation on the part of the government to the Indians." The Galvanized Yankees would have put it more forcefully, more succinctly: "Give it back to the Indians!"

In early June 1866, orders went up to Forts Berthold, Sully, and Randall, relieving the 4th U.S. Volunteers from further duties. The six companies were mustered out at Fort Leavenworth as they arrived, between the dates of June 18 and July 2.[10]

They had come to Dakota 10 years too soon. By 1876 the land was booming with settlers. Railroads were spanning its distances, and towns were springing to life across vast rich wheatlands. In splendid new forts along the Missouri, soldiers still served. From Fort Abraham Lincoln, Custer marched to glory. And the Indians were given back only a small corner of the territory "which never will be settled by the white man."

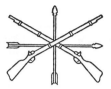

From the Cimarron to the Powder

VI

The spring months of the "bloody year on the Plains" were a difficult time for General Grenville Dodge, commanding the Department of the Missouri. Almost every day brought more reports of Indian troubles, and with these reports came a growing rumble of discontent from the state volunteer troops he was depending upon to bring peace to the Plains. As soon as the Civil War ended, discipline slackened, the men became discontented, desertions increased, regiments threatened mutiny. During the entire summer of 1865 there was a continual mustering out, distribution, and redistribution at the various Western posts.

Dodge informed General Grant that he needed 5,000 men. Grant sent him 10,000, but Dodge complained that "very few of them got into the campaigns from the fact that the troops would no sooner reach Fort Leavenworth than they would protest, claiming that the Civil War was ended and saying they had not enlisted to fight Indians. The Governors of their states, Congressmen and other influential men would bring such pressure to bear that the War Department would order them mustered out. . . . Three regiments of infantry, seven regiments of cavalry and three batteries of artillery that reported to me under order of General Grant were mustered out on the march between Fort Leavenworth and Julesburg."[1]

To restore his thinning ranks, Dodge turned hopefully to the source of his dependable 2nd and 3rd U.S. Volunteers—the military prison camps. Throughout the month of April he dispatched a constant flow of urgent messages to prison commandants at Alton, Chicago, and Columbus. "As soon as companies of 5th U.S. Volunteers are clothed and equipped send them to Fort Leavenworth. . . . How long before they can start? If you have no arms they can draw them here or at Fort Leavenworth. . . . Send those companies of the 5th U.S. Volunteers that are mustered in without delay to Fort Leavenworth. . . . Colonel Maynadier is organizing companies for the regiment at Columbus, Ohio. . . ." One point that Dodge emphasized was that the new regiments of Galvanized Yankees must be enlisted for at least three years.

On May 3, he issued a special order: "Colonel H. E. Maynadier, 5th U.S. Volunteers, with the officers and enlisted men of the regiment now at Alton, Illinois, will proceed by steamer without delay to Fort Leavenworth."[2] As the result of Dodge's energetic prodding, the 5th arrived in Kansas some months before the one-year-men of the 2nd Regiment were mustered out. When companies of the 2nd concentrated around Fort Larned in the summer, companies of the 5th moved out from Leavenworth as replacements along the Santa Fe Trail. On June 1, Colonel Henry E. Maynadier arrived at Fort Riley and established regimental headquarters.

Maynadier undoubtedly was the most experienced and best qualified of the commanders of the six regiments of Galvanized Yankees. After graduating from West Point in 1847, he served with the artillery, infantry, and quartermaster. In 1860 he accompanied General W. F. Raynolds' expedition up the Yellowstone, and held the rank of captain when the Civil War began. A native Virginian who remained loyal to the Union, Maynadier preferred and was given military assignments in the West. As commander of a mortar flotilla during the siege of Island Number Ten in the Mississippi River, he made balloon ascensions to study the effect of bombardments, using the information to correct gun elevations. For this he won a citation for gallantry and meritorious service. Before the end of his duty on the frontier with the 5th Regiment, he would earn another citation for "distinguished service while operating against hostile Indians and accomplishing much toward bringing about peace with hostile tribes."[3]

In recognition of Maynadier's abilities, Dodge placed him in command of the Fort Riley subdistrict which included Salina and

Ellsworth. As he was thus responsible for safety of travel over that section of trail, Maynadier's first action was to organize an efficient escort and courier service which kept the men of Companies E, F, and G out in the field much of the time. He assigned Companies H and I to wagon trains bound for New Mexico. After the Indian troubles along the Little Blue, he ordered Lieutenant Robert Jones to march Company A up the Republican River and establish a camp at Lake Sibley. "Keep constantly on the alert," Maynadier directed, "frequently sending out scouting parties to ascertain if there are any Indians in that section of the country, reporting constantly to these headquarters any movement."

Back in Fort Leavenworth, meanwhile, were two companies of the 5th which Maynadier would not see for more than a year. These were Companies C and D, and for them was reserved a very special mission—one of the most exacting and dangerous expeditions assigned to any Galvanized Yankees. On April 20, General Dodge had ordered the commandant at Fort Leavenworth to "select two companies from 5th U.S. Volunteers, under a major, if present; if not, under best captain, and send them to mouth of Niobrara river, Nebraska Territory, to act as escort to the party that are opening the wagon road from that point west. Fit them out with supplies for three months and transportation to haul them. When necessary they can get additional supplies at any post. I think there are boats serving here that will take them on. They should, if possible, be at post designated by 10th of May."[4]

As there was no major available, Captain George W. Williford was selected as the "best captain." His own Company D and Lieutenant James W. Marshall's Company C would comprise the escort. In the late war, Williford had commanded a company of the 9th Illinois Infantry, and saw almost constant battle action from Shiloh to late 1864, when he was mustered out to recover from wounds and physical exhaustion. By the spring of 1865, Williford was ready for more military service. Dodge liked what he saw in the captain's record, and commissioned him immediately to the 5th U.S. Volunteers.

Companies C and D were recruited at Alton, which was no ordinary prison camp. In addition to the usual Rebel prisoners, Alton's penitentiary walls held suspected spies, political prisoners, and a number of Galvanized Confederates—these latter being former Union soldiers who had been captured by the Confederates, then had taken the oath of allegiance to the Confederacy and joined the Confederate Army only to be recaptured by the Union Army.

Colonel Benjamin Grierson, famed Union cavalry leader, had captured most of these Galvanized Confederates in a single fight at Egypt, Mississippi, December 28, 1864. When Grierson sent them up to Alton prison, he informed the authorities there that the captives had been "recruited from Southern prisons into the rebel service, and most of whom, I believe, were induced to join their ranks from a desire to escape a loathsome confinement. I commend them to the leniency of the Government."[5]

Fortunately for these prisoners, the horrors of Andersonville were fresh in everyone's mind, the nation's press devoting much space to sufferings of Union soldiers in that prison pen. Also, some of the Galvanized Confederates had crept over to the Union lines the night before the fighting and informed the Union officers that their comrades would lay down their arms and surrender at the first attack. The government, therefore, was lenient, as Grierson had recommended it be, and instead of executing these men as traitors, chose to enlist them along with regular Confederate prisoners in Companies C and D of the 5th U.S. Volunteers.

The composition of the two companies was as heterogeneous as a Foreign Legion. By the time they left Leavenworth, the combined units had shaken down to 159 noncommissioned officers and enlisted men—90 being former U.S. soldiers, 69 former Confederate soldiers. Nineteen Irishmen, five Englishmen, four Canadians, three Germans, a Scotchman, Russian, Prussian, Norwegian, Dutchman, and Italian composed the foreign-born group. The Americans came from almost every state—23 Missourians, 15 Tennesseans, 13 New Yorkers, 11 Indianians, 11 Pennsylvanians, 11 Ohioans, eight Kentuckians, five Mississippians, five Virginians, three Georgians, three Marylanders, two each from Illinois, Louisiana, Massachusetts, North Carolina, one each from Alabama, Arkansas, Connecticut, Michigan, New Hampshire, and Rhode Island.

For that era—when most men on earth seldom traveled far from their places of birth—it was a remarkably cosmopolitan group. It also was a perfect model for the irony of civil wars, with their complexities of personal loyalties. Neighbors from Tennessee, Kentucky, Missouri, even Indiana, had been on opposite sides. And there were the foreign-born who had been fighting fellow country-men on alien soil.

What were these men before the tragic absurdity of war had taken them out of their normal pursuits? In a time when half the population earned their bread by tilling the soil, it was not surprising that 85 of them were farmers. Ten had been laborers, seven carpenters. There were also seven sailors, two seamen, and a boatman—who were somewhat out of their element on the dry Plains, plodding westward into the wilds of Dakota Territory. The others included five blacksmiths, four bakers, three printers, three teamsters, two clerks, two masons, two miners, a machinist, fisherman, engineer, mechanic, miller, plasterer, goldsmith, butcher, chairmaker, shoemaker, trimmer, merchant, cigarmaker, pattern-maker, sign painter, student.

Their average age was about 24. Privates John McKinney of Kentucky and David Malone of Tennessee were 43, the oldest. John Bunton of Missouri and S. W. Smith of Illinois were 17, the youngest. Compared to their descendants of a century later, they were small men. Only four were as tall as six feet; several measured only five feet, three inches. But they were durable men, determined to survive at all costs, some of them cynical after their war and prison experiences, loyal only to themselves, easy to discipline in time of danger, difficult to handle under the monotony of barracks routine.[6]

On April 30, Captain Williford marched them aboard the steam-boat *Jesse H. Lacy,* and they started up the Missouri on the first leg of their long summer journey. Three days later while the boat was docked at Nebraska City, Sergeant Jack Hale, 20 years old, formerly of the 143rd Pennsylvania Infantry, slipped ashore with six enlisted men; none of them returned. During the next week as the *Jesse Lacy* was chugging its way up to the mouth of the Niobrara, Corporal Martin Buzzard, formerly of the 2nd Pennsylvania Cavalry, and three enlisted men chose to go over the side and were seen no more.

In the second week of May, Williford was camped at the mouth of the Niobrara, awaiting the leader of the wagon-road expedition, James A. Sawyers. He was also wondering where he could obtain wagons and additional supplies for his men, none of whom had an extra pair of shoes or a spare uniform. Thirty civilian teamsters for the Sawyers expedition arrived a few days later, and then at last the leader himself appeared.

Sawyers was an ambitious citizen of Sioux City, eager to open a national road from his hometown to the Montana gold fields. For this purpose he had secured funds from the Interior Department, and was determined that the venture should succeed. Dismayed to find that his escort consisted only of infantrymen, he held up departure until he secured the promise of additional cavalrymen from nearby Yankton.

Early in June, Williford secured 25 wagons and 150 mules from a Sioux City freighter, but was unable to obtain clothing for his men. The mules were young and undersized, too small for drawing heavy wagons, but they were the only ones available. Meanwhile the expedition itself was assembling—engineers, guides, scouts, and five emigrant families who had decided to go West under the protection of the train. Surgeon Henry T. Smith also reported for duty; he would serve as physician for both military and civilian personnel.

During the three weeks delay, two corporals and five enlisted men joined the growing list of deserters from C and D Companies. And then at noon of June 13, Sawyers finally gave the order to move out.

They traveled westward along the south bank of the Niobrara, civilian guides and scouts in advance. Next in order of march was a platoon of Williford's infantrymen with a mounted howitzer; behind them rolled the military wagons, followed by another platoon of Galvanized Yankees. The second section of the train consisted of the expedition's wagons, followed by a third infantry platoon. In the last section were the emigrant families and their wagons, with a rear guard of infantrymen armed with another howitzer. The entire expedition included 53 men in Sawyers' group; about 20 men, women, and children in the emigrant group; and Williford's two companies of soldiers.

Delays were frequent, Sawyers halting the column at stream crossings to improve fords, sometimes to build a bridge. On the first afternoon's march they covered only four miles.

Next day they crossed Verdigris Creek, and sometime during that night, Privates Miles Shay and S. A. Myers decided they had seen enough of the West and deserted. On June 16 the promised cavalry escort joined the train—Lieutenant John R. Wood and 24 men of Company B, 1st Dakota. They reported to Williford, the senior officer, and he assigned them to riding the flanks. That night a thunderstorm stampeded the corraled herd, and the cavalrymen were busy until 7:00 A.M. rounding up strays.

On June 18, the train camped near the Ponca Agency. It was Sunday, but one of the Galvanized Yankees noted in his diary, "the religious element in the whole outfit appears to be dormant, as no chaplain accompanies the expedition."[7]

While most of the other soldiers were dozing the summer afternoon away, Private James Wilson, a 19-year-old New Yorker, and Private Richard Sneath, a 23-year-old Pennsylvanian, slipped out of camp, homesick for the East. These would be the last to desert on the march; the remaining 137 of the original 159 were ready for Montana and the gold fields. Only three of the deserters had been genuine Galvanized Yankees; the other 19 were former Union men who apparently had no use for any army—Union, Confederate, or frontier.

For the next 10 days the march was uneventful; then on June 29, as they neared Snake Creek, Williford's young mules began to give out. To lighten his loads, the captain cached a quantity of pickled pork and fish, and abandoned one wagon.

On July 1, the train spent the morning crossing Snake Creek. By noon the temperature reached 90°. "Next day we broke camp," teamster Albert Holman recorded, "and proceeded due west, hoping to be able to camp on the Running Water [Niobrara] that night, but every mile took us deeper into the sand hills and the sun of a July day pouring its hot rays upon the burning sand, glistened so that we were nearly blinded. By afternoon it was impossible to go but a few rods at a time, it being necessary to stop often and let the cattle breathe and rest, for the poor creatures were suffering so from want of water that their tongues protruded from their mouths, and several of them died. The men, too, were nearly prostrated from the heat, and in fact, some of them were so nearly overcome that they had to be placed in the wagons." The expedition's official thermometer reached 103° at noon, 106° at 2:00 P.M. Two of Williford's men collapsed from sunstroke.

Late on July 3 they were out of the worst of the sand hills, and found a campsite with plenty of grass, wood, and water—a good place to spend the Fourth of July. "We celebrated it, not only as the great national holiday," said Albert Holman, "but as a day of deliverance from the sand hills."[8]

Because of the continuing blasting heat, ceremonies were kept to a minimum. At noon Williford ordered his men bugled out for a short drill and inspection, one of the howitzers fired off a salute, and that was Independence Day on the Niobrara.

When they resumed march on July 5, the weather had moderated, and through most of the following week showers fell during the nights and the mornings were cool. On July 9, scouts sighted the first Indians, presumably hostile. Three days later, the forward guides skirmished with a small war party and captured two ponies from them.

The train was now moving along the fringes of the Black Hills, stronghold of Sioux and Cheyennes. Williford's men had walked the soles off their shoes, their uniforms were becoming threadbare, and they were not yet halfway to the Montana gold fields. Williford recalled Dodge's original order: "When necessary get supplies at any post." The nearest post—and the last post—was Fort Laramie, about 90 miles south. Each mile the train rolled now would take the escort farther from their last source of supplies.

On July 20 while in camp on Hat Creek, Williford informed Sawyers that he had no choice other than to send a detachment to Laramie for supplies; his men could not walk barefooted to Montana. Reluctantly Sawyers agreed. He offered the captain a wagon lighter than the standard army transports, and on the morning of July 21, Lieutenant Daniel Dana and 15 mounted men set out for Laramie. At Sawyers' request, Williford told Dana to make the journey there and back in 10 days. After that time, the train would break camp and resume march. If Dana was delayed, he would have to follow the trail until he overtook the column again.

Dana was in Laramie drawing supplies on July 26. Back in the camp on Hat Creek, Sawyers kept his road builders busy for three or four days grading approaches to a ford. When there was no more work to be done and the men began drifting off to hunt, fish, and prospect for gold, he convinced Williford that it would be advisable to move a few miles each day, to avoid the temptations of idleness.

On July 29 they reached the South Cheyenne, with the Black Hills in view off to the north. To keep his restless men occupied,

Sawyers sent a party on an all-day reconnaissance into the mountains. The weather was hot, in the high nineties again. They remained in camp one more day, waiting hopefully for Lieutenant Dana. Williford ordered signal fires lighted after dark, but there was no sign of the Laramie party.

About ten o'clock on the evening of August 1, after Sawyers had moved his wagons several miles up the Dry Fork of the Cheyenne, the camp was suddenly aroused by a cry of "Indians!" and the firing of several shots. "We were encamped in our usual careless way," said Albert Holman,

with only two men acting as corral guard. The soldiers, with their wagons, camped nearby. Their precautionary measures against danger in an Indian country were equally as lax as ours. . . . In the utter darkness, no one knew what to do and consequently did nothing, for all was commotion and confusion and then finally our attention was arrested by calls in the English language, from way out in the darkness, it was found that our "Indians" proved to be only the Laramie party which had overtaken us and in their exuberant joy of seeing our camp fires, had fired off their guns to which our two guards had responded by shooting directly at the foe as they imagined them to be. The members of the Laramie party narrowly escaped and then they realized the indiscreet method of announcing a safe return, and retreated from range of shot to halloo loudly for cessation of hostilities.

The near fatal incident proved of some value as a lesson to the expedition. "Never afterward in real danger," added Holman, "were we so badly frightened, nor did we ever so completely lose control of ourselves as at this time."[9]

Lieutenant Dana rode in somewhat abashedly to report to Williford that he had left the loaded supply wagon in Laramie with the quartermaster of one of General Connor's columns which would be marching north in a few days. The young lieutenant had been advised not to travel into the Powder River country with a loaded wagon guarded by only 15 men; it would offer too tempting a target for hostiles swarming in the wake of Connor's invasion, which was then in progress.

The barefooted men of Companies C and D accepted the disappointing news more philosophically than James Sawyers, who foresaw another irritating delay. From this day on, relations between Sawyers and Williford grew more and more strained. The captain insisted that he could not march his men without shoes; he would send Lieutenant Thomas Stull with some of the Dakota cavalrymen down to Old Woman's Fork to meet the supply column as it came up from Laramie.

When Sawyers angrily charged that Williford's mismanagement was costing him a delay of two weeks, the captain reminded him that the real delay had been at the mouth of the Niobrara when the escort was kept waiting almost a month while the road-building party was assembling.

Again the expedition resumed its short daily marches while a mounted detachment hurried south to meet the promised supply wagon. Lieutenant Stull and his cavalrymen waited at Old Woman's Fork until their assigned time ran out, then returned empty-handed to rejoin the train on August 9.

For the next three days, Sawyers' scouts and engineers floundered about the arid hilly country, suffering water shortages and pestered by cacti and rattlesnakes, searching for a route around Pumpkin Buttes to Powder River. On Sunday, August 13, they could take no day of rest because their water was gone. They moved out across a dry gulch, halting at noon without forming a corral. Some of the drivers unhitched their horses and turned them out on a grass slope.

A mile below the slope was a clump of trees, and 19-year-old Nat Hedges, thirsting for a drink, rode down to see if there might not be a water hole there. The boy had scarcely entered the thicket when a dozen shots rattled across the stillness of the day. At the same time the yipping wolf-like war cries of Cheyennes startled the nooning soldiers and road builders to their feet. "By the time every man had a gun in his hand, out rode fifty naked, red devils making for the horses. . . . Fire was instantly opened up. . . . The red men succeeded in stampeding the ponies, getting all but eight . . . withdrew a short distance from us and were dancing and yelling as only Indians can."[10]

No effort was made to pursue. Except for the 25 Dakotans, Williford had no mounted men. Roll calls of soldiers and civilians were hastily taken, and it was discovered that one man was missing, Nat Hedges. A volunteer party marched down to the thicket and found him dead, seven arrows in his chest, a bullet hole in his face, his skull bare from scalping. "He was a young man who had charge of the private freight train that accompanied the expedition," Sawyers wrote in his journal that day, "of much promise, being a genial and pleasant companion, and of very correct habits; his loss cast a gloom over the camp not soon dispelled."[11]

They placed Hedges' body in a wagon, redistributed the diminished teams, and traveled steadily until 9:00 P.M., corraling in darkness. The scouts reported Indian signs everywhere, and few men slept that night as they lay on their rifles beside the wagons.

When the sun rose on August 14, there was no evidence of hostiles, but every member of the party knew they were near, waiting for another opportunity to strike. The Indians struck before noon, the alert escort driving them away with steady volleys from their Springfields. Late in the day, young Hedges was buried in a coffin made from wagon boards; one of the women with the emigrant group furnished a winding sheet and a pillow.

In his journal entry for August 15, Sawyers noted: "Fine morning. The bluffs around at sunrise were covered with Indians to the number of 500 to 600, and fighting was commenced by their charging down over the plain and shooting into the corral."[12]

This would be the day when the division of authority between Williford and Sawyers would bring the train near to disaster. For eight weeks the two men had operated independently, Williford as commander of the military escort, Sawyers as commander of the civilians. Except for the friction over the Laramie expedition, they had kept out of each other's way.

But now that the train was surrounded by several hundred hostiles bent upon its destruction, Williford felt that he must take absolute command of its defense. He was confident that with his two howitzers he could stand off a long siege and eventually wear out the patience of the attackers.

Not everyone was so confident, however. Water was in short supply, and there was no forage for the animals. "A feeling of forlorn hopelessness seemed to spread over our entire party," said Albert Holman, "not from fear that the Indians could take us, but because of our inability to proceed, or to cope with and drive them away. . . . On the two highest hills, one north and one south, were gathered large numbers of Indians and from each group came the most hideous noises. They blew blasts from cavalry bugles, of which they had come into possession, danced, yelled, and taunted us in a most aggravating manner. They proved to be the Cheyenne Indians. Some few of them could speak enough English to call us all the vile names imaginable, very profane language to embellish their sentences."[13]

About noon the Cheyennes suddenly stopped their maneuvering and put up a white flag. Williford was skeptical of their good faith, but Sawyers was eager to bring the fight to an end so that he could start his wagons moving again. After some delay the captain reluctantly agreed to a parley in an open space between the corral and one of the wooded hills.

When Williford and Sawyers rode out of the corral with a small escort, they were surprised to see that the Cheyenne leader coming to meet them was wearing the blue uniform of a staff officer of the United States Army. A few moments later he was introducing himself in perfect English. He was George Bent, half-breed son of William Bent of Bent's Fort. At his side was his brother, Charles Bent.

In a way, the Bent boys were galvanized soldiers themselves. When they were in their late teens their father sent them to an academy in St. Louis, but before they completed their educations the Civil War began. As most of their white friends were pro-Southern, the Bents joined the Confederate Army. They marched off to Mississippi, were captured, then released to the custody of their father on their promise to remain in the West. Instead of becoming Galvanized Yankees, the brothers chose to be Galvanized Cheyennes, and late in 1864 drifted off to join their mother's people on Sand Creek.

They were there when Chivington massacred the village. Both survived, and swore eternal revenge upon their father's people for what had been done to the Cheyennes: *a little girl about six years old with a white flag on a stick; she had not proceeded but a few steps when she was shot and killed . . . one squaw cut open with an unborn child . . . White Antelope with the privates cut off . . . a soldier said he was going to make a tobacco-pouch out of them . . . a squaw whose privates had been cut out . . . a little girl about five years of age who had been hid in the sand, two soldiers discovered her, drew their pistols and shot her and then pulled her out of the sand by the arm . . . infants in arms killed with their mothers. . . .*[14]

George Bent had fought Chivington's soldiers fiercely; he was wounded, but escaped, and not long afterward he and Charley joined the Cheyenne dog-soldiers in their revenge war against all the bluecoat soldiers in the West. The brothers renounced the white blood of their father, let their hair grow to their shoulders, and somewhere along the way George had come into possession of the staff officer's uniform which he wore so arrogantly as he rode under the truce flag to meet James Sawyers and Captain Williford.

The Bents wanted to know why soldiers had come to kill Indians in the Powder River country. Williford replied that his soldiers had come to kill no one; they were escorting some white men who were building a road to Montana. The half-breed professed surprise. If he had known the party was peaceful, he said, he would not have attacked it. He added slyly that he could stop the fighting if the white men would give him supplies to distribute among the warriors—gunpowder, shot and caps, bacon, sugar, coffee, flour, and tobacco.

No, Williford replied coldly. If the Cheyennes wanted to fight, his soldiers would endeavor to satisfy them. If the Cheyennes wanted peace, they could go in peace, but he would not buy peace with presents.

Sawyers disagreed. He granted that no ammunition should be given the Indians, but what harm was there in giving them food and tobacco if they would let the train go on unmolested? Williford remained opposed. What guarantee was there the Cheyennes would keep their word? With full bellies, the warriors could keep the train surrounded; if they grew hungry they would soon go away to hunt. The two men argued bitterly, Sawyers insisting that he had the right to do what he pleased with his supplies.

In the end Williford had to admit that his orders gave him no authority to stop Sawyers from making an agreement with Bent's Cheyennes, but he wanted it on record that he was opposed to bribing the hostiles. He relinquished the parleying to Sawyers.

George Bent drove a hard bargain. After a long harangue, Sawyers delivered a full wagonload—about 3,000 pounds—of flour, sugar, coffee, and tobacco to the truce site.

As a considerable number of Cheyennes came off the hills to carry away the goods, Williford sent out an equal number of soldiers to keep order. According to one of the enlisted men, the captain also granted permission for his shoeless soldiers to barter for moccasins.[15] In a few minutes the two groups were mingled, milling around the wagon. Some of the warriors flashed rolls of greenbacks—the Bent brothers had taught them the value of paper money—offering as much as $25 for a single charge of powder. Taunts were exchanged; some of the Indians quarreled among themselves over division of the spoils. A melee followed, and shots were fired; two or three soldiers were slightly injured by wild flying bullets. It was a dangerous moment, but George Bent took his Cheyennes away before open fighting could start again.

The day was almost gone, and a short time later at retreat roll call, two of the Dakota cavalrymen were reported missing. Williford immediately sent out a search party, and just over a low knoll a few yards from where the melee had broken out around the truce wagon, they found the arrow-filled body of Private Anthony Nelson pinioned to the ground with a sharp-pointed pole. Until darkness fell they searched for Private John Suse, a Mexican, but he was never found or heard from again. "It was believed by his comrades that he had deserted to the enemy, as it was seen during the armistice that he had found an old chum and countryman among them."[16]

August 16 dawned with no Indians in view, and the train rolled out early. To Sawyers' great disgust, Williford insisted on extraordinary precautions, slowing the speed of travel. Williford's vigilance paid off late in the day, when a party of Indians drove in the pickets and made a dash at the herd; the soldiers beat them off and not an animal was lost.

Some time during that same day, the captain advised Sawyers that he could not take his ragged, shoeless soldiers much farther. Sawyers' reaction was to accuse Williford of cowardice; he noted scathingly in his journal: "Our escort commander began to grow faint-hearted, and all the officers except Lieutenant Marshall [D Company] were clamorous for the abandonment of the expedition and proceeding to Laramie as fast as possible."[17]

For the next two or three days, the Sawyers expedition was virtually lost, with hostile Indians hovering on its rear and flanks. In his journal, Sawyers claimed all credit for saving the train, belittling and damning Captain Williford for lack of cooperation. But according to General Dodge, to whom Williford reported, it was the captain who saved the expedition. "Captain Williford went simply as an escort to the party, and had no control whatever over it, and exercised none until he was obliged to do so in order to save his command, in which, by his superior ability and skillful management, he succeeded. General Connor sent word to Colonel

Sawyers . . . not to attempt to penetrate the country he was making for, as it was impracticable. No attention was paid, however, to General Connor's advice, or to that of all experienced guides who were consulted. The party pushed on, got into the Bad Lands on Powder River, and was there extricated and taken to Fort Connor by Captain Williford."[18]

In his own report, Williford briefly mentioned finding the trail of Connor's expedition on August 22. "On the 23rd our command was found to be only fifteen miles from Fort Connor, and received orders from General Connor to report with the detachment to that post for duty."[19]

Since Lieutenant Dana's departure from Laramie in July, the outside world had heard nothing of the expedition. "News from Sawyers' wagon route party has just come in," one of Dodge's staff officers wrote from Laramie on September 1. "They turned up on Powder River. They were lost for a month. The troops were in good health, but nearly naked."[20]

As there was no supply of shoes and clothing at Fort Connor, Dodge ordered Williford and his two companies relieved from further escort duty, replacing them with a detachment of cavalry from the base camp at the fort, and the Sawyers expedition continued on toward Montana.

In late August 1865, Fort Connor (which would soon be renamed Fort Reno) was only a few days old. The commander to whom Williford reported was Colonel J. H. Kidd of the 6th Michigan Cavalry, and the first duty assigned the U.S. Volunteers was construction work on the stockade and quartermaster building.

On September 8, General Dodge arrived on an inspection tour and heard the story of the Sawyers expedition directly from Williford. When the general asked the captain what he thought of the value of Sawyers' road, Williford replied sardonically: "It would be a good route if one half of the hills were inverted and dumped into the ravines."[21] Before Dodge left the fort, he showed his confidence in Williford by naming him post commander to replace Colonel Kidd, who would soon be marching south with his cavalry for mustering out.

And so, Companies C and D of the 5th U.S. Volunteers settled down for a long winter on Powder River. Williford inherited from the Connor expedition an experienced quartermaster, Captain W. H. Tubbs, and also acquired five mountain howitzers and a

12-pounder field howitzer, enough artillery to fend off any Indian attacks. He selected Lieutenant Marshall of D Company as his adjutant, Lieutenant Dana to command D Company, Lieutenant Stull to command C Company. Late in September when the withdrawing Connor expedition marched past the fort en route for Laramie, Captain E. W. Nash and his mounted Omaha Scouts were detached and assigned to Williford for cavalry service.*

Completion of barracks and storerooms before winter was the main objective, and the men worked long hours, cutting and hauling cottonwood logs from the Powder bottoms. Except for picket and guard details, military routines were virtually suspended during this critical period. Indians showed themselves frequently, but kept out of rifle range. The only fatality during October was an accident, Sergeant Peter Lee of Missouri "killed by the discharge of his own gun." By the end of the month, the men were in earthen-roofed barracks, and Williford issued his first Rules for the Post:

Reveille (roll call)	at Daylight
Breakfast Call	7:30 A.M.
Surgeon's Call	8:00 A.M.
Dinner Call	12:00 Noon
Retreat (roll call)	Sunset
Tattoo (roll call)	8:00 P.M.
Taps	8:30 P.M.

Bugle calls will be sounded five minutes before each of the above.

After tattoo no soldier will be allowed to leave his quarters without permission from his Company Commander and all loud talking will cease.

After taps the men will retire, talking will cease, and lights be extinguished.[22]

On November 6, some of Captain Nash's Winnebagoes took the horse herd four miles out of camp to graze. A band of Arapahos made a sudden strike, killed and mutilated one of the herders, stampeded a few horses. After that the Winnebagoes' vigilance became so strict and so deadly that hostiles in the area soon learned to keep their distance from the fort on Powder River.

The days grew shorter and colder. For lack of other recreation, gambling in the barracks became prevalent, and Williford felt compelled to issue a general order on November 15:

---

* Earlier in the year, Nash's 70 scouts had served with the 3rd U.S. Volunteers at Fort Kearney. The Omaha Scouts were mostly Winnebagoes, recruited from a tribe uprooted from their Minnesota homeland and who had been living on the Omaha reservation.

It having come to the knowledge of the Commanding Officer that the habit of gambling is freely indulged in by both non-commissioned officers and soldiers of this command and that in many instances pecuniary embarrassment has resulted therefrom, be it ordered that hereafter any non-commissioned officer or soldier convicted of gambling, shall if a non-commissioned officer be reduced to the ranks; if a soldier, be confined at hard labor, during the pleasure of the Commanding Officer; and all monies staked shall be confiscated and appropriated for the benefit and comfort of sick soldiers in hospital.[23]

As Williford must have foreseen, gambling did not stop, but he had to make an example of at least one man. The luckless one was Corporal Michael Kelly, 21 years old, former carpenter's apprentice of New York City. Mike Kelly's loss was 22-year-old Private John Ferguson's gain; Ferguson, a Canadian, won the lost stripes.

Blankets and winter uniforms, bacon and flour, came up the trail from Fort Laramie just in time for the first big snows, and from then on—through December and January—life became dreary and monotonous for the men in the stockade. Soon after New Year's Day, 1866, Williford received notification that the fort's name had been changed from Connor to Reno.

By February half the command was ill. Lack of vegetables in their diet brought on scurvy, and pulmonary diseases spread rapidly through the poorly ventilated barracks. Williford himself was ailing, with swellings in his face and legs which Surgeon Smith diagnosed as dropsy.

Within a few days of each other four men died in the hospital. Ephraim McClure, 26 years old, Missouri, farmer—of scurvy. M. K. Liggett, 20 years old, Mississippi, farmer—consumption. Thomas Kelly, 40 years old, Florida, seaman—typhoid fever. James Holt, 30 years old, Kentucky, farmer—congestion of lungs.

It seemed that spring would never come to the lonely post on the Powder. The weekly mail couriers from Fort Laramie—which was now headquarters for Maynadier's 5th Regiment—brought no news of their relief, and the men began to wonder if they might not be marooned at Fort Reno for the two years remaining of their enlistments. Early in March, Captain Tubbs and Lieutenant Marshall received transfer orders, leaving Williford short of officers. On March 24, Sergeant Owen Healy and a detail of 11 men took advantage of the situation and deserted. Several days later seven of them were picked up near Laramie and confined in the guardhouse there. On April 9, Sergeant Michael Enright of

Limerick, Ireland, and four men also departed without leave, and were not seen again.

By this time Williford was so seriously ill that Surgeon Smith recommended his transfer to a post with more adequate medical facilities. The captain left in an ambulance, could go no farther than Fort Caspar (formerly Platte Bridge Station). He died there April 29.

During May, Captain Nash acted as post commander. The first emigrant trains of the season bound for Montana came up the Bozeman Road from Laramie, and also from Laramie came new rumors and new orders. The rumors cheered the U.S. Volunteers; regular army troops were said to be en route from Fort Kearney to relieve them. The orders were for Captain Nash. He was to start marching his Omaha Scouts to Laramie for mustering out.

Lieutenant Dana, acting commander in place of Nash, also received new orders. He was to assign detachments of his men as escorts to wagon trains going to Montana. Some of the men assigned to these trains never returned to Fort Reno; also some of those at Reno who were not assigned to wagon trains decided to go to Montana on their own. At last, on June 28, Colonel Henry B. Carrington and a battalion of the 18th Infantry arrived with orders relieving the Galvanized Yankees from further duty at Fort Reno.[24]

"They were certainly glad to be relieved," one of Carrington's enlisted men recorded. "They had had no trouble with the Indians but had found the place far from being desirable as a permanent place of residence."[25]

Before departing from Fort Reno, the men of C and D Companies celebrated their second Fourth of July in the service of the United States Army. A review, patriotic orations, firing of salutes from the fort's field howitzer, completed the formal ceremonies. In the afternoon some of the boys imbided too freely of "tanglefoot" whiskey obtained from a portable road ranche in the vicinity. One fatal accident marred the holiday: Private Joseph M. Thompson, 25 years old, former carpenter from Davis County, Kentucky. The report of his demise was devoid of details: "Killed accidentally by discharge of a revolver by a soldier of the 18th Infantry."[26] Private Thompson had been a Rebel; the 18th Infantry was made up partly of green troops who were awkward at handling their weapons, partly of Union veterans who had marched through Georgia with Sherman. Perhaps it was an accident, perhaps not.

On July 6, Lieutenants Dana and Stull led their companies out of Reno for Fort Laramie, where they were to report to Colonel Maynadier for further assignment. Of the 137 men who had made the long march up the Niobrara, 104 still endured, ready for whatever the future held in store for them.

While C and D Companies were having their adventures along the Niobrara and the Powder, far to the south their comrades in other companies of the 5th U.S. Volunteers were also seeing a great deal of the Plains and the Rockies. From May through July of 1865, Company A remained camped at Lake Sibley on the Republican River; B, E, and F performed escort duties out of Salina and Fort Riley, G, K, and I moved farther west on the Santa Fe Trail, and a detachment of H Company traveled all the way to New Mexico with an army supply train.

In August, when Patrick Connor started north on the Powder River Expedition, he asked General Dodge for soldiers to replace those he was taking from stations along the Platte. As Indian hostilities in Kansas appeared to be coming to an end, Dodge decided to transfer Maynadier's regiment to Connor's district of the Plains. "I have ordered the 5th U.S., about 800 strong, to you," he informed Connor on August 15. "This with the 6th U.S. and what California infantry you have, is all the infantry we will have this winter . . . that portion of the 5th U.S. Volunteers with Colonel Sawyers' wagon party is ordered to report to you when he discharges them. They must be up in that country some place."[27]

Maynadier marched from Fort Riley on August 26 with six companies. H and I would come up later from Fort Dodge and Camp Wyncoop. On September 9, the 5th arrived at Fort Kearney, meeting for the first time Galvanized Yankees from the 3rd and 6th Regiments. After drawing rations, they traveled on west to Julesburg and camped for several days outside Fort Sedgwick, headquarters for the 3rd U.S. Volunteers, who were awaiting orders for mustering out. The boys of the 5th would have been pleased to move into the adobe barracks recently constructed by the 3rd, but orders from General Connor dispersed the regiment by companies to other stations. "The regimental staff will be held in readiness to move to Fort Laramie," Maynadier announced on September 20.[28] The colonel had been chosen to command that important post in Connor's absence. As events turned out, Maynadier would remain at Laramie throughout the crucial Indian peace negotiations of 1866, and was there when Colonel Carrington marched north to fortify the Montana Road.

Maynadier took only his headquarters staff with him to Laramie, sending Companies A, E, and F to Fort Halleck, G and K to Camp Wardwell, and B to Denver for quartermaster duties. In the spring of 1866, A and E were moved back east to Fort Kearney to replace Carrington's 18th Infantry battalion which had been there most of the winter. H, I, and K marched south to Fort Lyon, Colorado, the center of new Indian disturbances on the far western section of the Santa Fe Trail. G went to Fort McPherson. F replaced a company of State volunteers at Fort Collins, a key station on the Overland Stage Line north of Denver. Near Fort Collins ran a clear mountain stream, Cache La Poudre, and off to the west the Rockies "seemed to hang in the sky like clouds." Duties were light until late in the summer when half the company was detached and sent up the trail to help build a new post, Fort John Buford (later renamed Fort Sanders).[29]

The men of B Company meanwhile were out of the action, living like peacetime soldiers in Denver, where they worked in a quartermaster base, loading wagons and dispatching trains to all the army posts in the area. Their commander was Captain Thomas McDougall, a thoroughgoing officer who permitted no slackness among his men.*

When soldier details from other 5th Regiment companies came into Denver for supplies, they must have been envious indeed of B Company. In their off-duty hours, the B Company men had a booming town of 5,000 people for a playground. No dugouts, no sod houses, but solid brick buildings—stores, churches, a school, newspaper office, and the U.S. Mint. Gambling houses were wide-open until the small hours of the morning. "There was always a brass band in front and a string band in rear, so if one wanted to dance, he could select a partner of almost any nationality, dance a step, step up to the bar, pay two bits for cigars, drinks or both and expend his balance on any game known to the profession."[30] The B Company soldiers may occasionally have regretted being out of the action along the Platte line, but they had spent enough time

---

* After leaving the U.S. Volunteers, McDougall joined the 7th Cavalry, and was in command of the pack train at the Little Big Horn.

doing escort duty in Kansas to know they were the luckiest Galvanized Yankees of the entire 5th Regiment.

"It is impossible to conceive of a more dreary waste than this whole road is," General William T. Sherman wrote from Julesburg on August 24, 1866, "without tree or bush, grass thin, and the Platte running over its wide, shallow bottom with its rapid current; no game or birds; nothing but the long dusty road, with its occasional ox team, and the everlasting line of telegraph poles. Oh, for the pine forests of the South, or anything to hide the endless view."[31]

Sherman never liked the Plains country. He saw it first at its worst time of the year—the end of summer—when the roadway was a mass of powdery stifling dust and all color was faded from the land. He had come out on an inspection tour of military posts, and one of the decisions he had to make was how soon the 5th U.S. Volunteers could be mustered out. The regiment still had more than a year of enlistment service remaining, but Sherman was determined to replace all Volunteers with regular Army troops as soon as possible.

He was not impressed by the new post at Julesburg—Fort Sedgwick, with its adobe walls and earthen roofs and floors. "As lumber can be had . . . I have instructed that good roofs and floors be made. . . . There are a few of the 5th U.S. Volunteers left behind, their companies being out escorting surveying parties for the Pacific Railroad."

During that summer the shining rails of the Union Pacific had moved a mile a day up the Platte Valley, signaling the eventual end of Ben Holladay's Overland Stage Line, as well as much of the freight wagon traffic. "Fort Kearney is no longer of any military use, so far as danger is concerned," Sherman said,

and now that the railroad is passing it in sight, but with a miserable, dangerous and unbridgeable river between, it must be retained for the sake of its houses and the protection of wagon travel, all of which still lies to the south side of the river. General Wessells commands, and has two companies at Kearney, and two companies higher up at Plum Creek, where General Pope thought there was or might be danger from some roving bands of Indians that hunt buffalo to the south, over about the Republican. All these companies belong to the 5th U.S. Volunteers (rebel) that I want to muster out, and must muster out somehow this fall; but I will defer making an emphatic order till I look up the line farther, and see where other troops are to come from to protect the stock and property. At Kearney the buildings are fast rotting down, and two of the largest were in such degree of tumbling that General Wessells had to pull them down, and I will probably use it to shelter some horses this winter, and next year let it go to the prairie dogs. Same of the temporary station at Plum Creek.[32]

The two companies Sherman found at Kearney were A and E. Those at Plum Creek were the survivors of the late Captain Williford's Niobrara adventure, the men of C and D, who had been sent there from Laramie after their march from Fort Reno in July.

Commander at Plum Creek was Captain George M. Bailey, D Company, and his first problem was to halt an excess of drinking among his men. "In the future under no circumstances," he ordered on August 7, "will Ranchemen, Storekeepers or Sutlers be allowed to sell Spirituous, Ale or Malt Liquors to any troops of this command or to troops passing here. . . . Any offender will suffer loss of all Liquors in his possession. The Post Sutler will be allowed to sell Ale to the men in modest quantities."[33]

Undoubtedly the main reason for the drinking problem at Plum Creek was monotony—almost as bad as at Fort Reno, where liquor seldom had been obtainable. The expected Indian raids—which had been so frequent the previous summer when the 3rd Regiment was patrolling the Platte line—did not materialize. Aside from occasional uneventful escort rides over the dusty trail to Fort Kearney or Midway Station, there was little to break the deadly routine.

One bright event was the arrival of the wife of Corporal Patrick Welch. Her cheerful Irish face was a tonic; the men smartened up their appearances, and in no time at all Mrs. Welch was the unofficial camp laundress. It was a black day at Plum Creek when Corporal Welch was transferred to Fort Kearney. As soon as Captain Bailey realized the importance of having a woman in camp he urged General Wessells to return the corporal and his wife. "Corporal Welch does a great many things," Bailey explained, "and then I need the services of his wife as Laundress, there being none at the Post and the men do not get time to do their washing."

Late in August all of Company C was transferred to Fort Kearney, and again Bailey discovered he had lost another indispensable corporal, Russian-born Nicholas Korber, the post's only bugler. "Respectfully request he may be returned as soon as possible, as I have no one who can blow calls until he returns."[34]

In September there were rumors of hostile Indians lurking in the vicinity of Plum Creek. Bailey led out a scouting party, found no sign of Indians, reported to Wessells that the Indian scare had been invented by one Daniel Truman, who had a contract to bring out 4,000 railroad ties from Spring Creek for the Pacific Railroad. "I am of the opinion that Truman wants soldiers sent down with his wagons simply to save the hire of laborers." Bailey may not have been aware that timbered places on the Plains were usually Indian burial sites, and that peaceful tribes sometimes became violently hostile when these sacred places were logged. Before the matter could be settled, however, Company D received unexpected orders to move to Fort Kearney.

One of the last pieces of military business in the regiment's records concerned the case of Private George Washington Johnson, awaiting dishonorable discharge. An itinerant printer before the war, Johnson had joined a Confederate artillery, was captured by Sherman's army at Resaca, Georgia, and after becoming a Galvanized Yankee was made first sergeant of Company D. He was soon reduced to the ranks for drunkenness; he reformed briefly and was promoted to corporal, then reduced again on the same charge. He was of a sort found in all armies—the amiable, purposeless soldier, growing old in the service, fearful of the responsibilities of civilian life.

Private Johnson's poignant plea for mercy is presented as he wrote it:

Guard House, Fort Kearney
Sept. 18, 1866.

Gen'l H. W. Wessells,
   Hon. Sir
Circumstances alter cases, but never more so than in mine.
The Specification was false which charged me with being drunk two or three days. When I was only two days out of the Guard House, and on the morning of the second day, Capt. Bailey told me I was sober. I was hastened from work, or should have plead differently.
I served the U.S. in the 3d Infantry in Mexico under Scott, in the taking of Vera Cruz, Cero Gorda (where I was wounded,) Contrerass, Cheribusco (again wounded) three weeks after to Molin de del Ray and Chepultipec, from thence to the gates and taking of the city.
During the entire time I was Orderly Sergt of D Company. Returned and was discharged as such.
I am well aware of the position in which I am placed. I was driven to accept it, and am therefore compelled to adopt it. I am somewhat ad-

vanced in years. If you could consistently allow me to return to duty in any of the companies at this post, I will guarantee you will find me a soldier.

Obediently yours,
Geo. Wash. Johnson.

At the end of Johnson's letter was an indorsement by his commanding officer: "Private Johnson could be a splendid soldier if it were not that he always gets drunk when he has an opportunity of doing so."[35]

Regardless of how General Wessells may have decided the case, Private Johnson's army career was soon to be ended. A few days later orders came to muster out the entire 5th Regiment. Sherman had made up his mind that he could return the Galvanized Yankees to civilian life before winter. He reached that decision on the last day of September at Fort Lyon, where Companies H, I, and K of the 5th were garrisoned in unfloored, flat-roofed buildings subject to flooding. "Anybody looking through them," he commented, "can see full reasons for the desertions that have prevailed so much of late years. The quicker we get our garrisons and military establishments down to the regular army, the quicker we will secure economy."[36]

And so the 5th U.S. Volunteer Infantry Regiment came to the end of its service. Regimental headquarters and the seven companies along the Platte assembled at Fort Kearney and were discharged there by General Wessells on October 11. Companies H, I, and K had to wait a few weeks longer at Fort Lyon, then marched to Leavenworth, and were the last companies of Galvanized Yankees to be mustered out, November 11, 1866.*

* See Chapter XI for a more complete account of Company H.

From Camp Douglas

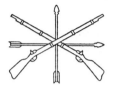

to Camp Douglas

1

"I'm going away, I'm going away, but I'm coming back if I go
ten thousand miles."

So went one of the popular songs of the Confederacy, and no soldiers deserved more to sing it than the men of the 6th U.S. Volunteer Infantry. The 6th was the last regiment of Galvanized Yankees
to be organized, following the 5th out of Fort Leavenworth by
about two weeks. While the 5th was replacing the 2nd Regiment
along the relatively peaceful Santa Fe route, the 6th moved up to
busy Fort Kearney to take over from the 3rd.

It was June 1865—two months after Appomattox—when the
6th reached the Plains country. State Volunteers who had been
guarding the Overland Mail and Pacific Telegraph lines were
being mustered out in haste to avoid mass mutinies and desertions.
In a matter of a few days, the 10 companies of the 6th found
themselves almost the sole guardians of 2,200 miles of telegraph
lines and stage roads.[1] From June until the spring of 1866, they
marched and countermarched over considerable areas of Nebraska,
Wyoming, Colorado, Kansas, and Utah, until some of them truly
must have traveled the 10,000 miles of their war song.

Six of the 10 companies of the 6th were recruited at Camp
Douglas, Illinois, two at Camp Chase, Ohio, two at Camp Morton,
Indiana. Regimental commander was Colonel Carroll H. Potter,
a young man who had received two years of training at West Point

before the Civil War. During the war, he won the rank of brevet
brigadier-general for meritorious service. To assist him in directing
the widely scattered operations of the 6th, Potter was assigned an
experienced lieutenant-colonel, William Willard Smith, who had
served during the war on General H. W. Halleck's staff in
Washington.

Unlike most other Galvanized Yankee commanders, Potter joined
his regiment before it left Camp Douglas for the West. Companies
organized at the Indiana and Ohio prison camps were transferred
to Camp Douglas, and in early April marched out to Camp Fry,
a training center which had been established in 1864 on the out-
skirts of Chicago for the Hundred Days' volunteers. There Colonel
Potter took command, treating the former prisoners as if they were
raw recruits, insisting that they be taught first how to stand at
attention and salute. Drums and bugles awakened the men each
morning and directed their daily round of activities, which included several hours of drill. Potter held frequent inspections, required coats and blouses to be always buttoned, saw that the grounds
were regularly policed and barracks kept neat and clean. He permitted no laxness among his company officers, held them responsible for all infractions committed by their men, and excused no
absences from any roll calls.[2]

Within two or three weeks, the 6th was a smart regiment, and
doubtless would have compared well with Colonel Dimon's highly
polished 1st. On April 27 General Dodge put in an urgent plea
for immediate transfer of the 6th for service on the Plains, and
two weeks later the regiment moved by rail from Chicago to Fort
Leavenworth, arriving there May 11. It was the first regiment of
Galvanized Yankees to reach the frontier intact and at full strength
—organized, trained, and officered. "I have the honor," Colonel
Potter proudly notified General Dodge, "to report to you for orders
. . . the 6th U.S. Volunteers, 950 enlisted men and 26 commissioned officers present for duty."[3]

Less than 24 hours later, Dodge ordered the Leavenworth commandant to "get the 6th U.S. Volunteers off for Kearney and
Julesburg as soon as possible." On May 14th the regiment marched,
and on May 31 arrived at Fort Kearney.[4]

During the early days of June, companies moved out rapidly
to relieve the hard-pressed 3rd Regiment at unguarded posts along
mail and telegraph routes. E Company took over the 80-mile route

east of Fort Kearney between Muddy Creek and Big Sandy. A, F, and G marched to Fort Laramie; H and I to Camp Rankin at Julesburg; K to Post Cottonwood; B farther west to Camp Wardwell; C and D remained at Kearney.

In recognition of Colonel Potter's experience, General Connor placed him in command of the South Sub-District, which included the Overland Mail Route between Forts Collins and Halleck, a section then suffering severe Indian raids almost daily. Conditions had become so bad, in fact, that the stage company was threatening to suspend service unless more military protection was guaranteed.

Potter transferred his headquarters to Denver on June 14, and began an energetic effort to make the route secure. By shifting his troops, he was able to restore armed escorts for each coach between all stations. "Instruct your non-commissioned officers," he directed post commanders, "to have two of the escort ride about 100 yards in advance of the coach; the other two post in the rear, keeping careful lookout for Indians or any signs of them."[5]

On June 27, Potter informed General Connor at Fort Laramie that he anticipated no more trouble along his section of the route. "I took through with me from Fort Halleck, with a government team, all the mails that were there, one entire wagon load, and returned from Sulphur Springs with a mail of nearly same amount returning east . . . had no trouble with Indians . . . if stock tenders from the Overland Mail Company will watch the stock while feeding on grass in the day, and keep them near the station, and at night place them in a corral, which I have ordered to be guarded every night, they will not lose so much of their stock."[6]

Three days later, Potter's optimism suffered a blow when he received reports of new Indian raids. One soldier was killed at Rock Creek, 60 head of stock lost. The raiders drove away all stock at Willow Springs. On July 4, the hostiles mocked the national holiday by striking at a strongly guarded herd outside Fort Halleck, sweeping away 14 of the best stage horses. That same day at Fort Collins, two companies of Kansas Volunteer cavalrymen almost mutinied when one of the 6th Regiment's staff officers, Major Henry Norton, ordered them up the road to pursue the raiders.

While Potter was endeavoring to clear up trouble west of Denver, the Indians began raiding along his line to the east. On July 6, Lieutenant-Colonel Smith reported from Camp Wardwell that wagon trains near Wisconsin Ranch were under attack, and that he was in urgent need of mounted men to retaliate. Potter was able to scrape together only a paymaster's escort of one sergeant and nine men, dispatching them to Smith with a cheery message to "do the best you can with the force you have. Whip the Indians if possible."[7]

In his reports to General Connor of these developments, Potter hinted that he needed more troops. Had he known how little military use was being made of his three Galvanized Yankee companies at Connor's Laramie headquarters, Potter might have been more demanding.

At Laramie, Companies A, F, and G spent most of July performing the same dreary garrison routines they had endured at Camp Fry. They listened to lectures on how to salute, what the proper uniform consisted of, and the necessity for maintaining a respectful attitude toward officers. Occasionally they escorted a logging train, or served on sawmill details[8]—all this at a time when their regimental commander down in Colorado Territory was desperate for men with arms to fight off Indian raids.

Connor probably was unaware of this misuse of the Galvanized Yankees. In July he was occupied in organizing his expedition to Powder River, and no doubt viewed Potter's stagecoach troubles as only a temporary annoyance which would soon be cleared up by a thrust at the Indians in their Powder River villages. As the time for the campaign neared, Connor began collecting all available mounted troops. He was especially eager to use his own California cavalry which he had left at Camp Douglas—a post overlooking Salt Lake City. After some deliberation, Connor decided to order the Californians from Utah to the Powder, and replace them with Galvanized Yankees.

Consequently, instead of sending more troops to Potter in Colorado, Connor advised the commander of the 6th U.S. Volunteers to transfer headquarters to Utah, taking along three companies of his regiment. At about the same time (early August) Connor ordered Companies H and I from Nebraska to replace cavalry along the harassed telegraph line west of Fort Laramie.

Potter selected Companies A, D, and F for the transfer to Camp Douglas, and then because he could not immediately relinquish his duties in Colorado, he assigned Lieutenant-Colonel Smith responsibility for marching the battalion over the arduous route to Utah.

One can easily imagine the shock to these former Confederates, who had survived the ordeal of Camp Douglas prison, when they suddenly learned they were under orders for a march to Camp Douglas. A majority of the soldiers of the 6th Regiment were Southern mountaineers, keen-witted but unblessed with a knowledge of much reading, writing, or geography, and then as now, army orders were never very explicit by the time they sifted down to the level of the enlisted men. It is quite probable that when the three companies marched out of Laramie for Utah many of these men believed they were on their way to the same wretched Camp Douglas from which they had been emancipated by taking the oath of allegiance. Even for those who knew it was a different place, the very name *Camp Douglas* created an image so repugnant they scarcely could have been blamed for not wanting to go there. As events proved, the two Camp Douglases were as different as hell and heaven. In 1865 the luckiest soldiers in the West were those privileged to be assigned to Camp Douglas, Utah.

Nevertheless, during the month's march across Wyoming and Utah, 35 of the 275 men of the three-company battalion deserted. Lieutenant-Colonel Smith ordered company commanders to compile descriptive lists, and he sent these out to military posts where passing wagon trains were inspected. Teamsters and wagonmasters were warned not to give any men on the lists employment, clothing, or money, nor aid them in any way in escaping to the States or the mining districts of the Territories.[9] Very few of these deserters, however, were ever apprehended.

On September 30, Smith's battalion of Galvanized Yankees reached Fort Bridger. They trailed on across the yellow-aspened Wasatch Mountains, passed through Echo Canyon, and at 2:30 P.M., October 9, marched into Camp Douglas, Utah, to receive the surprise of their lives.

Instead of the gray, rotting, cottonwood-log barracks they had known back on the Plains, they saw a military post built of white-painted frame lumber and solid stone. Out from the entrance marched the entire post command, headed by a brass band playing a stirring martial air. For the first and probably only time in the short history of the Galvanized Yankees, they were welcomed by a formal review of Union soldiers—men from California and Nevada.

While this astonishing performance was underway, the new-comers had a chance to observe their surroundings. Camp Douglas lay on a bench of land above Salt Lake City, with a breath-taking view of a long valley. Within the panorama lay the coppery ex-panse of Great Salt Lake, snow-capped mountains reaching to the clouds, and the town itself. From the heights, Salt Lake City re-sembled a fairyland village, with broad regular streets, handsome buildings, and gardens of trees and flowers. On the fringes were farmhouses with livestock grazing in green fields.

Camp Douglas seemed but a smaller model of this City of the Saints. Close-clipped grass carpeted a spacious parade ground. The post's streets were of smooth hard-packed gravel, and along the gutters ran perpetual streams of sparkling water diverted from a creek foaming down from the mountains.

This pleasant garrison was only three years old, having been founded by General Patrick Connor himself in October 1862. Ostensibly it was located as a base to protect the Overland Stage and Pacific Telegraph lines from Indians, but its principal objec-tive was to intimidate the Mormons, whose loyalties to the Union were in doubt and under aggravation as a result of recent anti-polygamy laws passed by Congress. Most Mormons also took a neutral attitude toward the Civil War, a position which by 1862 was considered by ardent Unionists as equivalent to disloyalty.

As highest-ranking representative of the United States military authority in Utah, Connor went about his duties with deadly seriousness. His viewpoint was typical of contemporary anti-Mormon sentiment among Westerners, some of whom regarded polygamy with even more distaste than secessionism. "General Connor never jokes," his friends said of him. One of his first acts was to mount a cannon on the Camp Douglas esplanade, facing down on Brigham Young's tabernacle.[10]

Relations between the military post and Salt Lake City's Mormon leaders were decidedly cool, of course, and when Connor began replacing temporary buildings with stone from nearby quarries, Brigham Young protested vigorously. The post was taking on too permanent an appearance to suit him. He demanded that the U.S. government abolish Camp Douglas, claiming that it was taking up valuable space within the corporate limits of Salt Lake City, that it was a constant annoyance to the inhabitants, and that its cavalry horses fouled the city's water supply.

The government, however, supported Connor, who continued to develop and improve the post, until it became virtually a luxury garrison. Among other cultural activities, he sponsored a camp newspaper, the *Union Vedette*, and ordered a special building erected to house its office and plant. The paper, "published by officers and enlisted men of the California and Nevada Volunteers," carried on a continuous feud with the Mormon press, one of its regular features being an editorial attacking polygamy or Mormonism.[11]

When the Galvanized Yankees arrived in October 1865 they knew nothing of this long-standing contention between military and church. Yet already they had become involved in the quarrel. Even before they set foot in Utah Territory, a Mormon elder referred to them publicly as "thieving, rascally 'galvanized' ruffians from the plains . . . intent on coming into Zion to sojourn here."[12]

The *Vedette* editor, recalling that Mormons had described California and Nevada soldiers as "rag-tag and bob-tail of society," was quick to reply: "Why is it that soldiers are so feared in Utah? Are the virgin daughters of Zion in danger from them?" He described the Galvanized Yankees as "a splendid looking lot of men; and have the reputation of being intelligent, disciplined and thorough soldiers . . . staunch and tough as Trojans. . . . The men who have fought bravely against the Union cause have shaken hands with the men who have fought for it, and 'the Union one and undivided' is again their joint motto. It is the policy of the truly brave to forget past differences, which the soldiers of Camp Douglas, who are now a mixed class, will endeavor to do. During the war they fought on opposite sides, but they are all members of the one *family of Americans*."

Evidently Mormons were not the only local critics of the 6th U.S. Volunteers, for later on the *Vedette* found it necessary to mention the "quiet, gentlemanly conduct of our Volunteers" in the face of some verbal abuse from citizens at Camp Douglas. "If these people take it upon themselves to provoke our Volunteers causelessly," the editor warned, "they will perhaps at sometime or other be made to know better."[13]

The Galvanized Yankees meanwhile were enjoying the unexpected comforts and delights of Camp Douglas. On weekday evenings they could attend a camp theater where the "best stock company in Utah" presented dramas, pieces, and parts. Admission for enlisted men was 50c. Between acts they could patronize the theater's refreshment stand, which served "pies, cakes, candies, fruits, choice temperance drinks, and sugars, all at reasonable prices." On Saturday evenings free dances were held in Camp Douglas Hall, girls from Salt Lake coming up for some "merry tripping of the 'light fantastic.'" Other amenities of the camp included a fruit wagon which rolled past the barracks every day, the services of an expert bootmaker, a dentist, and two "artists in the razor and hair brush business" who operated a "fashionable hair dressing salon" next to the theater.

In addition to all this, a jolly temperance group addressed a special invitation to "our comrades of the 6th U.S. Volunteers": "There is a flourishing lodge of Good Templars in Camp, in which we would like to have you enrolled as members. The regular meetings are held every Tuesday evening. Send in your names and help the noble cause which so many of the Californians and Nevadans are advocating. Do not be backward, you will be welcome. You will pass many pleasant evenings in their hall, besides being benefitted by becoming temperate soldiers."[14] Among the advantages of becoming a Good Templar, it was rumored, was the availability of young lady guests who "went around and kissed the boys to see if they have not been breaking the pledge." No records are available of the number of Galvanized Yankees who took the pledge and joined up.

After a few days of adjustment to this dreamlike existence, the boys of the 6th were given passes into town during their off-duty hours. A four-horse, double-decker omnibus ran regularly between camp and Salt Lake City, which was then a bustling capital of 20,000. Here they discovered liquor and cigar stores, bakeries, ice cream resorts, book and newspaper dealers, luxurious merchandise emporiums, and numerous saloons.

The Salt Lake Theater offered performances by well-known actors and actresses from the East. "Miss Alexander made a dashing appearance in unmentionables," the *Vedette* reported on October 16, "gallant and gallous, gay and festive." She was acting in *Our American Cousin,* a play which everyone wanted to see because President Lincoln had been enjoying it at the time of his assassination. For music lovers, there was still another theater, the Academy of Music, designed for perfect acoustics and furnished with elaborate stage scenery and a handsomely painted drop curtain. Admission prices ranged from $1.00 to $10.

The men in the ranks soon discovered one big flaw in their wonderful new world: the constant drain upon their pocketbooks. Opportunities to spend were numerous and seductive; their $16 per month simply would not stretch from payday to payday.

Life at Camp Douglas was by no means a continual round of easy-going enjoyments. Routine post duties became more onerous as many of the Californians and Nevadans, including the post commander, departed on long furloughs, leaving Lieutenant-Colonel Smith in command. Smith allowed no slackness. He held rigid inspections, sent the men out on wood-cutting details, and drilled them hard twice a day. That they soon mastered the requirements for "show" troops is indicated in a *Vedette* report of a Sunday dress parade held for local citizens: "The men of the 6th Infantry 'done' the manual of arms in a manner that pronounces them 'none behind' their comrades of the other battalions of this post."[15]

On October 26, after ending his campaign in the Powder River country, General Connor returned to Camp Douglas to resume command. He was received as a conquering hero. The 6th U.S. Volunteers and the post band paraded. A grand banquet was held for him, with all officers and "a majority of the (so-called) Gentiles of Salt Lake City in attendance. . . . The pleasant social company proceeded at once to do justice to the viands with which the tables groaned, and after which corks flew, champagne flowed, and toasts and responses became the order of the hour."[16] In addition to numerous ovations for the general, toasts were offered to the *Union Vedette,* the "brave Irish soldiers of our armies," and to the 6th U.S. Volunteers.

Saturday night, October 28, Camp Douglas Hall was elaborately decorated for a "sociale dance" in Connor's honor. The camp theater's stock company also scheduled a special performance of *Othello.* Connor, however, made only a brief appearance at the dance, avoided Shakespeare, and slipped away to Salt Lake to see the beautiful Julia Dean Hayne in *Peg Woffington.*

On the last day of the month, for the first time since their enlistment in the U.S. Army, the boys of the 6th were paid promptly and in full. In their affluent surroundings, they needed every dime received. All day, heavy snows fell on the nearby mountains, but the Galvanized Yankees felt no uneasiness over the approaching winter. They considered themselves lucky enough to feel sorry for those of their comrades who during the march across Wyoming had so foolishly deserted and missed out on all the pleasures and comforts of Camp Douglas, Utah.

2

During late autumn and early winter, the other seven companies of the 6th Regiment were engaged in much more rugged service in the hostile Indian country farther east. In November, Company B transferred from Camp Wardwell, Colorado, to Post Alkali, Nebraska, to patrol the dangerous run between Plum Creek and Julesburg. Companies C and E moved west from Fort Kearney to Plum Creek, Cottonwood, and Julesburg; then in December a detachment of E Company rushed back east to Columbus, Nebraska, to guard a pontoon bridge across Loup River. Company G remained at Fort Laramie. In September, H and I took over the heavily raided telegraph line west of Laramie, H being responsible for the section between Fort Caspar and Sweetwater, I the section between Laramie and Caspar. K remained at Cottonwood (Fort McPherson).[17]

In January 1866, an expedition marched out of Fort McPherson to punish hostiles who had been cutting telegraph wires and raiding ranches. K Company was involved in the campaign, which was under command of Lieutenant-Colonel Richard H. Brown of the 12th Missouri Cavalry. One of the more interesting, although not always accurate, accounts of this comic-opera affair was recorded by John Nelson, who was serving as a civilian scout.

The greater portion of the troops, Nelson said, "were Southern prisoners," who seemed to be more loyal to Colonel Brown than most of his Missourians. "The expedition was a hopeless one in many respects, and above all it ought never to have been sent out at that time of the year." After an unproductive 85-mile march in bitter weather, the colonel announced one evening his intention of making a long detour via the Platte, instead of returning directly to Fort McPherson. This caused much dissatisfaction among officers and men. "It was not surprising, therefore, that at mess, the same night, after the Colonel had left, a resolution was passed by the officers that the order should not be carried out."

According to Nelson, one of the lieutenants took drastic measures against his unpopular commander. The lieutenant buried a 10-pound shell in the sand under Colonel Brown's bed, and laid a train of powder to where it could be ignited outside the tent. "But the fuse did not ignite, and the next morning the Colonel was just as frisky as ever." He ordered tents struck, wagons loaded, and gave the command to march. "Much to the Colonel's surprise, however, the troops refused to move. The artillery, who were Southerners, were ordered to fire upon the men; but the entire command was of one opinion, and the artillerists were told that if they fired a shot they would be seized and blown to pieces from the mouths of their own guns. They thought better of it, and caved in."

The informal Colonel Brown yielded to the mutiny and started his column back directly for Fort McPherson. Along the way, Indians raided the livestock herd one night, but after a few minutes of fighting were driven off. "This was the only honor and glory that fell to Colonel Brown's lot during the campaign," Nelson reported. "We arrived at the fort the following day, and that evening I saw Colonel Brown receive a sound thrashing from a private soldier whom he had given permission to 'lick' him if he could. That seemed to wipe out all the grievances of the command, and the men received the Colonel back into their good graces again. This incident will show the military relations at that time existing between officers and men."[18]

It is difficult to assess the reliability of John Nelson's story. All or a part of K Company, 6th U.S. Volunteers, accompanied this expedition, but the records reveal nothing of any mutiny, nor do they indicate whether K Company troops were the artillerists named in the incident.

At Fort Laramie during these same weeks, the boys of Company G witnessed the unfolding of a poignant frontier episode involving a friendly Brulé chief, Spotted Tail, his daughter Fleet Foot, and Colonel Maynadier of the 5th U.S. Volunteers.

After Colonel Maynadier established headquarters for the 5th at Laramie and then assumed command of the post in the autumn of 1865, he spent much of his time laying the groundwork for the Laramie peace council of 1866. Maynadier's efforts to win the cooperation of Red Cloud and Spotted Tail met with little success, however, until March 1866, when word came down from Powder River that Spotted Tail's beautiful daughter, Fleet Foot, was dying

and that her father was bringing her to Fort Laramie to spend her
last days.

The Galvanized Yankees had never heard of Fleet Foot, but
they soon learned a good deal about her from a Virginia-born
frontiersman, Charley Elston. Elston had lived with the Sioux for
years, but in his old age came in to Laramie to spend the winters.
He liked to loaf around the sutler's store, talking with off-duty
soldiers. Elston said:

Fleet Foot won't marry an Indian. Her father's been offered two hundred
ponies for her, but won't sell her. She says she won't marry anybody but
a "capitan," and that idea sort of pleases her father for more reasons
than one. Among the Indians every officer, big or little, with shoulder-
straps is a capitan. With her it's a capitan or nobody. She always carries
a knife, and is as strong as a mule. One day a Blackfoot soldier running
with her father's band tried to carry her off, but she fought and cut him
almost to pieces—like to have killed him; tickled her father nearly to
death. The young bucks seem to think a good deal of her, but are all
afraid to tackle her. The squaws all know about her idea of marrying
a capitan; they think her head is level, but don't believe she will ever
make it.

She tried to learn to read and speak English once of a captured boy,
but the boy escaped before she got it. She carries around with her a little
bit of a red book, with a gold cross printed on it, that General Harney
gave her mother many years ago. She's got it wrapped up in a parfleche.
You ought to hear her talk when she is mad. She is a holy terror. She
tells the Indians they are fools for not living in houses, and making peace
with the whites.

One time she and Spotted Tail went in to Jack Morrow's ranch and
made a visit. She was treated in fine style, and ate a bushel of candy and
sardines, but her father was insulted by some drunken fellow and went
away boiling mad. When he got home to his tepee he said he never would
go around any more where there were white men, except to kill them.
She and her father got into a regular quarrel over it, and she pulled out
her knife and began cutting herself across the arms and ribs, and in a
minute she was bleeding in about forty places, and said that if he didn't
say different she was going to kill herself. Spotted Tail knocked her down
cold as a wedge, and had her cuts fixed up by the squaws with pine pitch;
and when she came to he promised her that she could go, whenever he
did, to see the whites. And she went; you bet she went. She would dress
just like a buck and carry a gun. White men would not know the difference.
They can't get *her* to tan buckskin, or gather buffalo cherries. No, sir.

In 1864, Fleet Foot saw Fort Laramie for the first time when
Spotted Tail brought her with him for the peace council of that
year. Captain Eugene Ware, 7th Iowa Cavalry, described her as
being tall and well dressed, about 18 or 20 years old. "During the

daytime she came to the sutler's store and sat on a bench outside, near the door, watching as if she were living on the sights she saw. She was particularly fond of witnessing guard-mount in the morning and dress-parade in the evening. . . . Among ourselves we called her 'the princess.' She was looking, always looking, as if she were feeding upon what she saw."[19]

When Maynadier learned in early March 1866 that Fleet Foot had died en route to Laramie, he immediately dispatched runners to meet the grieving Spotted Tail and inform him of the sincere sympathies of the fort's commander, and offering to honor the chief's daughter with a military funeral. In addition, Maynadier sent an ambulance with an escort of G Company, 6th U.S. Volunteers.

A few miles north of the fort, the Galvanized Yankees met Spotted Tail, his principal warriors, and a number of lamenting squaws. It was a cold sleety day, the landscape bleak, streams locked in ice, brown hills patched with snow. None of the Volunteers had ever seen Fleet Foot in life, yet they had been caught up in her legend, and being sentimental Southerners most of them were moved by the sight of the cortege. The dead girl had been wrapped in a deerskin, tightly thonged and creosoted with smoke; this crude pall was suspended between her favorite ponies, a pair of white mustangs.

Fleet Foot's body was transferred to the ambulance, her white ponies fastened behind, and the procession continued toward Fort Laramie. When Spotted Tail reached the Platte, Colonel Maynadier turned the entire garrison out to met the Brulé chief. He recorded:

After greeting him, I conducted him to the fort and to my headquarters. I then informed him that the Great Father offered peace to the Indians, and desired them to have it for their own benefit and welfare. That, in two or three months, commissioners would come to treat with them and settle everything on a permanent basis of peace and friendship. I sympathized deeply in his affliction, and felt honored by his confidence in committing to my care the remains of a child whom I knew he loved much. . . .

The chief exhibited deep emotions during my remarks, and tears fell from his eyes, a rare occurrence in an Indian, and for some time he could not speak. After taking my hand he commenced with the following eloquent oration: "This must be a dream for me to be in such a fine room and surrounded by such as you. Have I been asleep during the last four years of hardship and trial and am dreaming that all is to be well

again, or is this real? . . . We think we have been much wronged and are
entitled to compensation for the damage and distress caused by making
so many roads through our country, and driving off and destroying the
buffalo and game. My heart is very sad, and I cannot talk on business;
I will wait and see the counsellors the Great Father will send."

The scene was one of the most impressive I ever saw, and produced
a marked effect upon all the Indians present, and satisfied some who had
never before seemed to believe it, that an Indian had a human heart
to work on and was not a wild animal.[20]

Maynadier ordered his soldiers to erect a scaffold and fashion
a fine coffin. Fleet Foot's white ponies were slain, and their heads
and tails nailed to the scaffold so that "she could ride through the
fair hunting grounds of the skies."

As the sun sank next day, a military funeral procession marched
to the post cemetery behind Fleet Foot's red-blanketed coffin, which
was mounted on an artillery caisson. A 12-pounder howitzer rolled
behind the caisson, followed by G Company of the 6th U.S. Volunteers and other units at Laramie.

Officiating at the funeral was the former chaplain of the 2nd
U.S. Volunteers, Reverend Alpha Wright, who had remained at
Laramie as post chaplain after his regiment was mustered out in
November 1865. Chaplain Wright consulted with Spotted Tail as
to how he wanted services for his daughter conducted.

Spotted Tail gave Chaplain Wright the little book that General Harney
had given her mother many years before. It was a small Episcopal prayer-
book such as was used in the regular army. The mother could not read
it but had kept it as a talisman. Chaplain Wright deposited it in the coffin.
Then Colonel Maynadier stepped forward and deposited a pair of
white kid gauntlet cavalry gloves to keep her hands warm while she
was making the journey. The soldiers formed a large hollow square
within which the Indians formed a large ring around the coffin. Within
the Indian ring and on the four sides of the coffin stood Colonel Maynadier,
Major George O'Brien, Spotted Tail and the Chaplain. The Chaplain at
the foot read the burial service, while Colonel Maynadier and Major
O'Brien made responses. Spotted Tail stood silently at the head looking
into the coffin, grieving. When the services closed, Major O'Brien placed
a crisp one-dollar bill into the coffin so Fleet Foot might buy what she
wanted on the journey. Each of the Indian women came up, one at a
time and talked to Fleet Foot; some of them whispered to her long and
earnestly as if they were by her sending some hopeful message to a lost
child.   Each one put some little remembrance in the coffin; one put a
little looking-glass, another a string of colored beads, another a pine cone
with some sort of an embroidery of sinew in it. Then the lid was fastened
on and the women took the coffin and raised it and placed it on the scaffold.

The Indian men stood mutely and stolidly around looking on, and none of them moved a muscle or tendered any help. A fresh buffalo-skin was laid over the coffin and bound down to the sides of the scaffold with thongs. The scaffold was within the military square, and was also the twelve pound howitzer. The sky was leaden and stormy, and it began to sleet and grow dark. At the word of command the soldiers faced outward and discharged three volleys in rapid succession. They and their visitors then marched back to the post. The howitzer-squad remained, and built a large fire of pine wood, and fired the gun every half-hour all night, through the sleet, until daybreak.[21]

3

During that winter at Camp Douglas, Utah, Companies A, D, and F continued their routine garrison duties. On November 6, Colonel Potter arrived from Denver to establish regimental headquarters. He was duly serenaded by the band, and a week later Connor named him post commander, the general thenceforth devoting his energies to administration of the District of Utah.

Late in November as the result of a shooting quarrel in a Salt Lake "whiskey resort," good relations between the Galvanized Yankees and the Californians suffered a setback. A private of the 6th U.S. Volunteers fired a "fatal shot into the bowels" of a California infantryman. Colonel Potter sent California cavalrymen out in every direction to track down the murderer, but he was not apprehended. The Good Templars at Douglas seized upon the incident as an example of the evils of drinking. "Abstain from the beer or whiskey shop," they warned. "We hope to receive a large access in membership from the 6th U.S. Volunteers. Our temperance roll is open, and we will be pleased to see them come forward and proclaim themselves enemies to King Alcohol."[22]

On November 25, General Connor reviewed his troops, and announced that he was relieving all the Nevadans and two companies of Californians so that they might return to their respective states for mustering out. This left Camp Douglas with a majority of Galvanized Yankees.

Thanksgiving Day was December 7 that year, and the men celebrated quietly, with "Utah trout and Timpanogos turkey" as specialties of the holiday feast. In keeping with the 6th Regiment's new responsibilities, Colonel Potter ordered no liquor served, a decision which he may have regretted a few days later.

On the night of December 19, fire broke out among whiskey

barrels in the commissary warehouse. "The barrels exploded, scattering flame and destruction all around. The liquor flowed along the floors and becoming instantly ignited, the whole interior of the building, as if by magic, was a sheet of flame. . . . The camp was aroused and almost superhuman efforts exerted by Colonel Potter, the officers and men to save the stores and adjoining buildings."[23]

Not a drop of whiskey was salvaged, leaving Camp Douglas as arid as a desert. Considerable quantities of grain, sugar, bacon, and flour were also destroyed or badly damaged. For more than two weeks throughout a dry and sober Christmas and New Year's holiday, the fire smoldered, permeating the air with an aroma of scorched whiskey and grain. The editors of the *Union Vedette* hinted that Mormons had set the fire; the Mormons declared it was the will of Providence. The Good Templars made no public comment.

4

By winter's end almost all state volunteer troops in the West were mustered out. During the hiatus between their departure and the arrival of regular army companies, the Galvanized Yankees were thinly spread between Camp Douglas and Fort Kearney.

Early in April, Company F of the 6th was ordered east from Camp Douglas to garrison Fort Bridger, where Lieutenant-Colonel W. W. Smith had assumed command in January. Virginians in the company found a compatriot there in the person of the post trader, William A. Carter. Judge Carter was tall, spare, flaxen-haired, with white flowing beard and moustache, "a high-toned, intelligent and hospitable Virginia gentleman, universally popular with all who associated with him."[24] He was a sort of Galvanized Yankee, himself, having spent the war years at Fort Bridger making a fortune by trading with Indians.

Those who won the friendship of Judge Carter and were invited into his home must have felt they were back in the Old South. He had collected a fine library and subscribed to all the best papers and magazines. His beautiful daughters, who had been sent East for schooling, entertained the soldiers with music from a piano which had been hauled from New York across the Plains and the Rockies.

Although Fort Bridger lacked the amenities of Camp Douglas,

it was located in an attractive valley, green with cottonwoods and willows, perfumed by wild roses blooming along every creek. For those who liked hunting, game was abundant, deer and elk, and sage hens as large as turkeys. Fishermen could find brook trout in the snow-fed streams. Whiskey was plentiful, especially a cheap variety made locally and known as "Valley Tan." A venerable mountain man, Jack Robertson, who lived at Bridger and frequently regaled the F Company men with tales of his exploits, claimed that he drank Valley Tan instead of water to keep from freezing up in the winter time. "There is no such thing as *bad* whiskey," Robertson declared. "Some is better than others, but I never saw any bad whiskey."[25]

After they grew accustomed to Fort Bridger, the F Company soldiers did not especially miss the pleasures of Camp Douglas and Salt Lake City.

5

In late spring the first regular army units came marching from Fort Kearney, a battalion of the 18th U.S. Infantry to take over Camp Douglas.* Somewhat reluctantly, the 6th's regimental staff and Companies A and D departed from Utah and joined F Company temporarily at Fort Bridger.

Meanwhile B Company rushed 200 miles south (May 1866) from Post Alkali to Fort Wallace, Kansas, to assist in quelling Charley Bent's Cheyennes, who were raiding stagecoaches along the Smoky Hill route. E Company took over the mail run between Julesburg and Laramie and kept official communications moving to the Northern stations.

In June, Company A added 400 to its "ten thousand miles" by making a fast march east to Fort Halleck. This latter post was a rude contrast to Douglas and Bridger. It was a collection of log-and-mud huts under command of a regular Army officer, Major Henry R. Mizner, who had recently arrived with two companies of the 18th U.S. Infantry. Company F of the 5th U.S. Volunteers was already garrisoned there.

* The 18th U.S. was the first regular infantry regiment to take up posts on the Indian frontier following the Civil War. It was under command of Colonel Henry B. Carrington, who established headquarters at Fort Phil Kearny, near which occurred the Fetterman Massacre of December 21, 1866.

Mizner soon let the Galvanized Yankees know that their informal ways would not be tolerated at Fort Halleck. He issued strict regulations concerning care of weapons, limits of the post, and relations between enlisted men and officers. "Such appellations as Doc, Cap, Lieut, Sarge, and the like, not being military will not be tolerated under any considerations."[26]

The men of Company A had scarcely grown accustomed to this post when Mizner received orders to abandon it, march his command 70 miles east to Big Laramie River, and start construction of a new post, to be called Fort John Buford.* The 18th Infantry companies and the U.S. Volunteers celebrated the Fourth of July by marching 23 miles toward their new destination. Again, Major Mizner's orders were stringent:

No man will be permitted to leave the ranks unless sick, when he will be reported by a non-commissioned officer to the Surgeon in rear of the command; no man will be permitted to ride, and none except teamsters to place their arms or accoutrements in the wagons, except by direction of the Surgeon. . . . A detail of one non-commissioned officer and three men in addition with the cook of each company will form the guard for the three company wagons and this detail will not be permitted to leave the train.

The men will wear blouses and their clothing will be neatly packed in knapsacks and will be carried on the wagons. No enlisted man will be permitted to wear on duty any arms but those issued to him by his Company Commander. The rear guard will arrest and disarm all stragglers. No hunting parties will be permitted until the command is encamped. Reveille will be sounded at 4 o'clock A.M. and General at 5 o'clock A.M.[27]

On July 7, they reached the Big Laramie, pitched tents, and immediately began construction of the new fort. After looking over his men, Mizner selected a Galvanized Yankee from A Company, Sergeant William B. Nash, a 30-year-old carpenter of Dyer County, Tennessee, to direct the building work.

Throughout July, Mizner allowed nothing to interfere with the constant timber chopping, hauling, sawing, and hammering. He forbade all gambling, drinking, and the "pleasure riding of government horses." From Denver, he brought in laundresses to do all the washing, fixing prices at $1.00 per dozen items for officers, 75c per dozen items for enlisted men. Flannel sack coats and pants were 25c each, great coats 50c, regardless of rank of the owners.[28]

---

* Soon afterward the name was changed to Fort Sanders. This post was meant to guard the junction of the Denver stage line with the main Overland line to Salt Lake City.

Dissatisfied with construction progress, Mizner asked for more men, and H Company of the 6th was relieved from duty along the upper section of the Pacific Telegraph line. After adding another 225 miles to its marching record, H Company reached Big Laramie August 2.

Colonel Potter's headquarters staff meanwhile was adding 400 miles to its record, marching from Fort Bridger to Fort Sedgwick, where it arrived July 15 to establish final headquarters station for the 6th Regiment. About the same time C Company was relieved from duty at Sedgwick and assigned as escort to an engineer party of the Pacific Railroad operating out of Big Laramie Canyon. "Since last muster," Captain David Ezekiel reported August 31, "the company has marched 476½ miles for the month to the source of Lodgepole Creek and in and over the Black Hills, a spur of the Rocky Mountains—touching the following military posts, viz, Camp Collins, C.T. and Forts John Buford and Laramie, D.T."[29]

Just about the time the scattered companies of the 6th were becoming reconciled to the idea of spending two more years of service in constant marching from post to post, General Sherman appeared on his inspection tour. He arrived at Fort John Buford September 5. "We found Major Mizner there with two companies of the 18th and some detachments of the 6th U.S. Volunteers engaged in building the post. It was real cold, ice forming on the surface of the water and a heavy frost at night."[30]

Next morning, Sherman advised Mizner to start Companies A and H of the 6th to Fort Kearney, where they were to await orders for mustering out. As he moved on across Colorado to Fort Lyon, Sherman made up his mind to return every Galvanized Yankee in the West to civilian life before winter.

In early October, all but one company of the 6th Regiment arrived at Fort Kearney, and they were mustered out there on October 10 and 15. Not until late in the month was the perambulating Company B relieved from duty at Fort Wallace. The soldiers of that outfit completed the "ten thousand miles" of their Civil War song by marching all the way across Kansas to Fort Leavenworth for mustering out on November 3, 1866.

The Incredible Captain Shanks  VIII

John T. Shanks, commander of Company I, 6th U.S. Volunteers, apparently was the only Galvanized Yankee officer who had served with the Confederate Army. A small, dark-skinned, dark-haired, restless Texan in his early thirties, Shanks would have done well in the fifteenth-century Renaissance Italy of the Borgias, or the eighteenth-century London of William Hogarth. He was a proto-type of the clever and unscrupulous adventurers who thrived in the Gilded Age of the late nineteenth century in America. He always kept both eyes open for the main chance.

At the time of his capture in the summer of 1863, Shanks was riding with General John Morgan's Confederate cavalry on the famed raid across Indiana and Ohio. He had entered military service in 1861 at Austin, Texas, as a private. Within six months he had fought in some battles in Arkansas and was promoted to lieutenant. In 1862, because of his civilian experience as book-keeper and clerk, he was transferred to the subsistence department in Tennessee with the rank of captain.

Shanks later commanded a company in the Battle of Stone's River. After most of his men were killed or wounded and his company was consolidated with another, Shanks went to General John Morgan's camp near Murfreesboro in search of a new com-mand. Morgan needed no officers, but he agreed to add Shanks to his scouting company, a group of bravados who had little use for military rank. Among Shanks's associates during this period was Morgan's adjutant, George St. Leger Grenfell, a British soldier-of-fortune.

Morgan's raiders crossed the Ohio River into Indiana, July 8, 1863. Eleven days later, after a hard fight at Buffington Island, Ohio, Shanks along with several hundred other Confederate cavalrymen was taken prisoner. Shanks later claimed that he "represented himself to be a private," but actually he could not have done otherwise, for Morgan had never given him a commission and he wore no insignia of rank.[1]

Shanks and other enlisted men of Morgan's command were first confined in Camp Morton, Indiana; then on August 17 were transferred to Camp Douglas, Chicago. That his comrades thought well of him at the time is indicated by the fact that they elected him their sergeant-major. In this position he acted as spokesman for the Morgan group, and quickly ingratiated himself with the prison commandant, Colonel Benjamin Sweet. Sweet appointed Shanks postmaster for the latter's camp area, and when the clever Texan made it known that he was a first-class penman with several years of clerical experience, the colonel assigned him to headquarters as a clerk.

In a short time, Shanks was earning money on the side by performing clerical chores for Union officers and surgeons at Camp Douglas. These duties led gradually to special privileges. He was allowed to go into Chicago in the company of officers, and occasionally even attended theatrical performances. Shanks was one Civil War prisoner who knew how to gain and enjoy the amenities of life.

During the winter of 1863-64, Colonel Sweet permitted certain charitable persons of Chicago to visit Camp Douglas and present prisoners with warm clothing, blankets, and food. Shanks became well acquainted with a Mrs. Mary Morris, whose husband Judge Buckner Morris was a leader of the Sons of Liberty, a secret society which was plotting to deliver the states of Illinois, Indiana, and Ohio to the Confederacy. As Colonel Sweet would learn eventually, the conspirators' plans included the storming of Camp Douglas and release of prisoners of war there.

Shanks also met "the daughter of a well-known resident of Chicago," and fell in love at first sight. Although the young lady was not disloyal to the Union, she did not object to the Texan's romantic attentions. With his usual facility for enjoying the world's pleasures, John Shanks soon obtained permission to visit his sweetheart, in the company of a prison guard.[2]

Late in the summer of 1864, when President Lincoln gave his approval to plans for recruiting Confederate prisoners into the Union Army for service on the frontier, Shanks recognized a new opportunity for personal advancement. If he could raise his own company, perhaps Colonel Sweet would not only release him from prison but send him on his way westward with an officer's commission. He immediately applied to take the oath of allegiance, and became an earnest converter of Confederates into Galvanized Yankees. But his hopes were dashed, temporarily, when Lincoln limited enlistments to the two regiments organized at Rock Island.[3]

Meanwhile the Sons of Liberty and a group of Confederates in Canada were weaving a dark plot for the capture of Chicago. Camp Douglas was to be the primary target. Eight thousand prisoners there would be freed and given arms so that they could seize the city. The date selected was the day of the national elections, November 8, 1864.

On November 3, a Union secret agent known as Keefe appeared at Camp Douglas and informed Colonel Sweet of the plot. Sweet was not completely surprised. For months he had been aware that something was brewing. Later, he was to tell a writer for the *Atlantic Monthly* that he had suspected many of his prisoners were receiving and sending letters in code. They were "wild, reckless characters," he said, "fonder of a fight than of a dinner, and ready for any enterprise, however desperate, that held out the smallest prospect of freedom."[4]

Sweet, however, was surprised at the immediacy of the date set for action by the conspirators. He had only five days to find the leaders, establish proof of their guilt, and arrest them. As he pondered this pressing problem with Detective Keefe, Sweet suddenly thought of John Shanks. The Texan, he was certain, knew all about the plot, probably knew some of the conspirators, and might be persuaded to help in trapping them. Sweet decided to promise Shanks nothing in return for becoming a spy; yet some sort of reward would be vaguely implied.

The colonel summoned Shanks to his office, introduced him to Keefe, related the bare outline of the conspiracy, and then asked the Texan if he would help track down the schemers. Shanks is quoted as replying: "But I shall betray my friends. Can I do that in honor?"

Although he may have been a rogue, Shanks was also romantic. He asked Sweet's permission to confer for one hour with his sweetheart before making a decision. This was arranged, and the girl is supposed to have advised him: "Do your duty. Blot out your record of treason."[5]

Without further hesitation, Shanks agreed to the proposition. He knew that his spying mission would be extremely dangerous, but even his worst enemies never accused him of cowardice. Colonel Sweet described him at the time as having an "open, resolute face," and said that he had "that rare courage which delights in danger and commits heroic enterprises from pure love of peril."

To protect Shanks from being suspected by his fellow Confederates, Colonel Sweet arranged next day a cloak-and-dagger "escape" in a garbage wagon. The Texan informed his barracks mates that he was planning to escape by hiding in the rear of the wagon; he even asked them to aid him by engaging the driver in conversation while he crawled into the vehicle.

The plan worked perfectly. Sweet posted himself near the exit gate where the wagon was required to halt for guard's inspection. As it slowed to a stop, the commandant waved the guard aside. "Let the driver pass," he said, and the wagon rolled on through the gate.

In the wagon Shanks found a civilian overcoat to cover his Confederate uniform. Following instructions given him by Sweet and Detective Keefe, he went directly to the home of Mrs. Mary Morris. He told her and Judge Morris that he had just escaped from Camp Douglas and asked them for sanctuary. Mrs. Morris gave him $30 for railroad fare to Cincinnati and the address of a sympathizer there who would help him get into Kentucky.

This, however, was not what Shanks had been told to accomplish. His objective was to find other conspirators in Chicago. But he thanked the Morrises and left the house. To his surprise he found Detective Keefe waiting on the sidewalk. Had Keefe not been there, would Shanks have taken the train to Cincinnati? No one can say, of course, but it was clear that Sweet did not trust his spy.

Keefe informed Shanks that they were to go to 90 Washington Street, where Colonel Sweet was waiting for a report. The spy had learned nothing, of course, other than that the Morrises were sincere Confederate sympathizers, and this was already known. After marking each bill which Mary Morris had given him with a "Q," Shanks turned the money over to Sweet.

For two days Shanks was kept undercover while Keefe and Sweet tried desperately to ferret out the conspirators. Then, on November 6, he was given a new assignment. Keefe had observed several suspicious characters going in and out of a hotel, the Richmond House. Shanks was to go there and attempt to establish connections with them. For this mission he was given a suit of civilian clothes, a pair of derringers for protection, and $15 for expenses.

He walked boldly into the lobby, registered as John Thompson of Springfield, Illinois, and casually glanced over the list of guests. Most of the names had that oddly spurious quality of invented identities; then suddenly he recognized a familiar signature: George St. Leger Grenfell, the British soldier-of-fortune, General John Morgan's former adjutant!

Shanks immediately sent a note to Grenfell's room, stating that he was an old friend who would like to see him. Grenfell asked him to come up. Some weeks afterward when he was tried for conspiracy, Grenfell claimed that he did not remember Shanks and had only invited him to his room out of politeness. But the Texan swore that Grenfell received him cordially. "I told him I had just escaped from Camp Douglas," Shanks testified, "and was now in a precarious position. He expressed solicitude in my behalf. . . . He asked if the prisoners in Douglas would cooperate with any assistance from outside; I replied that they would."[6]

Grenfell then said he was not feeling well, the result of a hunting trip to southern Illinois, where he had been stricken with malarial fever. After a few minutes, Shanks excused himself and said he would return later.

About 9:30 that evening when Shanks again called upon Grenfell, he was introduced to two young men who were with the Englishman. They called themselves Fielding and Ware, and after Grenfell informed them that Shanks had just escaped from Camp Douglas, they began discussing plans for attacking the prison. Four simultaneous assaults were to be launched upon each side of the camp, each force to consist of 200 men. Where the 800 recruits were to come from was not made clear, but before the meeting adjourned, Shanks volunteered to lead one of the storming parties.

Shanks then invited Fielding to his room, sent for a bottle of whiskey, and until 1:30 in the morning the two men drank and discussed plans for the capture of Camp Douglas and an attack upon the city of Chicago. Would Shanks have betrayed Sweet and gone through with these wildly impractical schemes of his former comrades-in-arms? Again, no one can say. Certainly Colonel Sweet still did not trust him, for at 3:00 A.M., Detective Keefe and a provost guard burst into the rooms of Grenfell and Shanks, arresting both men. Keefe handcuffed the surprised Texan and hauled him off to close confinement in Camp Douglas. At the same time all over Chicago, other suspected conspirators were being taken into custody.

Whatever Shanks's real intentions may have been, he knew which way to jump for the benefit of John T. Shanks. He realized that he was the only witness against St. Leger Grenfell, and lost no time in letting Colonel Sweet know he would be available to testify against the Englishman.

When he was released to Sweet's custody, Shanks said: "The wonder to me now is how the Colonel could have trusted so much to a Rebel."

"Trusted!" Sweet replied. "Your every step was shadowed from the moment you left this camp till you came back to it in irons."

"Is that true?" Shanks seemed disappointed. "I didn't know it, but I felt it in the air," he admitted.[7]

A few weeks later the celebrated trial of George St. Leger Grenfell and seven other conspirators opened before a military commission in Cincinnati. John Shanks, who had failed to buy a ticket to Cincinnati with the money given him by Mary Morris, traveled there now at government expense. He was the leading witness for the prosecution.

During 10 weeks of testimony, defense lawyers dredged up a vast number of facts about Shanks's past life, dwelling upon his misdeeds in efforts to discredit him as a reputable witness. His father had been a respectable wagonmaker in Nacogdoches, Texas, where Shanks was born in 1832. At the age of 15, the boy began clerking in the county courthouse. As he grew older he worked as bookkeeper and salesman, managed a store, raised livestock. "I have a rancho in Texas," he boasted to the court. Along the way he became acquainted with the great Sam Houston; after Houston was elected governor of Texas in 1859, Shanks was rewarded with a position in the general land office at Austin. Somehow he won a reputation for toughness, and when he was charged with forging a land warrant, a gunman had to be employed to arrest him. The arrest was made aboard a ferryboat on the Trinity River without incident, and Shanks was taken to jail. He lost his case and was sentenced, then appealed and won. About this time the Civil War began, and Shanks enlisted. He told the court that he was a strong Union man and had joined the Confederate Army against his judgment because of strong local pressures.

He denied charges that he had left one wife in Texas, another in Mississippi, and had proposed marriage to a third woman in Tennessee.[8]

"The evidence of the witness Shanks had created quite a bit of excitement here," newspaper correspondents reported from Cincinnati in January 1865. By the end of March, John T. Shanks and St. Leger Grenfell were well known to Northern newspaper readers. When the trial ended April 6, prison sentences of varying lengths were given to the American-born conspirators. Grenfell, who may have been the least guilty of the lot, was sentenced to death. (The sentence was later commuted to life imprisonment on Fort Jefferson in the Dry Tortugas; in 1868 while attempting escape in an open boat, the doughty Englishman was drowned.)

Released from custody of the court, witness Shanks was returned to Camp Douglas on April 6, 1865. On that same day Colonel Sweet gave him his reward—the command of a company of Galvanized Yankees. Colonel Carroll Potter was at Douglas organizing the 6th U.S. Volunteers; two more companies were needed to complete the regiment.

Next day Shanks reported for duty at Camp Fry, near Chicago, and handed a written request endorsed by Sweet to Colonel Potter: "I have the honor to respectfully apply for the appointment to the position of Captain of Company I, 6th Regiment, U.S.V. Inf. now under your command." Potter approved it immediately, and sent him on to a physician, who asked him nine questions:

Have you ever been sick? When and of what diseases?
Have you any disease now, and what?
Have you ever had fits?

Have you ever received an injury or wound upon the head?
Have you ever had a fracture, or dislocation, or a sprain?
Are you in the habit of drinking? Or have you ever had the "horrors"?
Are you subject to the piles?
Have you any difficulty urinating?
Have you been vaccinated, or had the smallpox?

Shanks passed his physical examination, and was officially commissioned captain on April 21.[9]

Company I, which he would command during the following 19 months, was a Deep South unit. Mississippians, Alabamians, and Georgians made up half the muster roll. Tennesseans, Kentuckians, Missourians, and North Carolinians were next in frequency, with three or four men from each of the states of Louisiana, South Carolina, and Virginia. Shanks would get along very well with these men; Company I's losses from desertion were much lower than the average.

On May 11, the 6th Regiment arrived at Fort Leavenworth, and within 24 hours Shanks was in trouble with Colonel Potter for being late to drill. In defending himself, Shanks characteristically cast the blame elsewhere:

In obedience to your orders I have the honor to report the reason of my absence from company drill this morning was on account of the tardiness of the Post Quartermaster and not my own.

Early this morning I obtained permission from the adjutant to get my breakfast in the Fort, and draw a tent, with the view of returning as soon as I accomplished the object of my visit. When I returned my company was out at drill which I very much regretted. I assure you, Colonel, it is not my *intention* or desire to *evade* drilling my company and a strict compliance to all orders that have or may hereafter be assigned.

I am very respectfully
Your obt' servant
John T. Shanks
Commanding Co I, 6 U S V[10]

Two days later Company I moved out of Leavenworth with the regiment. Shanks's first order in the company book assigned George H. Campbell, 36 years old, McNairy County, Tennessee, and Elisha C. Powell, 28 years old, of Clarke County, Mississippi, as teamsters to drive the company's wagons to Fort Kearney.

At Julesburg, Company I began its first duty on the Plains under direct command of Colonel McNally of the 3rd Regiment. On June 22, McNally ordered Shanks to take 20 men and escort Leander Black's civilian wagon train on a round trip to Fort

Laramie. For the first time since his capture in Ohio, John Shanks was now a man on his own. And again he was soon in trouble with authority.

It was customary for wagonmasters to pay soldier escorts small sums of money for their services. As officer in command, Shanks received this money from Leander Black, but failed to pass it on promptly to his men. News of this omission somehow reached the ears of General Patrick Connor, after Shanks had returned the wagon train safely to Julesburg. Connor immediately sent a telegram to Shanks, demanding an explanation.

Fortunately for his future career as an officer of the Galvanized Yankees, this time Shanks had a plausible explanation:

I have returned to the enlisted men that accompanied Mr. Black's train the amount paid them for their services, etc. On my arrival at this Post, I was instructed by Col. C. H. McNally, commanding, to receive from Mr. Black the amount due each enlisted man, keep a correct account of the same, and furnish them with small amounts at a time to purchase such necessaries from the sutler as they might need. The Colonel's reasons for giving these instructions was to avoid as far as possible the purchase of ardent spirits by enlisted men from passing trains, and prevent the occurrence of so many desertions from the post. Acting under these instructions, I notified Mr. Black, stated to him the reasons they were so given, and since my return I have witnessed enough to convince me that Col. Mc-Nally's instructions to me was necessary to avoid the objects above stated. I have the honor to state farther that the money was not withheld from the men with the view of defrauding them, but to maintain the proper military discipline.[11]

On July 25, Sergeant Joseph Thompson, a 21-year-old farm boy of Roane County, Tennessee, and five privates from Mississippi were reported absent without leave from Company I. Captain Shanks immediately secured mounts for 22 men and went in hot pursuit. A day or so later the six would-be deserters were back at Julesburg in the guardhouse. Shanks was determined to keep his company intact for the duration.

In early summer, General Connor made his decision to replace the California cavalry at Camp Douglas, Utah, with companies of the 6th Regiment. Although Company I was not sent to Utah, it was ordered on August 16 to Laramie for reassignment. The new duties were made clear on August 31:

Captain John T. Shanks with his Company I, 6th U.S.V., will immediately take up the line of march westward on the line of the Pacific Telegraph and will make the following distribution of his command: 1 sergeant,

2 corporals and 15 privates at Horse Shoe Station; Lieutenant Griffin, 1 sergeant, 2 corporals and 15 privates at Deer Creek; 1 sergeant, 2 corporals and 15 privates at Platte Bridge; Headquarters and remainder of the company at Camp Marshall, D.T.[12]

Camp Marshall was a crude square of stables, barracks, and stockade built around a telegraph station at La Bonte, 66 miles west of Fort Laramie.* Except for scenery, wild game, and prowling Indians, La Bonte had little to offer in the way of diversions, but Captain Shanks soon established himself comfortably. From departing officers of the 3rd U.S. Volunteers and the 11th Ohio Cavalry, he collected a pair of mountain howitzers for defense, and three dogs, two cats, and two tame crows to relieve the tedium of his duties. His main responsibility was to keep the telegraph line open, but he preferred entertaining passersby and swapping stories with them.

One of the classic stories of La Bonte started with Jim Bridger. Bridger was cooking his breakfast there in a grove of trees when he glanced up and saw 250 bears sitting down and watching him. They had smelled bacon frying and came in as near as they dared.

"What did you do?" someone would ask Bridger.

"Oh, didn't do nothing."

"Well, what did the bears do?"

"Oh, they did nothing, only they just sot around."[13]

As a result of this story, a common saying around that part of the North Platte country was that soldiers stationed at La Bonte "only just sot around." Captain Shanks, however, did more than just sit around. He enjoyed himself while doing it, as the diary of Captain B. F. Rockafellow testifies. Rockafellow, of the 6th Michigan Cavalry, was returning with one of the columns of Connor's Powder River Expedition, and stopped at Camp Marshall on the night of September 21.

Shanks's hospitality and generosity almost overwhelmed Rockafellow. He enjoyed the good dinner and choice cigars, but being a teetotaler had to use deception to make Shanks believe he was drinking whiskey instead of water. "It worked well and the very hospitable gentleman was not displeased. Captain Shanks is the Texan who rendered such valuable assistance to the Govt. in ex-

* The post was named for Captain Levi G. Marshall, Company E, 11th Ohio Volunteer Cavalry Regiment, who supervised its construction in the autumn of 1864.

posing plans of the traitors in the Chicago Conspiracy. He is about 1 H P size with dark complexion, eyes, hair and whiskers. Was Capt in rebel service. Served on Genl. Bragg's staff, and served under Morgan in Kentucky. He led column which drove in pickets within four miles of Cinn."

Next day, Rockafellow added one more intriguing item about his host. "Capt Shanks aroused us from sweet slumbers to dress by a large crackling fire and then being well treated were invited out to a good breakfast. . . . He expects his lady from Chicago. She was threatened with insults and efforts made to capture or kidnap her, to cause her to divulge his part in the great conspiracy."[14]

As a result of Shanks's cordiality and his luck in staying out of trouble for a few weeks, he won the confidence of his superiors at Laramie. On October 20, he was given command over all troops between Forts Laramie and Caspar, a section which included not only 6th Regiment infantrymen but several detachments of the 11th Ohio Cavalry. (Some of the Ohio cavalrymen, as has been noted, were also Galvanized Yankees, a few of them former comrades of Shanks, captured as was he while raiding with Morgan across Ohio.)

During that autumn most of Shanks's Indian problems were concentrated at Horse Shoe Station, which was usually the first stopping place for travelers bound west from Fort Laramie. One of the big raids occurred on November 25, when a party of Sioux attacked the station and ran off 30 head of horses. In an attempt to discourage further raiding at Horse Shoe, Shanks sent Lieutenant W. W. Swearingen of the 11th Ohio and 20 mounted men to strengthen the garrison.

Winter soon settled down over the North Platte country, and blizzards helped pacify the hostiles. The weather also kept soldiers confined to their cramped quarters. To keep in touch with his scattered stations, Shanks sent telegrams up and down the line. Occasionally he made telegraphic reports to Laramie headquarters, most of them routine, but on December 31, Colonel Maynadier must have been startled to receive this one: "I was shot today by a private of L Company, 11th Ohio Volunteer Cavalry while in the discharge of my official duties. Wound not dangerous. After shooting me, man tried to escape, was pursued by my orders and mortally wounded. Jno. T. Shanks, Captain."[15]

Shanks's assailant was Private Thomas Ferrier, a 22-year-old farmer from Calloway County, Missouri. Ferrier was not a Galvanized Yankee. He had enlisted in the Union Army at St. Louis, in August 1863, and was sent to Fort Laramie, where he was assigned to the 11th Ohio.

Ferrier was still alive on January 4 when Lieutenant Henrie W. Brazie, acting provost marshal, arrived from Fort Laramie to investigate the shooting incident. After five days of questioning witnesses and parties involved, a puzzled Lieutenant Brazie returned to Laramie with several depositions.

I found so many reports in circulation that it was impossible to form an opinion as to the merits of the case and it became necessary to take the statements of the principal actors in the affair. The only thing not satisfactorily explained by these statements is the shooting of Private Ferrier, which from all I could learn was entirely unjustifiable, it appearing that he was shot after he was in the custody of the party sent to arrest him. . . . The wound of Captain Shanks was inflicted by a pistol shot, fired by Private Ferrier which took effect in his left shoulder. The wound of Private Ferrier is also a pistol shot, entering his head near the left temple and passing out above the right eye. The shot was fired by Private Roy, Company I, 6th U.S. Volunteers, and so close to his head that the powder was blown into the flesh.

With these explanations, Lieutenant Brazie appended the depositions, and suggested that they would give his superiors "the same grounds to form an opinion as I have, and therefore I will advance none."

Captain Shanks in his statement said that on entering the cavalry mess room he had found Ferrier and Private W. S. Foster of L Company engaged in a fight. When he ordered them to desist, Foster obeyed, but Ferrier "peremptorily refused." The captain then ordered Ferrier to his quarters, but he again refused to obey.

I then ordered Corporal Bowers of same Company to arrest him and take him to his quarters and keep in custody until he became quiet and sober. Some ten minutes afterward I passed out the mess room door of my detachment, and stopping in the door to give some instructions to one of the cooks, the aforesaid Private Ferrier came out of the cavalry company quarters, with a revolver in his hand, and not thinking he intended shooting me I paid but little attention to him. Suddenly he fired on me, the ball entering the left side of my neck and lodging in my left shoulder, partially paralyzing my left arm. I fell to the ground insensible, Ferrier attempting his escape through the back gate of the corral. After being carried to my quarters I then became sensible, and was notified of Ferrier's escape. I ordered a sufficient number of my men to pursue him and capture him at all hazards. After pursuing him about a mile from the post, Sergeant Johnson who was in charge, reports he was overtaken by them, and ordered to surrender, which he refused to do, saying he would die first. One of the men fired on him, the ball entering the left temple and lodging in his right eye.

The first enlisted man questioned by Lieutenant Brazie was Corporal Elijah Rushing of Company I, who stated that on the day of the incident, New Year's Eve, he was ordered by Captain Shanks to issue a gallon of whiskey to each of the two detachments at Camp Marshall. "I issued first a half gallon to each of them. About an hour afterwards I went into the mess room. Ferrier was cursing Foster, backing him into the commissary room."

Corporal Rushing approached them and said: "Gentlemen, stop this fight."

"Damn you, who are you?," Ferrier retorted. "I can whip Foster or any of his friends."

Corporal Rushing replied: "Sir, I have not insulted you. I want you to stop this fuss."

About that time Shanks appeared, and Ferrier told the captain that Company L had been imposed upon ever since it had been at Camp Marshall.

"Who has imposed on Company L?," Shanks asked.

"Corporal Rushing and Foster," Ferrier replied, and added: "Captain Shanks, I am a man from the bottom of my feet to the top of my head."

From this point on, Corporal Rushing's account was virtually the same as Captain Shanks, but there were some discrepancies in the story told by Corporal Bowers of L Company. Bowers said that the 15 Ohio cavalrymen were given a full gallon of whiskey, of which they used two-thirds in making toddy. He added that Ferrier and Foster began quarreling over a canteen of whiskey, and that when Shanks ordered him [Bowers] to take Ferrier to his quarters, the captain had "his pistol in his hand cocked." Bowers said that Ferrier willingly locked arms with him and they walked to the cavalry barracks. "On entering the door we unlocked arms and I moved on into the quarters. He stopped and seizing a pistol stepped to the door again and fired on Captain Shanks."

To assure Lieutenant Brazie that there was no ill-feeling toward Shanks among the Ohio men, Bowers added: "I would further state that the Captain has been very kind to us, showing no difference between our men and his own, always giving almost anything we asked of him."

Private Foster, the soldier with whom Ferrier was scuffling, said that when Corporal Rushing attempted to stop them, Ferrier told the corporal "to mind his own business. . . . Captain Shanks came in and had a long conversation with Ferrier and then went out. We all thought everything was quieted but pretty soon Captain Shanks came into the kitchen with a revolver out which it was drawn on Ferrier. I do not know but I heard Captain Shanks say to Ferrier, 'You have wakened up the wrong man.' Ferrier spoke up and told Captain Shanks, 'You have the advantage of me now.' "

Foster also added that when the shot was fired, he heard Shanks cry out: "I am a dead man! Company I, do your duty!"

As Foster was one of the telegraphers at Camp Marshall, he returned to the office, and not long afterward Shanks summoned him to his quarters to give him the message which was telegraphed to Fort Laramie that evening. "I was in Captain Shanks' room when Roy, I Company, 6th U.S. Volunteers, came in and told Captain Shanks, 'I have got your man,' holding a pistol in one hand and shaking Captain Shanks' hand with the other." When Foster asked Roy if Ferrier had been shot, Roy replied: "He is and I shot him. When they run on Captain Shanks, they run on Company I."

In presenting these depositions, Lieutenant Brazie expressed the opinion that the statement of Sergeant William Johnson of Company I "comes nearer explaining the circumstances than any other I could procure."

Johnson's story of the altercation in the mess room was about the same as the others, except that he added considerably more profanity in recalling the remarks of the men involved. After the shooting of Shanks, Sergeant Johnson said that in obedience to the captain's orders he started in pursuit of Ferrier with five or six men. "About a quarter mile from the post we separated, Corporal Stacy of my company and myself going together. We followed down the creek about a half mile and turned back up it again. After going about a quarter of a mile, I saw two men about ten steps apart going in the same direction as ourselves. When I got up in about ten steps of them they turned face to face and were talking. As I went across the creek I says to Ferrier, 'You have shot the Captain and you have got to go to the quarters with me.' He turned his back to me, and was shot. Before being shot he refused to surrender, whereupon Private Frederick Roy fired on him, seeing that Ferrier was armed with his pistol buckled around him."

At the end of his official report of January 9, Lieutenant Brazie stated that a surgeon was in attendance on Private Ferrier "and pronounces the patient out of danger and in his opinion will survive."

Ferrier died the next day. The case was closed with the notation "by reason of gun shot wound."[16]

In the life of John Shanks there never seemed to be any long periods of tranquillity. The wound which he believed not dangerous became infected and he was ill for most of the winter. Things began to go badly. His easy relations with Fort Laramie were never the same after the shooting of Ferrier. Headquarters chastised him for not sending reports regularly, for not keeping the mails moving smoothly over his section, for not saving empty gunny sacks, for not reading the Articles of War regularly to his men, and for visiting Laramie without permission.

On January 27, 1866, he received an order to "take prompt measures to secure a large and abundant supply of ice for the use of the troops during the coming summer. Where ice houses have not already been built they will be constructed without delay." At blizzard-ravaged La Bonte, ice was the last thing Shanks or his men were interested in, but three weeks later he received a curt order to report "what steps have been taken to secure a supply of ice for next summer."[17]

To take some of the paperwork off his desk, Shanks assigned his lieutenant, James V. Griffin, to command Company I and Camp Marshall, and devoted his flagging energies to matters concerning other stations in his section.

About this time the telegraph line also became a constant annoyance. Civilian operators quit, blizzards snapped poles, and inspectors from the Pacific Telegraph Company arrived and demanded troop escorts.

On March 9, a severe windstorm flattened several miles of poles between La Bonte and Horse Shoe, severing communications. As he made a reconnaissance of the damage and assigned repair details, Shanks must have realized for the first time the enormity of the task which had confronted the original builders of the line some five years earlier.

For some reason, chroniclers of the Old West have generally ignored the drama of that first telegraph line. The Overland Mail, Pony Express, and Pacific Railroad have become fixed in Western legend, but the Pacific Telegraph has been lost in the maze of history. It was built in 1861, a decade before the first railroad, and was overshadowed by onrushing events of the Civil War.

As in the building of the transcontinental railroad, construction of the telegraph was organized as a race between competing companies, one moving eastward from California, the other westward from Nebraska. The first company to reach Salt Lake City would receive a prize of $40,000.

An engineering genius, Edward Creighton, was in charge of construction from Nebraska westward. He employed 80 men, purchased 700 cattle for beef, loaded 75 ox-drawn wagons with wire insulators, tools, and provisions. Dividing his workmen into three crews, he assigned one group to digging holes, another to cutting and setting poles, the third to stringing wire.

The race began on July 4, 1861, the contract requiring completion within two years. Three months and 20 days later, October 24, Creighton strung his last roll of wire into Salt Lake City and won the prize. The Californians came in two days afterward, and telegraphic communication was established between the Atlantic and Pacific. President Lincoln sent the first message, the Governor of California responded, and Brigham Young dispatched greetings in both directions. Rates were set at $6.00 for the first 10 words, each additional word 75c, which explains why news bulletins from the East published in Western newspapers were models of language economy.

Creighton's most difficult problem was securing suitable poles across long stretches of treeless plains. Specifications called for poles 20 feet long to be sunk four feet in the ground, and in some places they had to be hauled more than 100 miles. Creighton had surveyed his route, however, locating sources of supply in advance, and he distributed his timber cutters and oxen so they were always in the right places at the right times.

Creighton furnished his workers with good tents and large quantities of excellent food cooked on portable stoves. The diggers averaged about 12 miles per day, digging 24 holes per mile, but the pole crew gradually fell behind and was still 150 miles from Salt Lake when the last hole was dug.

Fortunately for the line builders, the Indians exhibited more curiosity than hostility in 1861. At Deer Creek—later to be one of Captain Shanks's stations—a Sioux delegation confronted the diggers when they arrived and made a mild protest. The Sioux had heard correctly that the poles were to stand as tall as three men, but they also had been told that wire was to be strung closely from top to bottom. Such a fence, they declared, would keep all the buffalo and other game from their favorite hunting grounds. When the superintendent assured them that only one wire was to be strung along the top of the poles, the Indians seemed relieved.[18]

To prevent possible Indian interference with the line, Creighton arranged for visiting chiefs along the route to inspect the instruments and receive mild electric shocks, which might lead them to dread the strong medicine of the wire. One chief, however, was skeptical of the white man's magic. Captain Eugene Ware told of how this Indian persuaded his warriors that it would be a good thing to have some telegraph wire up in their village to fasten ponies to. "They cut off nearly a half-mile of wire," Ware said, and all the Indians, in single file on horseback, catching hold of the wire, proceeded to ride and pull the wire across the prairie toward their village. After they had gone several miles and were going over a ridge, they were overtaken by an electric storm, and as they were rapidly traveling, dragging the wire, by some means or other a bolt of lightning, so the story goes, knocked almost all of them off their horses and hurt some of them considerably. Thereupon they dropped the wire, and coming to the conclusion that it was punishment for their acts and that it was "bad medicine," they afterwards let it alone. The story of it, being quite wonderful, circulated with great rapidity among the Indians.[19]

By the time the Galvanized Yankees came into the West, however, the Indians had overcome their fear of the white man's humming messenger wires, and would often rip out long sections, sometimes cutting down poles and burning them. Another enemy of the telegraph was the buffalo, especially on open plains where there were no trees for animals to rub their itching hides against. After a dozen or so shaggy buffaloes scratched themselves against a slender pole, it would often fall to the ground. In an effort to stop this, sharp spikes were driven into the poles, but the spikes seemed only to add to the bliss of the scratching monarchs.

The long section of telegraph line which Captain Shanks had to repair in March 1866 was more vulnerable than most because the builders had used pine poles instead of cedar, and after five years of use the wood was beginning to rot. New poles had to be cut and barked, and new holes dug in hard frozen earth. But the captain knew that every newspaper editor west of La Bonte would be publishing acidulous comments about the telegraph's military guardians if too much time elapsed before service was restored. He worked his men hard for three days, and messages began flowing East and West again.

A month later another crisis confronted Captain Shanks. Five men deserted at Horse Shoe Station, presumably gone up the Bozeman Trail to the Montana goldfields. Shanks wanted to track them down, as he had done successfully at Julesburg, but could not obtain permission to take a small detachment into the dangerous Indian country north of the Platte. These were the only men lost to I Company by desertion during its period of service.

In June, orders came for all 11th Ohio Cavalry units to proceed to Fort Laramie for mustering out. Shanks took over the Ohioans' horses, mounted half his men, and prepared to guard his section with reduced forces. Fortunately the Indians were temporarily peaceable; many were gathering at Fort Laramie for treaty negotiations organized by Colonel Maynadier.

Marching westward from Fort Kearney was Colonel Henry B. Carrington and the 18th U.S. Infantry, regular Army troops, some of them bound for Utah, some for the Powder River country where Carrington would establish headquarters at ill-fated Fort Phil Kearny. By an odd coincidence, Carrington had been one of the chief prosecutors of the Chicago conspirators, but there is no record that he and Shanks met in the West. Carrington crossed the Platte 10 miles east of La Bonte at Bridger's Ferry, operated by a squaw-man, Benjamin Mills. A detachment of the 11th Ohio had left there a week before Carrington arrived, and Shanks had not yet replaced them. As Carrington's wagons pulled in for the crossing on June 20, Mills informed the colonel that Sioux had raided there 24 hours earlier.

Carrington immediately let it be known that Bridger's Ferry was a critical point on his supply line. During the next few months hundreds of wagons had to be transported across it to sustain operations along the Bozeman Trail. Shortly afterward, Shanks received orders to move his headquarters to the Ferry. Henceforth its defenses would have equal importance with the telegraph line.

To go with him to Bridger's Ferry, Shanks selected his favorite sergeant, 23-year-old Clark Suggs of Newton County, Mississippi, Corporal John Spriggs of Mobile, Alabama, and 19 dependable privates. He placed small howitzers at opposite landings, established vigilant guard routines, and the Sioux soon learned that Bridger's Ferry was no place for raiding.

Shanks and his boys passed a pleasant summer, the captain as usual finding ways of obtaining little luxuries which made life more enjoyable for the detachment. Some of the last references to his military career appear in records of the 18th Infantry at Fort Phil Kearny, where boards of survey inquiring into supply shortages reaching that post noted that such items as soap and coffee had been "requisitioned" from wagons passing Bridger's Ferry, Captain Shanks commanding. One mysterious disappearance never solved was a consignment of porter, meant for use by surgeons at the fort as a tonic for invalids. Of 258 bottles, 205 had disappeared somewhere between Laramie and Phil Kearny.[20] Wagons carrying the bottles of mildly alcoholic brew passed Bridger's Ferry in September, just about the time John Shanks received orders to prepare Company I for mustering out.

In what better way could he and his boys have bid farewell to their service as Galvanized Yankees than in festive toasts over bottles of U.S. Army porter? On October 11, 1866, one day after all the enlisted men of his company were mustered out at Fort Kearney, John T. Shanks relinquished his commission. So ended his fantastic career as soldier of the Confederacy, prisoner of war, spy for the Union, and captain of U.S. Volunteers.

Ohioans from Dixie:

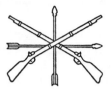

The Powder River Expedition

IX

As has been noted, a considerable number of former Confederates were enrolled in the 11th Ohio Cavalry Regiment. The first battalion of the 11th—all Ohioans and staunch Unionists—arrived at Fort Laramie in May 1862. Late the following summer the second battalion (Companies E, F, G, and H) traveled from Ohio across the Plains to join the regiment; on its rosters were a few former Confederates. In June 1864 at Fort Laramie, Companies I, K, and L were organized from surplus recruits assigned the regiment, including Galvanized Yankees enlisted from prisoners of war.

Among the men in Company E were several former Confederates and Confederate sympathizers. Because most of them used false identities, it is impossible to trace the origins of these Galvanized Yankees. Several were Kentuckians who had been active in Ohio with the Knights of the Golden Circle, an organization opposed to the war policies of President Lincoln. Some had probably joined up for the sole purpose of traveling westward, then deserting at the first opportunity and disappearing into mining areas in search of their fortunes. Most were very young, 18 to 21.

In September 1863, Company E stopped for about a week at Fort Kearney while en route to Laramie. One night several of the soldiers rode over to a Dobytown saloon for drinks and a few games of chance. Among them was an Ohio lad who had enlisted as Benjamin Monroe. His real name was Benjamin Monroe Connor, but he had received a medical discharge from an Ohio infantry regiment, and as his Southern comrades had done, changed his identity so that he would not be rejected for cavalry service in the West.

While sitting in a saloon, Connor overheard a group of E Company men plotting a mutiny. "I observed from their dialects that these men were Southerners. . . . I listened as intently as I could without betraying my interest, and gathered that their intention was to get as many soldiers as possible to join them in a mutiny when we reached Julesburg." There were four ringleaders—Patrick Gray, William Crawford, and two Kentuckians who had enlisted under the same *nom de guerre* of John Sullivan. Their plan was to give the secret grip of the Knights of the Golden Circle to every soldier in E Company to test out those who might be favorable to the mutiny. "I was among rebels dressed in Union uniform. These men had joined the Northern army to escape being drafted to fight directly against the South, knowing that the 11th Ohio was enlisted for service in the Indian country. . . . I rode along silently behind the bibulous crowd, taking in every word of the treasons a few of them planned so boldly, yet uncertain how I should act in the matter. I was only twenty years old at the time, and timid."[1]

For several days, Connor kept his dangerous knowledge to himself. Company E resumed march for Julesburg, and every night he observed the plotters discussing their conspiracy. At last one evening he gathered courage and went to see the commanding officer, Captain Levi Marshall, and told him everything he knew.

Next morning at company formation, Marshall placed the two Sullivans, Gray, and Crawford under arrest, disarmed and dismounted them, and ordered them to walk the remaining 300 miles to Fort Laramie.

At Laramie, the four troublemakers were court-martialed and sentenced to three months hard labor. During this period, young Connor's duties along the telegraph line brought him occasionally to Fort Laramie, where he would see the prisoners shackled in ball and chain, chopping wood or policing the post. He wondered if they had guessed the identity of their betrayer.

In the spring of 1865, the four men were released and assigned to Ben Connor's detachment at South Pass. Connor stayed clear of them, and was not aware that they were still plotting mutiny. Suddenly one day in May, the two Sullivans and Gray resisted the authority of Lieutenant John Brown. This time no court-martial was necessary. Brown ordered them shot to death in the act of mutiny.[2]

"Many men in our command were from Kentucky and a few had come from other Southern states," Connor said. "In case the mutiny had come to a head, bloodshed would have been unavoidable. . . . Not all the Southerners were disloyal by any means."[3] A short time after the shooting of the three mutineers, one of the loyal Southerners warned Connor that the surviving fourth member of the group, Crawford, had somehow discovered that he (Connor) was the one who had reported the original conspiracy to Captain Marshall.

"I felt that Crawford would either kill me or I would be compelled to kill him. . . . So one day I started out hunting, as I had often done before, leaving the post with a horse, a gun, and a saddle, but this time never to return."[4] (Ben Connor spent the remainder of his long life in the West, as a miner, cowboy, and respectable stockman. He was so remorseful of his act of desertion that he never returned to Ohio.)

In late summer of 1864, Captain Henry E. Palmer was ordered to report for a special assignment at Fort Leavenworth "to take command of a detachment of the 11th Ohio Cavalry, sixty men, every one of them lately Confederate soldiers with John Morgan on his raid into Ohio." Palmer was to conduct these men to Fort Kearney and there turn them over to Captain J. L. Humfreville of the 11th Ohio.

On August 8, as Palmer and his detachment were nearing Big Sandy Station, they met several freighters and stagecoach passengers on horseback, fleeing a band of raiding Cheyennes. Palmer listened to the fugitives' stories of massacres farther west, then decided to march on. His 60 Kentucky cavalrymen were experienced raiders themselves, and had volunteered to fight Indians. They camped that night on the Little Blue, with Indians all around them on distant hills.

Next morning the former Morgan men saw at firsthand the savage results of a hostile Indian raid. They were among the first to reach the smoking ruins of the William Eubanks ranch.* "We

* See pages 33-34 for the story of Lucinda Eubanks.

found the bodies of three little children," Captain Palmer recorded, "who had been taken by the heels by the Indians and swung around against the log cabin, beating their heads to a jelly. Found the hired girl some fifteen rods from the ranch staked out on the prairie, tied by her hands and feet, naked, body full of arrows and horribly mangled."[5]

At adjoining ranches they discovered similar scenes of death and desolation. Farther along the trail they came upon an abandoned wagon train. "The teamsters had mounted the mules and made their escape," but the Cheyennes had ripped off wagon covers and strewn goods all along the road.

Ironically, one of the minor depredations committed by the Indians must have reminded the Morgan men of the day they were captured at Buffington Island, Ohio. When the Confederates had discovered they were surrounded, they scattered their stolen booty recklessly, spinning out bolts of cloth in long streamers across an Ohio wheat field. Now, a year later on a Nebraska prairie, they saw similar bolts of cloth unwound by Indians beside an abandoned wagon train.

By this time troops summoned from nearby posts and stations were arriving to restore order along the trail, and Captain Palmer and his 60 cavalrymen continued their march westward. At Fort Kearney, Captain Jacob Humfreville, commanding Company K, was waiting to take the new arrivals into the 11th Ohio Cavalry.*

Captain Humfreville's Company K was headquartered at Fort Laramie until the autumn of 1864, then was moved west to Fort Halleck, a stage-line post at the base of Elk Mountain. The winter was a bitter one, with severe blizzards and violent winds. On February 17, a sergeant and a private of Company K were frozen to death near Bear Creek. Post duties were light, however, and Arapahos in the neighborhood were temporarily peaceable. The Indians camped around the fort and drew rations occasionally from the quartermaster.

One of the Ohio boys, Private Charles Adams, later recalled how the Arapahos would gather on a long bench outside post

---

* Company K's Descriptive Book lists five Southern-born soldiers, two from Kentucky, and 25 foreign-born, Irish, German, etc. If all 60 of Captain Palmer's party were Morgan men, they must have been scattered through several companies of the regiment, used false names and places of birth, or remained as unassigned recruits.

headquarters. "Any one could sit with them and smoke," he said. "I often smoked with them. They considered it a grand insult if anyone sat with them and refused to smoke. . . . They had a long stem pipe—did not put it in the mouth but against the lips. They would commence at the right of the line, take a few puffs and pass to the next without turning their heads."[6]

Soldiers at Fort Halleck also were fascinated by the Arapaho children's grasshopper roasts. "When they had a bed of hot coals and ashes, they would make a place and put the hoppers in and cover them up. This would burn the wings and legs off and when they got hot they would pop like corn. When they were roasted to suit them, the children would sit around and rake the hoppers out with sticks and appear to enjoy them as much as peanuts."[7]

With the arrival of spring, most of the Arapahos dismantled their tepees and went away. By summertime they had resumed their old habits of raiding stage stations for livestock.

In June 1865, Captain Humfreville sent a detachment of K Company up to Sage Creek to help pacify these hostiles. During a running fight on June 8, George Bodine and Perry Stewart were killed, William Caldwell wounded. "The Indians hate red-haired men," Charles Adams noted. "Bodine's hair was very red. He had fourteen arrows in his body."[8]

Whether by chance or design, the two Ohio companies selected by General Connor to accompany him on the Powder River Expedition were E and K. Toward the end of June, Connor ordered the scattered detachments of these companies to assemble at Fort Laramie. On the Fourth of July an order was issued permitting the sutler to let the men have whiskey without an order from the officers. According to Private Adams, the result was "a free for all drunk."

For a month the Ohio companies camped at Laramie with other units of Connor's column awaiting supplies from Fort Leavenworth. No supplies had arrived by August 1, but Connor could wait no longer. He had organized his punitive expedition in three columns, their movements timed so that all would arrive simultaneously on Rosebud River in the heart of the hostile Indian country. The rendezvous date was September 1. Two Missouri regiments under Colonel Nelson Cole were moving westward from

Omaha, and Colonel Samuel Walker's 16th Kansas Cavalry had
to be set in motion to avoid a mass mutiny.*

Leaving the stage and telegraph lines in the care of the 3rd,
5th, and 6th U.S. Volunteer Infantry, Connor started north with
a limited reserve of ammunition and no rations except hardtack.
But in his column were the best cavalrymen then soldiering in
the West. He also had Captain Frank North's Pawnee Scouts,
Captain E. W. Nash's Omaha Scouts, and seven excellent guides,
including Jim Bridger and Mitch Boyer.

Bridger may have offered suggestions in the drafting of Connor's first general order, August 2, but it also reveals the general's
shrewd understanding of cavalry requirements, the strengths and
weaknesses of horses and men:

The following rules will be observed in this command.

No galloping of horses on the march will be allowed, and officers will see
that the utmost care is taken of the animals.

Horses will not be saddled in the morning until Boots and Saddles is
sounded at these Head Quarters.

Horses will be brought inside the lines at sundown, or when stable call
is sounded, and securely hobbled and tied.

On the march, when a halt is made, officers will see that the girths of
the saddles are loosened, bridles taken off, and the horses allowed to graze.

In case of night attack, the troops will surround their horses, and if the
enemy is not close up to the horses, and cannot be seen, the men will lie
or kneel down so as not to make a mark for the enemy.

No man is to remain behind, or quit the ranks for any purpose whatever,
without permission from the Captain, or Officer commanding his company.
Officers are never to give permission to any man to quit the ranks, excepting on account of illness—or some other absolutely necessary purpose.

Officers must be particularly attentive to prevent the men from going out
of the ranks for water. When this is required the column will be halted.
The canteens must be filled before starting.

Whenever the bugles sound the Halt for the head of the column, the call
will be repeated by the bugles along the line.

Firing of arms on the march or in camp, without orders, is strictly
prohibited. When arriving at camp in the afternoon, the horses will be
allowed to run with the lariats on about fifteen minutes to give them an
opportunity to roll before being hobbled.

The Officer of the Day will accompany the guard on the march, and will
see that the train is kept well closed up.

This order will be read to every company in the command.'

* The Kansans claimed their enlistments ended with the Civil War's ter-
mination, and became so obstreperous that artillery had to be turned on
them to enforce order.

After some difficulty in crossing the Platte, Connor's troops moved swiftly northward. On August 14, they camped on Powder River, and Connor ordered the first timbers cut for construction of a permanent fort, which for a short time bore his name, then was changed to Fort Reno. While scouting this area on August 21, Captain Marshall's Company E ran into a band of Indians; in the sharp skirmish which followed they killed two of the enemy. Next day Connor detached from his forces both Ohio companies, a company of 7th Iowa Cavalry, the Indian scouts, and two six-pounder guns, and started on a forced march into the Tongue River Valley.

They reached the Tongue August 28 and camped. Late in the evening, the Pawnee Scouts came in to report a hostile Arapaho village of 250 lodges down the valley. Connor immediately ordered a night march.

Captain Henry Palmer, who had brought the Morgan men west from Fort Leavenworth and was accompanying this expedition as quartermaster, rode in the advance with Frank North's Pawnee Scouts. He was the first man to sight the hostile village.

Just before me lay a large mesa . . . all covered with Indians' ponies, except a portion about one-half mile to the left, which was thickly dotted with Indian tepees full of Indians. . . . General Connor then took the lead, rode his horse up the steep bank of the ravine, and dashed out across the mesa as if there were no Indians just to the left; every man followed as closely as possible. At the first sight of the general, the ponies covering the tableland in front of us set up a tremendous whinnying and galloped down toward the Indian village, more than a thousand dogs commenced barking and more than seven hundred Indians made the hills ring with their fearful yelling.[10]

Charles Adams, riding with K Company, said that Connor made a short speech to the men just before the charge:

Should we get in close quarters [Connor instructed them] the men should group in fours and stay together and use their guns as long as possible and under no circumstances use their revolvers unless there was no other chance. We were told to make every shot count, and be sure to leave one shot for ourselves and rather than fall into the hands of the Indians to use it as it would be preferable to falling in their hands. I have wondered how many would have taken their lives. I thought then and still think if I had gotten in a tight place and had one shot left I would have tried to get an Indian then take my chances. . . .

As we neared the village the command divided, some turning to the right, others to the left. The Indians had some of their tepees down and packs on their ponies and some of the ponies were so heavily packed that when they tried to run the packs pulled them over and they could not get up.

The squaws, papooses, dogs, and ponies all ran to save themselves. The women and children would run to the white men for protection, knowing they would receive no favors from the Pawnee Scouts. . . . The Indians ran to a high point and tried to rally but could not stand long before our carbines. We ran them four or five miles when our horses began to tire and we gave up the chase."[11]

Captain Humfreville of Company K admitted the fight was not a complete victory. "After eleven o'clock we were on the retreat, followed by the Indians, who fired upon us the entire night. . . . Never have I seen troops undergo such hardships as we experienced during the forty hours of this march and battle."[12]

The soldiers suffered several casualties. Captain Palmer said,

One of our men, a member of the 11th Ohio Cavalry, formerly one of John Morgan's men, a fine looking soldier with as handsome a face as I ever saw on a man, grabbed me by the shoulder and turned me about so that I might assist him in withdrawing an arrow from his mouth. The point of the arrow had passed through his open mouth and lodged in the root of his tongue. Having no surgeon with us a higher grade than a hospital steward, it was afterwards within a half hour decided that to get the arrow out from his mouth, the tongue must be, and was, cut out. The poor fellow returned to camp with us, and this late date I am unable to say whether he lived or died."[13]

This unfortunate Galvanized Yankee was identified by Charles Adams as "Ed Ward, alias John Johnson, a member of Company K."* Private Adams also described the incident somewhat differently: "The arrow had gone through his lip and tongue and in his jawbone a half inch. He was off his horse and hold of the arrow with both hands trying to pull it out. I went on and when we came back, he had pulled the shaft off leaving the spear in his mouth which was so tight they had to get some kind of pullers to get it out."[14] (Ed Ward, alias John Johnson, recovered, and was mustered out with his company a year later.)

As soon as the village was cleared and a few howitzer charges were fired after the retreating Arapahos, buglers sounded recall. One man had been killed, seven wounded. Enemy casualties were

---

* At least four "Wards" were enrolled in Morgan's regiments, any one of whom might have been Ed Ward. The K Company Descriptive Book states "John Johnson's" age in 1865 as 20, his birthplace as Hamilton, Ohio. Hamilton was only a few miles north of the Kentucky border, and a few Ohioans and Indianans with Southern family ties are known to have served with Morgan. The place of birth given by Ward also could have been false.

estimated at 63. Three hundred horses and ponies, 200 tepees, and immense quantities of pemmican and buffalo robes had been captured. "We found many things in the villages that had been taken from emigrants. One found a buckskin poke with $40 greenbacks in it."[15] Connor ordered tepee coverings and buffalo robes heaped in piles and burned.

In accordance with the plan of operation, the column was to move next against more formidable Sioux and Cheyenne encampments farther north. But Connor must first unite with Colonel Cole's Missouri cavalry and Colonel Walker's Kansas cavalry, somewhere on the Rosebud.

On the morning of September 1, the advance troops heard a cannon shot, but no one could be certain from which direction the sound came. As this was the day fixed for a rendezvous of the three columns, Connor ordered Captain Marshall to take E Company and 20 of the Pawnee Scouts and make a rapid reconnaissance toward the Rosebud in search of Cole and Walker.

After a four-day circuit, E Company rejoined the column. They had found no signs of the other forces. Next day, September 6, Connor decided to turn back over the route he had come in order to find grass for his horses. On September 7 he went into camp to restore his mounts, and the following morning sent out two scouting parties in search of the missing columns. Captain North and the Pawnees moved toward Powder River; Captain Humfreville and Company K, north toward the Rosebud.

K Company started out in a heavy rain which turned to snow. By the time they reached the Rosebud the storm had become a blizzard. They found no sign of human beings, red or white, and horses and men were exhausted when they returned to Connor's camp September 11.[16]

A few hours later the Pawnees rode in with an ominous report. They had discovered several hundred dead horses undoubtedly belonging to Cole's command. Some of the animals had been shot, others appeared to have frozen to death on the picket line. All were in an emaciated condition.

Connor was now greatly concerned over the fate of the Cole and Walker columns. He dispatched numerous scouting parties into the Powder River Valley, and at last on September 19, Captain North and his Pawnees found both Cole and Walker and their surviving troops. The cavalrymen were all on foot and near starvation, some offering the Pawnees as much as $5.00 for a single hardtack biscuit. For days the two combined columns had been under constant harassment by Sioux and Cheyennes, suffering severe casualties, and had been floundering about the Powder River country completely lost. Connor described them "as completely disgusted and discouraged an outfit of men as I ever saw."[17]

The demoralization of these two columns of the expedition led the *Fort Kearney Herald* to comment later: "Whether the command of 1600 men failed to proceed to the appointed rendezvous from the gross incompetence of its commanders or insubordination among the troops is a question upon which the public is at present in the dark."[18]

To recuperate his forces, Connor returned to the permanent base which bore his name only to receive on September 24 orders from his department commander relieving him of his command. The Powder River Expedition was ended. For the Morgan men it had been a campaign more arduous than any they had ever experienced under their dashing Kentucky commander.[19]

The Galvanized Yankees in Companies E and K, 11th Ohio Cavalry, now returned to Fort Laramie. When they arrived there early in October, they learned that supplies so sorely needed for the expedition had arrived from Leavenworth during their absence.

For the following year they continued to serve as cavalry adjuncts to U.S. Volunteer Infantry detachments guarding stage and telegraph lines across the Plains. In July 1866 they were mustered out. A quarter of a century later some of them may have attended one of the grand reunions of the regiment in Columbus, Ohio, and heard Governor William McKinley tell them they could take pride in being veterans of the last state volunteer regiment to be mustered out of service.[20]

X

Blizzard March

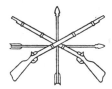

In August 1864 when Colonel Charles Dimon's 1st U.S. Volunteer Infantry Regiment was en route to the Missouri River forts, a battalion of four companies was detached at Chicago and sent to the Minnesota district. Settlers in that area were still fearful of a repetition of the bloody Indian massacres of 1862, and General Pope assigned the companies to four different forts.

For a year, A Company served at Fort Abercrombie, F at Fort Wadsworth, G at Fort Ripley, and I at Fort Ridgely. All were under command of Lieutenant-Colonel William Tamblyn. This was a most uneventful period of service for these men. Aside from occasional messenger duties between forts, they spent most of the year performing monotonous garrison chores. Although they lived fairly comfortably and suffered no tragic losses from scurvy, they also missed the exciting adventures of their comrades along the Missouri.

In July 1865, Lieutenant-Colonel Tamblyn was ordered to begin assembling his companies at Fort Snelling for mustering out. Company I arrived there first, and on July 30, Captain Richard Musgrove, the commanding officer, began preparing his final rolls. "A week or so later," he wrote, "I presented the completed rolls to the mustering officer, when I was surprised to be informed that . . . a telegram received during the night from General Pope . . . had directed our muster-out to be suspended, and that my company and the other three companies of our battalion be retained in the service until further orders. Some of my men were sorely disappointed, but made no trouble."[1]

Travel orders were not received until early October. Their first destination was Fort Leavenworth. Lieutenant-Colonel Tamblyn put his four companies aboard a Missouri River steamer, and a few days later they disembarked at Hannibal, Missouri. From there they journeyed by rail to St. Joseph, and then again by boat to Fort Leavenworth. On October 21, they went into camp outside the fort, and soon learned that they had been selected to guard the stations of a new stage line across far western Kansas.

This new route was the creation of David A. Butterfield, who had raised $6,000,000 in the East to establish competition with the Ben Holladay stage-line monopoly. It was known as the Butterfield Overland Despatch, and was to run from Atchison to Denver by way of the Smoky Hill River Valley in Kansas.

On September 23, 1865, Butterfield arrived in Denver on the first coach run, and announced the beginning of regular daily service. Nine days later, hostile Indians made their first strike, near Monument Station in western Kansas. A westbound coach was surrounded and a sharp fight resulted. Finally the coach had to be abandoned, the travelers cutting the horses loose and racing to safety. Western newspapers editorialized: Will the Smoky Hill Route Be Abandoned?[2]

Butterfield immediately denied any intentions of abandoning the route, but he did ask for military assistance. On October 4, General Grenville Dodge boarded an eastbound coach in Denver to have a close look at the practicalities of guarding the new line.

Dodge evidently recognized the advantages of the Smoky Hill route. It was 116 miles shorter than the Holladay route from the Missouri River to Denver, and much more grass was available for horses. The only thing lacking was military protection. Soon after General Dodge arrived in Atchison, Butterfield announced that his stagecoaches would be protected by Army escorts.

The escorts would consist of the four companies of 1st U.S. Volunteers, supplemented by detachments of the 13th Missouri Cavalry. Late in October, Lieutenant-Colonel Tamblyn was ordered to march 225 miles west to Big Creek and establish a new post to be called Fort Fletcher. (The name was later changed to Fort Hays.) Companies F and G would garrison Fort Fletcher.

Company A under Captain Hooper B. Straut would march another 100 miles westward to Monument Station. Captain Richard Musgrove's Company I was assigned to the farthest point west, Pond's Creek Station, 50 miles beyond Monument.

On November 1, Tamblyn set his column in motion. It consisted of 108 six-mule–team wagons loaded with rations, grain, ammunition, and lumber to supply his 250 men. "Rain fell most of the time during the first two or three days, and the roads were heavy, the soil being clayey, similar to that of Virginia, but the mud soon disappeared with the appearance of the sun and we then made about twenty miles each day."[3] On November 4, they camped on the Potawatomi reservation, 80 miles from Leavenworth, and two or three days later marched into Fort Riley to rest for a day.

At Salina we passed the last dwelling house on the frontier. Here was located a public house, on the outside of which was spread an immense piece of canvas on which was lettered: THE LAST CHANCE TO PROCURE A SQUARE MEAL. The price was one dollar. We looked inside at the small table spread in the middle of the room that constituted the first story, and concluded we would let the last chance pass and trust to army supplies for our next meal, rather than partake of a meal in that place.

Here we left the habitations of civilized man behind us, and entered that vast tract of country called the Great American desert, the domain of the Indians, the buffalo, the antelope, the deer and the wolf.[4]

On November 20, the column reached Big Creek, previously selected as a fort site because of the availability of timber and water. Lieutenant-Colonel Tamblyn ordered half the wagons unloaded, laid out locations for barracks, and established Fort Fletcher as new headquarters for the last battalion of the 1st U.S. Volunteers. (Back in Leavenworth, Colonel Dimon had arrived with the other six companies from Fort Rice, and was preparing to muster them out.)

After a two-day rest, Companies A and I resumed march with the remaining wagons of supplies. "The first three days out, the weather was fine, the trail in good condition, and we covered a longer distance than usual. A vast number of buffalo were in sight, and we killed two or three to furnish meat for the men of our commands."[5]

About noon on November 26, Straut and Musgrove decided to go into camp and rest the remainder of the day, as it was Sunday.

Three hours later, a band of mounted Indians swarmed down on a herd of grazing stock, sending 57 mules flying wildly across the plain. Captain Musgrove mounted some of his men and started in pursuit, but the raiders and the stolen mules were already out of sight.

After a conference between the two captains, it was decided to transfer the contents of nine wagons to others in the train, and abandon the empty ones. "The afternoon and night passed without further alarm, but towards night a smoke was seen a few miles to the west, which we understood to mean that the Indians were at work at a ranch just west of us and so the events of the morrow proved."[6]

As luck would have it, Companies A and I had run head-on into one of the year's worst raids in western Kansas—Cheyennes led by the half-breed Bent brothers, who were still wreaking vengeance on all white men in retaliation for the Sand Creek Massacre.*

Next morning before starting out, Straut and Musgrove told the teamsters to be ready to corral the wagons at the first signs of an attack. They also ordered wagon covers rolled back, and posted two soldiers in front of each one with rifles at ready.

After a few miles, Musgrove sighted a party formed in a circle not far down the trail. "I took a dozen men and advanced under cover of a ravine," he said, "intending to fire on them without warning, but I discovered that the party consisted of six white men and two women."

They were Butterfield employees from Castle Rock Station, fleeing from Cheyenne raiders. Livestock belonging to the company had been run off by the Indians, but the ranchers had made their escape. They reported that when they passed near Downer's Station during the night, they had seen buildings blazing and heard screams, but had not dared offer assistance; the Indians were too numerous. When the column reached Downer's, they found three dead men.

The body of one lay in front of the ranch, stripped of all clothing, and from his chest protruded more than twenty arrows. . . . Not far away lay another, also nude, his body pierced with many arrows, his tongue cut out, and he was otherwise namelessly mutilated. In the rear of the ranch a still more sickening sight met our view. Here the fiends had made a fire . . . and across the yet smouldering embers lay the body of a man

---

* See pages 129-132 for an account of the Bent brothers' attack on two companies of the 5th U.S. Volunteers earlier in the year.

half consumed from the knees to the shoulders. The arms were drawn to the chest, the hands clenched, and every feature of the face indicated that the man had died in agony. Without doubt he had been burned alive.[7]

This was only the beginning of a day of appalling discoveries. As the two companies continued westward, they found a succession of mute witnesses to the cruelty of the raiders. Always there had been torture and mutilation.

When night fell, Straut and Musgrove corraled their wagons and kept an alert watch until dawn, fully expecting an attack. They were still 40 miles from Monument Station, Company A's destination, but the two captains decided to try to cover the distance in one day. The march proved uneventful except for immense herds of buffalo which kept crossing the trail in front of them, heading south for winter grazing. As dusk fell they reached Monument, and to their great relief found there a detachment of the 13th Missouri Cavalry, quartered in adobe huts and dugouts.

Next morning, Captain Straut had his first look at the place where he was to construct dugouts for his new headquarters. The camp site lay on the west bank of the Smoky Hill, with a broad stretch of waving prairie grass extending for a mile or more along the bottomland. Beyond were the eroded clay formations known as "monuments," which gave the station its name.

The morning was spent in unloading Company A's supplies; then, late in the afternoon, a stagecoach arrived. It was a special coach carrying Butterfield's general superintendent, William R. Brewster, and several Eastern newspaper reporters whom he had invited to make the journey. Among them was Theodore R. Davis, special artist for *Harper's Weekly*. Brewster's mission was to show the newspapermen the safety and efficiency of the new stage line. Unless he had waited for the winter blizzards, he could not have chosen a more untimely week for the demonstration.

The travelers passed a quiet night at Monument, but before they could depart the next morning, a band of mounted Indians made a sweep at the mule herd. This time Captain Musgrove was ready for them. He ordered his men into firing positions and gave the raiders a shower of bullets. "The result was highly satisfactory, and to veterans of the hard fought battles of Virginia extremely ludicrous. The savages instantly whirled, threw themselves on the sides of their ponies farthest from us and were off with even greater speed than they had come."[8]

The Indians, however, refused to leave the vicinity. They kept out of rifle range until their numbers had grown to 400 or 500, then began circling the adobes, occasionally dashing in close. Determined rifle fire drove them away. Late in the afternoon, the dry prairie grass on the bottomland burst into flames. The Indians were trying to drive the soldiers out with smoke and fire.

Artist Theodore Davis later sent *Harper's Weekly* a series of on-the-spot drawings of this incident. "The strong breeze," he wrote, "brought the smoke and flame rapidly down, nearly reaching the adobe before we could check the fire by beating it down and out with our blankets."[9]

Soon afterward the attackers retired from the scene, and Superintendent Brewster announced that the coach would depart. This act of bravado did not go unnoticed by the officers at Monument, but they understood that Brewster was attempting to impress upon his guests that a stagecoach could pass unmolested through western Kansas.

As for Captain Musgrove, he had no intention of taking his slow-moving supply wagons across 50 miles to Pond's Creek until he had scouted the trail. Waiting until the next morning, he started out with a reconnaissance party of 12 men mounted on mules. They saw a few Indians watching them from distant hills, but no attack was offered.

About noon, as Musgrove was nearing a stock-tender's ranch, he noticed an abandoned stagecoach standing beside a corral. A moment later a man stepped out of a dugout; he was followed by seven or eight others. They were Superintendent Brewster and his guests, marooned after a chase by Indians. Although they had managed to reach the safety of the dugout, they had lost their team to the raiders. (Brewster, who had been so anxious to impress the newspapermen, must have been chagrined a few weeks later when Theodore Davis' exciting drawing of a Butterfield stagecoach in flight before Indians filled a full page of *Harper's Weekly*.)

"These men regarded my party as their deliverers," Musgrove said, "and gladly accepted my proposition to return to Monument with us. We rested our animals, partook of hardtack and coffee, and were on the point of starting east, when we observed horsemen approaching from the west."[10] The patrol proved to be a detachment of Company A, 13th Missouri Cavalry, under Captain DeWitt C. McMichael. The Missourians, who were to share duties with the Galvanized Yankees at Pond's Creek, were marching to meet Captain Musgrove's company, which was overdue.

After a consultation, McMichael agreed to use some of his horses to pull Brewster's coach on to Pond's Creek. Musgrove then returned to Monument with his squad, and on his arrival issued orders to Company I and the wagon drivers to prepare to march for Pond's Creek at dawn. "We pushed ahead as rapidly as possible, all the time using the utmost vigilance to guard against a surprise. Our constant preparation for trouble may have been observed by the Indians and thus saved us from an attack. After an hour's rest at noon for man and beast and for feeding the mules with grain rather than allowing them to graze, we again pushed on and arrived, late at night, at Pond's Creek."[11]

Pond's Creek Station—which was later to become Fort Wallace—was one mile from Smoky Hill River, on a low bluff surrounded by a treeless plain. The Missourians had already begun construction of dugouts, and as soon as the men of Company I unloaded their wagons they began digging similar excavations. They dug 8 by 10 foot holes six feet into the slope, covering them with poles, brush, and earth. Gunny sacks served as entrance covers.

The first order of business between Captains Musgrove and McMichael was to compare dates of muster. As McMichael proved to be the ranking captain, he assumed command of the new post, which was garrisoned by 120 men—70 Missouri cavalrymen and 50 U.S. Volunteer infantrymen. Musgrove was not impressed by the discipline of McMichael's troops. One of the cavalry lieutenants, he noted, had lost his voice because of a bullet that passed through his neck when he was trying to quell a disturbance among his men.

"Life at Pond's Creek Station was decidedly dreary. By the time quarters were completed winter had set in." Only the arrival of stagecoaches broke the daily monotony, and soon they were running on irregular schedules. After Superintendent Brewster's unfortunate experiences with the Eastern newspapermen, Butterfield had persuaded the army to provide escorts for all coaches crossing the Western division of his line, but by December passenger traffic dwindled, and service was cut to triweekly departures. When the first snowstorms swept down from the Rockies, the coaches stopped running entirely.

The snows also meant trouble for Pond's Creek and Monument.

The soldiers had brought only enough rations to last until mid-winter, and unless additional wagons could get through they would face starvation. To make matters worse at Pond's Creek, a large part of the rations were found inedible. Pork and bacon were spoiled and the hardtack was mildewed. As a deep snow cover remained on the ground, the horses also began suffering for lack of forage.

About a week before Christmas, a buffalo herd was sighted several miles out. Captains McMichael and Musgrove selected their best marksmen, saddled up, and went for a hunt. They brought in eight buffaloes. The meat was a welcome addition to the sparse diet of the post, but by Christmas Day it was all gone. No other herds were seen, and McMichael believed it unlikely that more would appear before spring.

On New Year's Day, 1866, the two captains made an inventory of their provisions and estimated that even on short rations the Pond's Creek garrison could subsist for only 15 more days. A few days later, with the frigid weather showing no sign of relenting, McMichael announced that he had decided to make his way East through the snow with his mounted men, leaving Musgrove's infantrymen to hold the station until relief could arrive.

"I regarded this as cowardice on his part," Musgrove recorded, "and involving a positive peril to my command. . . . I therefore sent him a written protest against his proposed course of action. Immediately on reading my communication, he strode into my tent, evidently excited, and prepared to finish me then and there."

Musgrove managed to calm the hot-blooded Missourian, but could not persuade him to change his mind about withdrawing the cavalry. On January 8, McMichael with an escort of eight men started for Monument, after issuing orders for the remainder of his company to follow the next day if he had not returned. "As soon as the captain left the post," Musgrove said, "I assumed command and forbade any one leaving the post except by orders issued by me. But Captain McMichael was evidently ill at ease. After he had been gone a few hours, he returned to the post, assumed command, and issued orders for the evacuation of the station."[12]

After waiting one more week in hopes that a supply train would reach Pond's Creek, McMichael ordered all remaining supplies loaded in two six-mule wagons, and on the morning of January 18, the 120 men began a 50-mile march to Monument Station.

Drifted snow had obliterated the trail, and much of the time they had to travel by dead reckoning. Horses and mules stumbled into deceptive hollows; shovels had to be used frequently to keep the wagons rolling.

They made only 12 miles the first day, and when darkness fell the men had to bivouac in the snow. "Those who had them spread rubber blankets upon the snow with woolen blankets on those, on which they lay down and covered themselves with other blankets. No faces were left exposed and the more the snow drifted over those beds the warmer were the occupants. Each morning long rows of snowy mounds looked like a graveyard in winter, but there was life there, and without the roll of drum or the bugle note the snow would heave and from the mounds men would issue, shake the snows from their bodies and their beds and prepare for another day's tramp."[13]

Each day their difficulties increased. Horses and mules began to fail for lack of forage, and one by one the animals were left to die along the track. On the second day out, wolves and coyotes appeared in the wake of the column, a gathering host of scavengers, depressing the spirits of the struggling soldiers.

"Most of the time," wrote Musgrove, "the weather was intensely cold—how cold we could not determine, as there was no thermometer in the party, but one night a mule was frozen to death while tied to the tongue of a wagon, and water left in an iron kettle was frozen to a solid mass and the kettle broken." Contemporary newspapers attest to the bitter weather of January 1866 in western Kansas. A Santa Fe stage arriving in Kansas City reported crossing the Arkansas River on the ice. Twenty wagon trains west of Fort Zarah were snowbound, their teams dying of cold and starvation. Snow was two feet deep at Salina. "Winter is severe on the plains."[14]

When they reached Monument Station they found Company A nearing the end of its provisions, and Captain Straut needed no persuasion to join his men to the hegira. Next day the enlarged column resumed march; almost a hundred miles of deep snowdrifts lay between them and Fort Fletcher, the nearest source of supplies.

A day or so later a blizzard struck. "The air was full of falling snow, driven by a pitiless and unceasing gale, but fortunately, we were . . . where we had a small quantity of fuel and therefore did not attempt to move."[15]

At last, after 16 days on the trail from Pond's Creek, and with practically all rations exhausted, the half-frozen column reached Fort Fletcher. There the men's hopes for nourishing food were quickly dashed. For a week, Lieutenant-Colonel Tamblyn's garrison had been existing on parched corn and had nothing else to offer the starving men from the West.

Tamblyn was pessimistic about prospects of immediate relief. In spite of intense cold, Indians had been harassing travelers between Fort Fletcher and Salina. Only a few days before, six employees of the Butterfield line had been attacked by a war party at Walker's Creek. Two men were killed, the other four badly wounded. Tamblyn ordered Captain William Bleadenhiser to mount 25 men of G Company and go in pursuit, but winds had already drifted over the tracks on hard-packed snow, and the raiders vanished.[16]

The officers' consultation at Fort Fletcher after arrival of the column from Pond's Creek was grim in its implications. Salina was 80 miles to the east, and even if the men could march that far on parched corn, there was little likelihood that the garrison there could feed them.

Then, on the first day of February, a miracle occurred. A supply train appeared on the eastern horizon; the wagons were loaded with rations for the three posts, enough to last at least a month. Tamblyn ordered everything unloaded at Fort Fletcher. As no stagecoaches had been running since December, he saw no reason to jeopardize the lives of the men in A and I Companies by ordering them back to their isolated stations.

"The first requisite at Fort Fletcher," said Musgrove, "was winter quarters. These the men set about building at once without waiting to recover from the fatigue of the late march. Fortunately there was a fringe of timber along the creek, and the art of building log cabins was well known to the men, so it was but a few days before the men were housed in comfortable cabins about eight by ten feet, four men to each."[17]

Unfortunately the soldiers of A and I Companies did not have long to enjoy their new quarters. Toward the end of February, the Butterfield Overland Despatch announced resumption of service, and the first coach from Atchison brought orders for Captains Straut and Musgrove to reoccupy Monument Station. A few hours later Captain Edward Ball and a company of the 2nd U.S. Cavalry arrived at Fort Fletcher. These regular cavalrymen were to relieve the 13th Missouri from further duties in western Kansas, and Captain Ball's headquarters would be Pond's Creek.

On March 1, the two companies of Galvanized Yankees started westward again, Captain Ball's cavalrymen serving as escorts. On March 6, they reached Monument. Captain Straut's men moved into their old quarters, and for the third time in three months Captain Musgrove's men had to construct new quarters for themselves. However, no sooner were they comfortably housed at Monument than a new set of orders arrived. Company I was to report back to their original station, Pond's Creek.

They found Pond's Creek bustling with springtime activity. Captain Ball had relocated the site a mile and a half northeast of the slope where the men had built dugouts, and there were rumors that a permanent fort would soon be built (Fort Wallace). This time there was no problem of constructing quarters. Tents were issued to the men, and although details were assigned routine activities, a new and more pleasant period now began for the men of Company I. As Captain Musgrove put it, "beyond the inevitable camp guard, there were no military duties to perform, and if the men were present at roll call night and morning, there were no restrictions on their movements."[18]

Meanwhile coaches were beginning to run again, but the Indians and the blizzards had almost wiped out Butterfield's resources. When his rival, Ben Holladay, offered to buy the line in April, the Overland Despatch quickly sold out. Perhaps Butterfield saw doom coming for all stagecoach lines in the steel railroad tracks pushing across both Nebraska and Kansas. Holladay, however, announced grandly that under his ownership the Smoky Hill division would become an express route between the East and California. The Galvanized Yankees served as guardians for Holladay's express coaches during part of their brief period of glory, but the world was changing. Both organizations would be mustered out of existence before the end of 1866.

In that springtime of their last period of service, the 1st U.S. Volunteers discovered that the Great Plains could be congenial as well as inclement. Under a warming sun the harsh landscape changed to delicate shades of green. The ice-locked prairie was transformed into a garden of wildflowers, filled with an abundance of game. There was time for hunting buffalo and antelope, for observing the antics of prairie dogs and jackrabbits. They discovered that not all Indians were hostile. And they learned the lore of the West from one of its best teachers, a seasoned scout named Bill Comstock.

Comstock was employed at Pond's Creek as official guide and interpreter. According to legend, he was the man sought by Ned Buntline, a dime-novel writer, to become the model for a character to be known as Buffalo Bill. Buntline, however, arrived too late—the Cheyennes had killed Comstock, so the novelist took William F. Cody instead. Comstock was much more of the genuine article than Cody. A grandnephew of James Fenimore Cooper, he grew up in the frontier tradition and had spent most of his life in the West. He was a bullwhacker, miner, Indian trader, trapper, buffalo hunter, and then a scout for the Army.

Before he came to Pond's Creek, Bill Comstock had known Galvanized Yankees at Fort Halleck, where he distinguished himself by capturing a desperado named Bob Jennings. Jennings had killed one Hod Russell, and then when a posse went to arrest him, he wounded the leader and escaped into the mountains above Fort Halleck. According to Charles Adams, a soldier stationed at Halleck, Jennings sent word to the commander, Captain J. L. Humfreville, that he would kill him or anyone else who tried to arrest him.

There was a hunter there named Billy Comstock who said he would get him for $1,000. No get him, no pay. So there was a bargain to that effect. Comstock took ten or twelve Indians and started off as though on a hunt. They found Jennings out in the mountains sitting by a tree, his big hocken [Hawken] rifle leaning against the tree and his belt and two big revolvers on the ground beside him. The Indians told him one of their ponies was lame and asked Jennings if he would see if he could tell what was the matter. He did not suspicion any trickery and when he took up the foot the Indians all piled on him and wound a rope all around him and had him good and fast.

He was taken to the post and kept a while in the guardhouse and then taken out and hung to a large sweep used to swing meat out of the reach of bears and wolves. . . . The large end was so heavy it took two or three men to hold it down. When all was ready the Captain asked him if he had anything to say. He commenced to say, "Hurrah for Jeff Davis and the Southern Confederacy," but before he got it all out the Captain said, "turn him loose," and away he went. The large end of the sweep was so heavy that when it struck the ground it threw him the length of the rope above the pole, and when he dropped down there was just a quiver and all was over.[19]

Presumably Bill Comstock received his $1,000.

At Pond's Creek, Comstock was a main attraction for the boys of Company I. "One of the diversions of the camp," said Captain Musgrove, "was listening to his tales of experience, his narrow escapes . . . the scenes of horror he had witnessed. . . . Bill Comstock had a wonderful ability at trailing a party of Indians or a single warrior. He could easily read all the 'signs' left by them for the information of other Indians, could interpret the meaning of one, two, or three columns of smoke used in telegraphing between different parties, and, after a party had passed could tell with remarkable accuracy, by examining the trail, how many were in the party."[20]

Another admirer of Comstock was the *Harper's Weekly* artist, Theodore Davis, who spent considerable time in western Kansas after his adventures on the Butterfield stagecoach. "No Indian was ever half so superstitious as Will Comstock. He had his 'medicine' horse, 'medicine' field-glass, 'medicine' everything, in fact. Even Will's evil-looking dog was 'medicine,' and had a 'medicine' collar. . . . Yet for all this, Will Comstock is fearlessly brave. He is quiet and unassuming in manner, small in size, and compact in proportion. He is one of the best riders in the Plains, with which he is probably more familiar than any other white man who roves over them."[21]

To the Galvanized Yankees, Comstock must have seemed imperishable. Yet only two years after they knew him during that spring of 1866 at Pond's Creek, he died at the hands of treacherous Cheyennes a few miles north of Monument Station.*

Early in May, one of the new Holladay express coaches brought unexpected orders from Fort Leavenworth. All companies of the 1st U.S. Volunteers were to march there for mustering out. †

* For an excellent account of the life of William Comstock, see "Will Comstock—the Natty Bumppo of Kansas," by Dr. John S. Gray, *Westerners Brand Book,* Chicago, February 1962.

† Company I, 1st U.S. Volunteers, was replaced at Pond's Creek by another company of Galvanized Yankees—Company B of the 6th U.S. Volunteers, Captain James Gordon, commanding (see Chapter VII). Company B served there until October 1866. In July, the station's name was changed to Fort Wallace, and it soon became one of the more active cavalry posts in the West, such names as Custer, Keogh, Benteen, Beecher, and Forsyth being associated with it. During the period the 6th U.S. Volunteers were

"The march was uneventful," said Captain Musgrove. "At Monument Station my company was joined with that of Captain Straut, and we proceeded together to Fort Fletcher. Here we joined the two companies there, and all proceeded under command of Colonel Tamblyn to Leavenworth." On May 22, 1866, the last man of the battalion was mustered out. "At St. Louis," Musgrove concluded his chronicle, "I secured transportation for my men to their several places of abode in the Southern states."[22]

So ended the longest period of service of any of the Galvanized Yankee organizations—22 months of soldiering from Virginia to Minnesota and the Great Plains of Kansas.

there, it was a 2nd Cavalry post. One of the officers of the latter organization, Lieutenant George A. Armes, recorded some of the excitement and color of the first days of Fort Wallace in *Ups and Downs of an Army Officer*. One of Armes's close friends, often mentioned in the book, was Lieutenant R. E. Flood, second in Command of Company B and the post quartermaster. The Galvanized Yankees of Company B. spent much of their time digging stone out of a nearby quarry for construction of the new fort.

Last Man Out

XI

In May 1866 when Lieutenant-Colonel William Tamblyn's battalion of 1st U.S. Volunteers closed out its record of longest service, there were still three other regiments of Galvanized Yankees on the frontier. The 4th Regiment, organized some three months later than the 1st, was mustered out in June. The 5th and 6th Regiments, organized seven or eight months after the 1st, served on until autumn. Not until November 13, 1866, were the last three companies disbanded—H, I, and K of the 5th Regiment—after 20 months of service.

Of all the Galvanized Yankee companies, H Company was the most peripatetic. From the day it was organized at Camp Douglas, Chicago, in April 1865 with a strength of 97 men, until early November of 1866 when its surviving 30 members marched into Fort Leavenworth to be discharged, H Company was forever wayfaring. It was also in a constant state of fragmentation, with detachments marching off on all sorts of major and minor missions. In the course of its journeyings, H Company operated in five different army districts. Its members saw most of the military posts of Kansas, Colorado, and Nebraska, and one of its detachments had the distinction of being the only Galvanized Yankee unit to serve in New Mexico—as escort to a wagon train.

H Company also had one of the highest rates of desertion of any company, although it is quite likely that some of the men so listed on its rolls may have simply become lost. Detachments returning from long marches usually found that the company had been transferred, perhaps 200 or 300 miles, and by the time they reached that new headquarters, the chances were that half the company had gone to one place and the other half somewhere else. The opportunities for striking off on one's own in such cases were no doubt tempting. In its 20 months of traveling, H Company lost 67 men, but only two by death, one by honorable discharge.

On April 28, 1865, H Company reached Fort Leavenworth from Camp Douglas prison, and three days later 22-year-old Charles H. Hoyt, "mustered from civilian life by virtue of a commission from the Secretary of War," took command with the rank of first lieutenant.[1] Judging from records of the company, it appears that Hoyt leaned heavily upon his 30-year-old sergeant-major, John C. McDade, a Confederate veteran from Pike County, Alabama.

H Company was primarily an Alabama-Georgia outfit, soldiers from those states representing about half the strength. Most of them had been captured in the Confederate Army's last defeats around Nashville and Chattanooga during 1864, and most were seasoned veterans of the Civil War.

On May 1, arms and equipment were issued to H Company, and the men began daily drills. On May 3, Hoyt received an order from headquarters to participate in the establishment of a chain of sentinels about the post: "The main object making this necessary [the order read] is thereby to prevent: 1st: The coming in of lewd women and others. 2nd: To keep soldiers within our lines and prevent loafing about. 3rd: To give men and officers a chance to practice thoroughly outpost and picket duty."[2]

For two weeks, H Company did its share of guarding Fort Leavenworth from "lewd women and others," and then on March 18 "took up the line of march" with the regiment, bound westward for Fort Riley. On May 28, the regiment marched into Riley and set up a tent camp. First duty for the H Company men was to dig latrines 50 yards from the camp guard line—12 feet long, five feet deep, three feet wide. Being a young man of modest sensibilities, Lieutenant Hoyt had the sinks screened with tree branches on the side facing the camp.

During the following week the company drilled, marched in dress parades, and awaited further orders. The orders came on

June 5. Companies H and I were to march immediately as escorts for a wagon train bound for New Mexico. When they reached Fort Dodge, the two companies would relieve the 2nd U.S. Volunteers on duty there; a detachment of H Company would then proceed with the train to New Mexico.[3]

As ranking officer, Lieutenant Frederick Hubert commanded the combined companies. The train consisted of 175 wagons and 150 head of cattle, and for the first few days Lieutenant Hubert permitted the men to walk beside the wagons in a loose route march. On June 14, when the train went into camp at Spring Creek, company roll calls revealed 12 men missing, lost, or deserted.

Hubert at once drew up a stern set of orders to be read to the men. Henceforth the two companies would alternate as rear guard, marching in formation, and be charged with the duty of rounding up stragglers. No soldiers would be allowed to leave the column without permission of the commanding officer.[4]

The train moved on to Fort Ellsworth, turned southwest, and followed the Santa Fe Trail past Forts Zarah and Larned. When buffalo herds were sighted, Lieutenant Hubert organized hunting parties to procure fresh meat for the command. As they approached Cimarron Crossing, they ran into some of the roving bands of Kiowas that had been making life miserable for the 2nd U.S. Volunteers at Fort Dodge.

On June 29, about 40 hostiles charged into one of the train's cattle herds, killing two Mexican herdsmen. "As soon as the cry of Indians rang through the camp," Lieutenant Hubert recorded, "I had the mule herd driven in, formed my men for the defense of the camp, and doubled the pickets around it. The Indians, satisfied with the mischief done, struck across the road and made for the river. They did not succeed in driving off any stock, notwithstanding the immense amount of stock in the command. . . . If I had had any means to pursue the devils they would not have gone away unpunished."[5]

Upon arrival at Fort Dodge on July 1, they were given a hearty welcome by Major William F. Armstrong and his 2nd U.S. Volunteers, who were eager to leave the dugouts they had constructed there during the spring.

H Company was not to spend much time at Fort Dodge, however. Major Armstrong, who had been fighting off Kiowas for a month, decided that a mere detachment of H Company was insufficient protection for the westbound train. He ordered Lieutenant Hoyt to take his entire company as escort to Fort Lyon. The commanding officer there could then decide what force would be necessary for the remainder of the journey.

So it was that H Company marched another 175 miles west to Fort Lyon, arriving there in mid-July. As Indians were not troublesome on the route south to New Mexico, Lieutenant Hoyt detached a few of his men to continue with the wagon train, and turned back for Fort Dodge with the rest of his company.

When he reached Fort Dodge, new orders were waiting. H Company was to turn about and march back west over the same trail for 100 miles and occupy Camp Wynkoop.[6]

Camp Wynkoop was 60 miles down the Arkansas River from Fort Lyon, and was about as lonely a place as a soldier could find in all of Kansas in 1865. It had been established in May 1864 by Major W. W. Wynkoop, then commanding at Fort Lyon, as a picket camp for observation of Indian or Confederate movements, but was soon abandoned.[7] As it was a halfway point between Forts Dodge and Lyon, the Army decided to send a company of Galvanized Yankees there to give military assistance to wagon trains.

Lieutenant Hoyt and his men had no horses, however, and they could offer little protection to trains passing through that wasteland of sand hills and blowing dust. After about six weeks of ineffectual duty—during which time they must have wondered if the Army had forgotten their existence—they received notice that the 5th Regiment was moving north to Nebraska. H Company was to abandon Camp Wynkoop and march to Fort Kearney by the most direct route.

They headed north across the untracked High Plains into hostile Cheyenne territory, crossed the Smoky Hill, and turned eastward along the Solomon. It was late October before they reached Fort Kearney only to discover that their regiment had moved on west to Julesburg and Laramie.

For lack of any other orders, the post commander at Kearney instructed Lieutenant Hoyt to distribute his company along the line of unguarded stations east of the fort as far as Little Blue. No sooner had Hoyt accomplished this and established headquarters at Spring Station, than orders from his regiment finally reached him. H Company was to report for duty at Camp Wardwell, Colorado.[8]

When the company was reassembled and started on the 250-mile march to Wardwell, Sergeant McDade reported 17 men missing. No one seemed to know where or when they had gone; they could have been lost or misplaced at any of a dozen stations. Lieutenant Hoyt never made any great effort to find them, and the missing soldiers doubtless made even a lesser effort to find their company. They were listed on the rolls as deserters.

In mid-December, the wanderers managed to settle down in winter tents at Camp Wardwell, but after New Year's Day various detachments were on the road again, performing messenger and escort duties to Denver and Julesburg. The last week of January in bitter cold weather, Lieutenant Hoyt and a platoon had to take a group of prisoners to Denver for courts-martial.[9]

H Company spent three months at Camp Wardwell, and the men evidently liked the place; only one desertion occurred. But springtime brought the inevitable marching orders. With I and K Companies, which were also stationed on the Julesburg-Denver trail, H Company was ordered to Fort Lyon "to form a permanent garrison."

From what they had seen of Fort Lyon back in the summer of 1865, Lieutenant Hoyt and his men had no desire to return there, but on April 1 they started south along the valley of Bijou Creek, struck the Denver-Santa Fe road, and marched into Fort Lyon three weeks later.

Even in springtime the flat-roofed, stone-walled buildings of Fort Lyon had a bleak look about them. The post had been built on the flats of the Arkansas River, and the only vegetation was a fringe of slender willows along the banks. At Fort Lyon there was no place to go and nothing to see. The enlisted men's quarters had no flooring, and every time rain fell, water would flow inside and remain for days on the hard-packed earth.

The post was under command of an aging lieutenant-colonel of the 2nd Cavalry, Enoch Steen, who believed in rigid discipline and harsh punishments for infractions of the rules. After a few weeks at Fort Lyon, the men of Company H would have welcomed a transfer to anywhere. But no orders came.

On June 9, Lieutenant-Colonel Steen gave them an unexpected holiday to honor the recent death of General Winfield Scott, and on the Fourth of July, after a dress parade, they enjoyed another half-day of rest. But on all other days their waking hours were spent drilling, policing, guarding, and standing inspections.

Lieutenant Hoyt, who was as much a civilian at heart as were his men, endured the monotonous existence until July 19, and then submitted his resignation "for private reasons."[10] By this time his company had dwindled to less than 40 men, and he must have realized that the captaincy which his command originally warranted would never be forthcoming.

After Hoyt departed in mid-August, H Company became largely the responsibility of Sergeant-Major McDade, who reported to Lieutenant A. O. Ingalls of K Company. Six weeks later when General Sherman arrived at Fort Lyon on his inspection tour of Western posts, he was so appalled by what he saw that he recommended the post be abandoned. The quarters, he said, were not fit for human habitation. "Anybody looking through them can see full reason for the desertions that have prevailed so much of late years."[11] Sherman ordered the 2nd Cavalry transferred to Fort Laramie, the three companies of Galvanized Yankees to be mustered out.*

H Company still had one more long stretch of Western country to cross—500 miles to Fort Leavenworth. On October 15, with I and K Companies, the Alabama-Georgia boys started east along the Santa Fe Trail, every step marched a step nearer home—for those who were going home.

Their delayed mustering out enabled them to benefit from a recent War Department ruling. They could keep their knapsacks, haversacks, and canteens—all for free. If they wanted to retain their well-used Springfield muskets they had to put $6.00 on the line. Revolvers were $8.00, swords $3.00. Those who elected to stay in the West probably chose revolvers.

At Fort Leavenworth on November 13, 1866, they became civilians again. These were the last of the Galvanized Yankees.

* In June 1867, Fort Lyon was relocated on a sandstone bluff 20 miles up the Arkansas from its old site.

XII

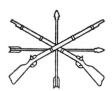

A Note on the Galvanized Confederates

Early in the Civil War the Confederate States of America had a far Western frontier, but its importance rapidly diminished, and as the Confederacy was never engaged in war with Indian tribes, its government could not offer prisoners of war their freedom in exchange for frontier service.

The Confederate Army did recruit, however, several hundred Galvanized Confederates (sometimes confusingly called Galvanized Yankees) from prison camps. As early as March 1863, General John Pemberton queried the Confederate Secretary of War, James A. Seddon, as to possibilities of enlisting Union soldiers held as prisoners of war in Mississippi. Seddon's reply left the responsibility largely to Pemberton: "Use your discretion with regard to men taken as prisoners of war. Enlist if any are willing. Let any willing take the oath of allegiance. Put any willing to work. Parole and dismiss toward their own country such as you may deem safe."[1]

Pemberton apparently never enlisted any of his prisoners. He probably never found time to do so, because during the next few weeks he was too much occupied with defending Vicksburg from the vigorous assaults of General Grant, and surrendering to him on July 4.

Not until late in 1864 did the Confederate War Department make any serious effort toward recruiting soldiers from prison camps. On September 13, General Samuel Jones reported to General Braxton Bragg from Charleston, South Carolina: "Many

Yankee prisoners now here profess to be highly indignant with their Government for not exchanging them . . . and they express an earnest desire to take the oath of allegiance, and many of them to join our army if we will permit them. Can anything be done in that way?"

Bragg forwarded the inquiry to Secretary Seddon, who replied: "A battalion or two might be formed of the foreigners—the Yankees are not to be trusted so far, or at all."[2]

Two weeks later from Macon, Georgia, General M. J. Wright notified Secretary Seddon that there were "a thousand or more" Irish and other foreign-born Union prisoners under his jurisdiction who desired to enlist in the Confederate service. "Shall it be done?" Wright asked.

"The enlistment of Irish and other foreign prisoners, as proposed, is sanctioned," Seddon ruled on September 30, and Wright immediately ordered that all foreigners willing to take the oath be placed in a separate camp to await specific instructions for enlistment.[3]

The first camp selected for concentration of recruits was at Florence, South Carolina. On October 12, Lieutenant-Colonel W. D. Pickett made an inspection of the camp, reporting his findings to General W. J. Hardee at Charleston:

They are mostly foreigners, and are generally good-looking men, and I doubt not will make good soldiers. They are woefully destitute in clothing and blankets, and their wants should be at once supplied. I recommend that they at once be placed in the field, either as an organization or scattered in old commands. I understand several hundred more foreigners can be enlisted, and if you will take Western men, 1,500 to 2,000 more can be enlisted. About 50 of them already enlisted are old gunners and seamen, and are anxious to go in the Navy. I recommend that they be allowed to do so.

When Hardee forwarded this report to Seddon, the Secretary of War evidently had some misgivings about immediate enlistment of these former enemies. For the time being, he directed, the recruits should be "detailed for work at their respective trades."[4]

Meanwhile other hard-pressed Confederate commanders, eager to fill up their rosters, began beseeching Richmond for permission to recruit from prison camps. The competition became keen, one general complaining that 1,100 of the prisoners enlisted at Florence "have been carried away to some place unknown to me by one of General Hardee's inspectors."[5]

Early in November, Seddon granted permission for "enlistment of a battalion of infantry from prisoners of war at Millen, Andersonville, and other points in Georgia," and soon afterward extended this to any military prisons in the Eastern theater of war. That the recruiting efforts were productive is indicated by a November report of the commandant at Camp Lawton, Georgia, who noted 349 prisoners enlisted in Confederate service.[6]

All this activity behind the Confederate lines soon came to the notice of the Union Army. On November 11 and 12, special reports were sent to the chief of staff, H. W. Halleck, from Union Army Headquarters, Department of the South, Hilton Head, South Carolina. The commanding general of the department, J. G. Foster, had taken testimony from several Galvanized Confederates who had escaped at the first opportunity and made their way back to the Union lines.

One of these men was Sergeant James D. Salsbury, Company K, 3rd New York Volunteer Infantry Regiment, who had been captured near Petersburg, Virginia, May 24, 1864. In his statement, Salsbury said "that to save his life and health he enlisted in the 47th Georgia Volunteers, knowing it was stationed at James Island, so that he could desert and come to our lines." Salsbury also told General Foster there were 150 former U.S. soldiers who had taken the oath of allegiance to the Confederate States of America and enlisted in that same regiment.

After questioning other men who had escaped, Foster estimated that there were "between 1,300 and 2,000 U.S. soldiers who have taken the oath of allegiance to the Southern Confederacy; 400 of them have arms and are on James Island; the others are in camp at Summerville. They are clothed in the C.S. Army uniform."

General Halleck immediately forwarded this information to General Grant with the notation: "Advices from other sources indicate that many of our foreign troops and substitutes, prisoners of war, are joining the rebel cause."[7]

About the same time that Grant was thus apprised of the situation, his opponent across the lines at Petersburg, General Robert E. Lee, also became interested. On November 14, Lee wrote Seddon that General J. G. Martin had informed him that 2,000 or 3,000 foreigners held as prisoners of war at Salisbury, North Carolina, could be enlisted in the Confederate Army.

He [Martin] also states that authority for this purpose has been given to several persons by the War Department and that the company officers are to be elected by the members of the company. If they are taken from among themselves I fear they may be neither effective nor reliable. How would it answer to organize these men into the Regular Army, with officers appointed by the President, and the whole under one good officer? The men would then be placed in camp, instructed, and disciplined. By the spring they would make a valuable addition to the Army. General Martin thinks that by proper management this force could be increased to 7,000 or 8,000.

In a lengthy reply, Seddon outlined his attitude toward prison recruitment, the steps he had already taken, and those he proposed to take. "I have given to officers supposed to be competent . . . permits to raise battalions, directing them to prefer Irish and French, and to enlist no citizens of the U.S. The latter, especially native born, I hold in great distrust." Seddon explained that he preferred to form battalions instead of regiments because he "doubted the expediency of having so many of this material together as a regiment required." The Secretary agreed with General Lee that the practice of permitting enlisted prisoners to elect their officers from among themselves was dangerous, and promised that it would no longer be permitted.[8]

The high hopes of General Lee for a "valuable addition" to his army from prisoners of war must have been considerably dampened on Christmas Eve, 1864, by a message from General Hardee at Charleston:

Colonel Brooks' battalion composed of Federal prisoners of war enlisted from prisons into the Confederate service, was found at Savannah to be utterly untrustworthy. The men deserted in large numbers and finally mutinied, and were narrowly prevented from going over in a body to the enemy. The ringleaders were shot and the remainder sent back to prison. These men were selected with great care, and were principally foreigners, and this is, therefore, a fair test of such troops. I recommend that all authority to organize similar commands be revoked.[9]

Three days later at Egypt Station, Mississippi, General Benjamin Grierson's Union Cavalry Division was facing a defensive position held by the 10th Tennessee Infantry and other Confederate regiments. After nightfall several soldiers dressed in Confederate uniforms made their way into the Union lines at a point held by the 3rd Iowa Cavalry and surrendered. They reported that they were former Union soldiers who had been prisoners of war at Andersonville. They told Colonel John Noble of the 3rd Iowa that they had enlisted in the Confederate Army to save themselves from death by starvation and disease, and that they had taken an oath they no longer remembered, with the design and determination to join the Union Army at the first opportunity. They also informed Noble that about 300 more Galvanized Confederates were with the 10th Tennessee, and that "many of these men would not resist in battle."[10]

Next morning when Grierson ordered an attack, the 3rd Iowa and 2nd New Jersey cavalry regiments bore the brunt of the fight with the 10th Tennessee. When the battle was over, the Union forces were victorious; they had also taken 500 prisoners, 254 of them former Union soldiers. According to Colonel Noble, the assurance that the Galvanized Confederates would not resist "proved true in many instances, although the fight was a severe one." The commander of the New Jersey regiment, however, reported that when his men came within range of the 10th Tennessee skirmish line, "they opened a heavy fire, killing three officers and 20 men and wounding 74 others, that he then made a charge, when they threw down their arms and surrendered."[11]

General Grierson ordered all the former Union soldiers shipped north to Alton, Illinois, for internment in a special prison designed for spies, political subversives, and deserters. In his report of their capture, Grierson explained that he believed they were induced to join the Confederate Army "from a desire to escape a loathsome confinement. I commend them to the leniency of the Government."[12]

For a few weeks the fate of these captives was in doubt, the judge advocate general being inclined to bring them individually to trial as deserters. But by this time the war was nearing its end, and in St. Louis, across the river from Alton, General Grenville Dodge was energetically seeking recruits for his 5th and 6th U.S. Volunteer Infantry regiments.

It was largely through Dodge's efforts that these special prisoners once again became Union soldiers. These were the Galvanized Confederates who became Galvanized Yankees in Companies C and D of the 5th U.S. Volunteers, and marched under Captain George Williford with the Sawyers Expedition to Powder River. (The end of their story is told in Chapter VI.)

In the meantime the Confederate Army had not entirely abandoned plans to recruit more prisoners of war into its ranks. About the same time that General Hardee completely rejected any further use of such recruits, General D. H. Maury, commanding in the lower Mississippi Valley, requested permission to give the experiment a trial in his department.

Secretary Seddon was extremely cautious in his reply, advising Maury not to place such recruits in new organizations, but to scatter them among veteran regiments. "In one case in which a new battalion was formed from such material," Seddon warned, "a conspiracy was discovered; and although it was promptly crushed, yet it was found expedient to disband the battalion." Seddon repeated the instructions he had given other commanders: "Recruit chiefly among the Irish. Men born in the U.S. should not be received unless known to have sincere and positive predilections for the South. Natives of the Southern States may be received more freely."[13]

As the war rushed to its end, harassed Confederate commanders in the East became involved in petty quarrels over available prisoner recruits. On January 17, 1865, General Zebulon York complained to General Lee that Lieutenant-Colonel John G. Tucker, commanding the First Foreign Battalion, had recruited prisoners promised to him in North Carolina. York's message was passed around through higher headquarters, accumulating indorsements while Grant was delivering his final hammer blows at the army of the Confederacy. The Confederate War Department at last decided that Lieutenant-Colonel Tucker's First Foreign Battalion had priority over York's brigade.[14]

Meanwhile General Sherman's victorious Union army had been rolling north from Savannah, freeing thousands of prisoners. By the time York received his reply from Lee, Sherman was threatening North Carolina, and nothing seemed of less importance than the Galvanized Confederates.

Notes

I. Introduction

1. Ware, p. 401.
2. Root, p. 505.
3. Waters, p. 62.
4. *Union Vedette,* April 12, 1865.
5. *Rocky Mountain Herald,* July 2, 1927.
6. Mackey, p. 649.
7. OR, Ser. I, vol. 48, pt. 2, p. 1228; Dodge, p. 63.
8. Ibid., pp. 751-52, 1239.
9. *Frontier Scout,* Aug. 17, 1865.
10. *Union Vedette,* Oct. 10 and 12, 1865.
11. *Frontier Scout,* June 15 and Oct. 12, 1865.
12. Ware, p. 401.
13. Sturgis, pp. 268-69, and from information supplied by Roy Brandon, Halls, Tennessee.
14. Goss, p. 225; Grigsby, p. 182.
15. OR, Ser. II, vol. 8, p. 358.
16. Butler, vol. 3, p. 557.
17. Bowles, p. 11.

II. "Bloody Year on the Plains"

1. OR, Ser. III, vol. 4, p. 680.
2. *Collected Works of Abraham Lincoln,* vol. 7, p. 531.
3. OR, Ser. III, vol. 4, p. 740.
4. Ibid., p. 744.
5. Ibid.
6. Ibid., 756.
7. Minnich, p. 30.

8. Ibid.
9. OR, Ser. III, vol. 4, p. 940.
10. OR, Ser. I, vol. 48, pt. 1, p. 761.
11. 2nd and 3rd U.S.V.I. Regts. Order Books, Feb. 1865.
12. *New York Times,* Aug. 19 and Sept. 21, 1864; Bailey, p. 66.
13. Taylor, p. 59.
14. H.Q. Dist. of North Kansas. Spec. Ord. 47, March 7, 1865.
15. 3rd U.S.V.I. Regt. Letter Book, March 1865.
16. OR, Ser. I, vol. 48, pt. 2, p. 60.
17. 3rd U.S.V.I. Regt. Order Book, May 1865
18. Ibid.
19. Hull, p. 35.
20. O'Rielly, Henry. Memorial of . . ., N.Y., Jan. 8, 1858. Broadside.
21. OR, Ser. I, vol. 48, pt. 2, pp. 709-10.
22. 3rd U.S.V.I. Regt. Letter Book, May 1865; Co. D, 3rd U.S.V.I. Regt. Order Book, June 1865.
23. 3rd U.S.V.I. Regt. Letter Book, May 1865; Co. C, 3rd U.S.V.I. Regt. Order Book, June 1865; OR, Ser. I, vol. 48, pt. 1, pp. 282-84.
24. OR, Ser. I, vol. 48, pt. 2, p. 523.
25. Ibid., pt. 1, pp. 273-74.
26. Ibid., pp. 279-80.
27. Ibid., pt. 2, p. 670.
28. Ibid., pt. 1, p. 282.
29. Ibid., pp. 316-17.
30. Bowles, pp. 10-23.
31. Watkins, p. 245.
32. Co. A, 3rd U.S.V.I. Regt. Order Book, May–June 1865; Richardson, p. 331.
33. Dixon, p 18.
34. Meline, pp. 42-43.
35. Dixon, p. 21.
36. U.S. Congress, 39th, 2nd sess. Senate Report 156, 1867, pp. 90-91.
37. Co. I, 3rd U.S.V.I. Regt. Muster Rolls and Record of Events, May–Nov. 1865.
38. 3rd U.S.V.I. Regt. Letter Book, July 19, 1865.
39. *Union Vedette,* July 20, 1865.
40. Co. I, 3rd U.S.V.I. Regt. Spec. Ord. No. 4, July 24, 1865.
41. Diary of Lieutenant William Y. Drew in Hebard and Brininstool, vol. I, p. 183.
42. Walker, p. 338.
43. Diary of Lieutenant William Y. Drew in Hebard and Brininstool, vol. I, p. 189.
44. Walker, p. 338.
45. OR, Ser. I, vol. 48, pt. 1, p. 357.
46. *Union Vedette,* Aug. 4, 1865.
47. For more complete accounts of the Platte Bridge Fight, see *Caspar Collins,* by Agnes Wright Spring, and *Fort Caspar,* by Alfred J. Mokler.

48. *Union Vedette,* Aug. 11, Oct. 24, and Nov. 14, 1865.
49. Young, p. 43.
50. Dodge, p. 86.
51. Cos. A, C, E, and F, 3rd U.S.V.I. Regt. Muster Rolls and Record of Events, May–Aug. 1865.
52. 3rd U.S.V.I. Regt. Letter Book, Sept.–Oct. 1865.
53. 3rd U.S.V.I. Regt. Order Book, Nov. 29, 1865.
54. Cos. E and G, 3rd U.S.V.I. Regt. Descriptive Books.
55. 2nd U.S.V.I. Regt. Order Book, March 1865.
56. Minnich, p. 36.
57. Root, p. 505.
58. Ryus, p. 162.
59. Root, p. 508.
60. 2nd U.S.V.I. Regt. Letter Book, June 1865.
61. OR, Ser. I, vol. 48, pt. 1, pp. 311-12.
62. Co. G, 2nd U.S.V.I. Regt. Spec. Ord. 42, Fort Dodge, June 14, 1865.
63. Cos. F and I, 2nd U.S.V.I. Regt. Order Books, May–Aug. 1865.
64. *Army and Navy Journal,* vol. 2, July 29, 1865, p. 773.
65. *Frontier Scout,* Sept. 7, 1865.
66. Mackey, p. 649.
67. *New York Times,* Sept. 15, 1865.
68. H.Q. Dist. of the Upper Arkansas. Gen. Ord. No. 33, Aug. 18, 1865.
69 OR, Ser. I, vol. 48, pt. 2, p. 1219.
70. Mackey, p. 649.
71. 2nd U.S.V.I. Regt. Order Book, Oct.–Nov. 1865.

III.   OATHS AND ALLEGIANCES

1. Stanley, pp. 200-206.
2. OR, Ser. II, vol. 1, p. 170.
3. Ibid.
4. OR, Ser. II, vol. 4, p. 615.
5. Stanley, pp. 208-10.
6. OR, Ser. II, vol. 3, pp. 788-89.
7. Ibid., vol. 4, pp. 162-63.
8. Ibid., pp. 233, 343.
9. Ibid., p. 417.
10. Ibid., pp. 499, 522, 542-43, 546-47, 550.
11. Ibid., pp. 563-70.
12. Ibid., pp. 593, 598.
13. Ibid., p. 621.
14. OR, Ser. II, vol. 5, pp. 240-41.
15. Ibid., p. 446.
16. *Indianapolis Journal,* June 12, 1863; *Indianapolis Sentinel,* June 15, 1863.
17. OR, Ser. II, vol. 6, p. 31.
18. OR, Ser. III, vol. 3, p. 722.
19. OR, Ser. II, vol. 6, p. 808.
20. Ibid., vol. 7, p. 823.

21. Malone, p. 46.
22. OR, Ser. III, vol. 4, pp. 191-92, 200; 1st U.S.V.I. Regt. Order Book, March 28, 1864.
23. Keiley, pp. 55-67.
24. Malone, pp. 45-49.
25. Atwood, p. 364.
26. Diary of Captain Robert Benson, as reproduced in *Month at Goodspeed's,* vol. 33, Jan.–Feb. 1962, pp. 94-95.
27. OR, Ser. I, vol. 41, pt. 2, p. 619; H.Q. U.S. Army in the Field, Virginia, Spec. Ord. No. 82, Aug. 28, 1864.
28. OR, Ser. III, vol. 4, p. 1037.
29. Ibid., p. 1185.
30. Army and Navy Journal, vol. 2, Aug. 27, 1864, p. 6.
31. OR, Ser. III, vol. 2, p. 1203.

IV.   SOLDIERING ON THE WIDE MISSOURI

1. 1st U.S.V.I. Regt. Order Book, Aug. 9, 1864.
2. Musgrove, pp. 156, 158.
3. Ibid., pp. 158-59.
4. OR, Ser. I, vol. 41, pt. 2, pp. 737, 813.
5. Dimon Letters, Aug. 29, 1864.
6. 1st U.S.V.I. Regt. Order Book, Sept. 8, 1864.
7. William Dowdy, Co. E, 1st U.S.V.I. Regt., Record of Military Service and Transcript of Court-Martial.
8. Dimon Letters, Aug. 29, 1864.
9. Butler, vol. 5, p. 10.
10. OR, Ser. I, vol. 41, pt. 3, p. 219.
11. *Frontier Scout,* June 29, 1865.
12. Dimon Letters, Sept. 29, 1864.
13. *Frontier Scout,* June 29, 1865.
14. Ibid.
15. Ibid., July 13, 1865.
16. Ibid., June 29, 1865.
17. OR, Ser. I, vol. 41, pt. 1, p. 155.
18. Drips, p. 97.
19. 1st U.S.V.I. Regt. Letter Book, Oct. 31, 1864.
20. Dimon Letters, Oct. 14, 1864.
21. *Frontier Scout,* June 29, 1865.
22. OR, Ser. I, vol. 41, pt. 4, p. 65.
23. *Frontier Scout,* June 29, 1865.
24. 1st U.S.V.I. Regt. Order Book, Oct.–Nov. 1864; Dimon Letters, Oct. 22, 1864.
25. 1st U.S.V.I. Regt. Order Book, Nov. 14, 1864.
26. Dimon Letters, Nov. 27, 1864.
27. 1st U.S.V.I. Regt. Gen. Ord. No. 5, Fort Rice, Nov. 28, 1864.
28. Dimon Letters, Nov. 24, 1864.
29. 1st U.S.V.I. Regt. Order Book, Dec. 10, 1864.

30. Ibid., Dec. 11 and 22, 1864.
31. *Frontier Scout,* June 22, 1865.
32. 1st U.S.V.I. Regt. Order Book, Jan. 6, 1865.
33. OR, Ser. I, vol. 48, pt. 1, p. 637.
34. 1st U.S.V.I. Regt. Order Book, Feb. 1, 1865.
35. Dimon Letters, Feb. 14, 1865.
36. 1st U.S.V.I. Regt. Gen. Ord. No. 8, Fort Rice, March 3, 1865.
37. Dimon Letters, Dec. 14, 1864.
38. *Frontier Scout,* July 27, 1865.
39. 1st U.S.V.I. Regt. Order Book, March 25 and 30, 1865.
40. Dimon Memorandum Book and Diary, April 12, 1865.
41. *Frontier Scout,* June 22, 1865.
42. Dimon Memorandum Book and Diary, May 12, 1865.
43. OR, Ser. I, vol. 48, pt. 2, p. 434.
44. *Frontier Scout,* June 29, 1865.
45. OR, Ser. 1, vol. 48, pt. 2, p. 851.
46. Ibid., p. 961.
47. *Frontier Scout,* June 15, 1865.
48. Coe Collection, Yale University Library.
49. *Frontier Scout,* June 22, 1865.
50. Ibid., July 6, 1865.
51. OR, Ser. I, vol. 48, pt. 2, p. 1091.
52. Drips, pp. 131-32.
53. OR, Ser. I, vol. 48, pt. 2, p. 1091.
54. Dimon Letters, Aug. 6, 1865.
55. *Frontier Scout,* July 27, 1865.
56. Ibid., Aug. 3, 1865.
57. Ibid.
58. Ibid., Aug. 10, 24, and 31, 1865.
59. Ibid., Sept. 7, 1865.
60. OR, Ser. I, vol. 48, pt. 2, pp. 1228-29.

V.   "GIVE IT BACK TO THE INDIANS"

 1. Butler, vol. 5, pp. 152-53.
 2. 4th U.S.V.I. Regt. Order Book, April–May 1865.
 3. OR, Ser. I, vol. 48, pt. 2, p. 647.
 4. *Frontier Scout,* Sept. 14, 1865.
 5. Co. C, 4th U.S.V.I. Regt. Muster Roll and Record of Events, July 1865.
 6. U.S. Congress, 39th, 2nd sess. House Exec. Doc. 23, Washington, 1867, p. 43.
 7. 4th U.S.V.I. Regt. Letter Book, Nov. 1865–March 1866.
 8. U.S. Congress, 39th, 2nd sess. House Exec. Doc. 23, Washington, 1867, p. 43.
 9. Butler, vol. 5, p. 687.
10. 4th U.S.V.I. Regt. Order Book, June 1866.

VI. From the Cimarron to the Powder

1. Dodge, pp. 78-80.
2. OR, Ser. I, vol. 48, pt. 2, pp. 58, 149, 306.
3. Co. A, 5th U.S.V.I. Regt. Order Book, June 1865.
4. OR, Ser. I, vol. 48, pt. 2, p. 146.
5. OR, Ser. II, vol. 8, pp. 124-26.
6. Cos. C and D, 5th U.S.V.I. Regt. Descriptive Books and Muster Rolls.
7. St. Louis *Missouri Republican,* Oct. 30, 1865.
8. Holman, pp. 13-14.
9. Ibid., p. 15.
10. Ibid., p. 17.
11. U.S. Congress, 39th, 1st sess. House Exec. Doc. 58, 1866, p. 22.
12. Ibid.
13. Holman, pp. 18-19.
14. U.S. Congress, 39th, 2nd sess. Senate Rept. 156, 1867, p. 96.
15. St. Louis *Missouri Republican,* Oct. 30, 1865.
16. Ibid.
17. U.S. Congress, 39th, 1st sess. House Exec. Doc. 58, 1866, p. 23.
18. OR, Ser. I, vol. 48, pt. 1, p. 340.
19. Ibid., pp. 388-89.
20. *Union Vedette,* Oct. 12, 1865.
21. Hafen and Hafen, *Powder River Campaigns,* p. 190.
22. Cos. C and D, 5th U.S.V.I. Regt. Fort Connor, D.T., Order Book, Oct. 28, 1865.
23. Ibid., Gen. Ord. No. 6, Nov. 15, 1865.
24. Ibid., Order Book, Jan.-July 1866.
25. Gatchell, pp. 48-52.
26. Co. D, 5th U.S.V.I. Regt. Descriptive Book.
27. OR, Ser. I, vol. 48, pt. 1, p. 354.
28. 5th U.S.V.I. Regt. Order Book, Sept. 20, 1865.
29. Co. F, 5th U.S.V.I. Regt. Order Book, July-Aug. 1866.
30. Young, p. 71.
31. U.S. Congress, 39th, 2nd sess. House Exec. Doc. 23, 1867, p. 6.
32. Ibid., p. 5.
33. Co. D, 5th U.S.V.I. Regt. Plum Creek, N.T., Gen. Ord. No. 2, Aug. 7, 1866.
34. Co. C, 5th U.S.V.I. Regt. Order Book, Aug. 28, 1866.
35. 5th U.S.V.I. Regt. Order Book, Sept 18, 1866.
36. U.S. Congress, 39th, 2nd sess. House Exec. Doc. 23, 1867, p. 18.

VII. From Camp Douglas to Camp Douglas

1. *Union Vedette,* July 15, 1865.
2. 6th U.S.V.I. Regt. Order Book, April 1865.
3. OR, Ser. I, vol. 48, pt. 2, pp. 222, 405, 411.
4. 6th U.S.V.I. Regt. Order Book, May 1865.
5. OR, Ser. I, vol. 48, pt. 2, p. 921.
6. Ibid., p. 976.

7. Ibid., p. 1060.
8. Cos. A, F, and G, 6th U.S.V.I. Regt. Order Books, July 1865.
9. 6th U.S.V.I. Regt. Order Book, Nov. 28, 1865.
10. *Union Vedette,* Jan. 20, 1866.
11. Ibid., Aug. 1865–Jan. 1866.
12. Ibid., Oct. 9, 1865.
13. Ibid., Oct. 10 and 12, 1865.
14. Ibid., Oct. 21, 1865.
15. Ibid., Oct. 17, 1865.
16. Ibid., Oct. 28, 1865.
17. 6th U.S.V.I. Regt. Order Book, Sept. 1865–Feb. 1866.
18. O'Reilly, pp. 258-87.
19. Ware, pp. 572-76.
20. U.S. Secretary of the Interior. Annual Report, 1866, p. 207.
21. Ware, p. 576.
22. *Union Vedette,* Nov. 13, 14, and 27, 1865.
23. Ibid., Dec. 20, 1865.
24. Waters, p. 58.
25. Ibid., p. 59.
26. Co. A, 6th U.S.V.I. Regt. Order Book, June 22, 1866.
27. Ibid., July 3, 1866.
28. Ibid., July 9 and Aug. 19, 1866.
29. Co. C, 6th U.S.V.I. Regt. Muster Roll and Record of Events, Aug. 1866.
30. U.S. Congress, 39th, 2nd sess. House Exec. Doc. 23, p. 12.

VIII.   THE INCREDIBLE CAPTAIN SHANKS

1. Brown, D. A., *The Bold Cavaliers,* pp. 286-87.
2. *Atlantic Monthly,* vol. 16, 1865, p. 115.
3. OR, Ser. III, vol. 4, pp. 740, 756.
4. *Atlantic Monthly,* vol. 16, 1865, p. 109.
5. Ibid., pp. 115-16.
6. U.S. Congress, 39th, 2nd sess. House Exec. Doc. 50, Washington, 1867, p. 35.
7. *Atlantic Monthly,* vol. 16, 1865, p. 120.
8. U.S. Congress, 39th, 2nd sess. House Exec. Doc. 50, Washington, 1867, p. 62.
9. John T. Shanks, Co. I, 6th U.S.V.I. Regt. Record of Military Service.
10. Ibid.
11. Ibid.
12. Co. I, 6th U.S.V.I. Regt. Order Book, Aug. 31, 1865
13. Ware, p. 297.
14. Diary of Captain B. F. Rockafellow, in Hafen and Hafen, pp. 194-95.
15. John T. Shanks, Co. I, 6th U.S.V.I. Regt. Record of Military Service.
16. Thomas Ferrier, Co. B, 11th Ohio Volunteer Cavalry Regt. Record of Military Service.
17. Co. I, 6th U.S.V.I. Regt. Order Book, Jan.–Feb. 1866.

18. *New York Times,* Dec. 12, 1861; Harlow, pp. 309-16, 490-97.
19. Gleed, pp. 19-41.
20. Brown, D. A., *Fort Phil Kearny,* p. 136.

IX. OHIOANS FROM DIXIE: THE POWDER RIVER EXPEDITION

1. Crawford, pp. 39-41.
2. *Official Roster of the Soldiers of the State of Ohio,* vol. XI, Akron, 1891, pp. 562-63.
3. Crawford, p. 75.
4. Ibid., p. 77.
5. Palmer, p. 197.
6. Adams, pp. 12-13.
7. Ibid., p. 12.
8. Ibid., pp. 8-9.
9. Co. E, 11th Ohio Cavalry Regt. Order Book. H.Q. Powder River Indian Expedition, North Platte, Gen. Ord. No. 1, Aug. 2, 1865.
10. Palmer, pp. 214-15.
11. Adams, pp. 14-15.
12. Humfreville, pp. 356-57.
13. Palmer, p. 216.
14. Adams, p. 15.
15. Ibid., p. 16.
16. *Union Vedette,* Jan. 20, 1866.
17. Grinnell, pp. 212-13.
18. *Fort Kearney Herald,* March 2, 1866.
19. Fairly complete documentary accounts of the Powder River Expedition may be found in *Powder River Campaigns,* by LeRoy R. and Ann W. Hafen.
20. Adams, p. 20.

X. BLIZZARD MARCH

1. Musgrove, p. 178.
2. *Union Vedette,* Oct. 5 and 26, 1865.
3. Musgrove, p. 182.
4. Ibid., pp. 183-84.
5. Ibid., p. 186.
6. Ibid., pp. 186-87.
7. Ibid., p. 188.
8. Ibid., p. 191.
9. *Harper's Weekly,* April 21, 1866, pp. 249-50.
10. Musgrove, p. 194.
11. Ibid., p. 195.
12. Ibid., p. 198.
13. Ibid., pp. 199-200.
14. *Union Vedette,* Jan. 18 and 26, 1866.
15. Musgrove, p. 200.
16. G Co., 1st U.S.V.I. Regt. Order Book, Jan. 1866.

17. Musgrove, p. 202.
18. Ibid., p. 219.
19. Adams, pp. 9-10.
20. Musgrove, p. 218.
21. Davis, p. 303.
22. Musgrove, p. 120.

XI.   Last Man Out

1. Charles H. Hoyt, Co. H, 5th U.S.V.I. Regt. Record of Military Service.
2. Co. H, 5th U.S.V.I. Regt. Order Book, Fort Leavenworth, May 3, 1865.
3. 5th U.S.V.I. Regt. Order Book, June 1865.
4. 5th U.S.V.I. Regt., H.Q. Detachment, Spring Creek, Kansas, Spec. Ord. No. 3, June 14, 1865.
5. 5th U.S.V.I. Regt., H.Q. Detachment, Fort Dodge, Muster Roll and Record of Events, July 1865.
6. Co. H, 5th U.S.V.I. Regt. Order Book, July–Aug. 1865.
7. OR, Ser. I, vol. 34, pt. 3, pp. 565, 712.
8. Co. H, 5th U.S.V.I. Regt. Order Book, Oct.–Nov. 1865.
9. Ibid., Jan. 26, 1866.
10. Charles H. Hoyt, Co. H, 5th U.S.V.I. Regt. Record of Military Service.
11. U.S. Congress, 39th, 2nd sess. House Exec. Doc. 23, 1867, p. 18.

XII.   A Note on the Galvanized Confederates

1. OR, Ser. II, vol. 5, p. 845.
2. Ibid., vol. 7, p. 82.
3. OR, Ser. IV, vol. 3, p. 694; OR, Ser. II, vol. 7, p. 900.
4. OR, Ser. II, vol. 7, pp. 974, 1014.
5. Ibid., p. 1086.
6. Ibid., pp. 1113-14.
7. Ibid., pp. 1121-23.
8. OR, Ser. IV, vol. 3, pp. 822-25.
9. OR, Ser. II, vol. 7, p. 1268.
10. Ibid., vol. 8, pp. 124-26.
11. Ibid., p. 554.
12. Ibid., p. 358.
13. OR, Ser. IV, vol. 3, pp. 1011-12.
14. Ibid., vol. 2, pp. 1029, 1083.

Sources

As there is a paucity of published materials on the Galvanized Yankees, this work is of necessity based largely upon original records of the six regiments concerned. Regimental letter, order, and roster books of the 1st, 2nd, 3rd, 4th, 5th, and 6th U.S. Volunteer Infantry in the National Archives furnished most of the detailed information. To clarify or expand certain incidents, the order and descriptive books of many companies, and service records of several individual officers and men, were also consulted.

In addition, the *Official Records of the Union and Confederate Armies* were useful for the organizational period of late 1864 and early 1865, and for military operations in the West on departmental, district, and sub-district levels.

Only one published account by an officer of the Galvanized Yankees was located, Captain Richard Musgrove's *Autobiography,* privately printed in a very limited edition for his family. This, with the manuscript diary and personal letters of Colonel Charles Dimon in the Western Americana Collection, Yale University Library, furnished much human interest material for the two chapters concerning the 1st Regiment.

Two newspapers proved to be quite useful sources, the *Frontier Scout* and *Union Vedette.* Both were soldier newspapers, the former being published at Fort Rice, Dakota Territory, the latter at Camp Douglas, Utah. The *Frontier Scout* was filled with activities of the Galvanized Yankees at Rice as well as at other Missouri River forts. The *Union Vedette,* while primarily interested in Camp Douglas matters, also received telegraph news from the East, and it was common practice for military telegraphers along the Platte section guarded by Galvanized Yankees to dispatch items to the *Vedette,* especially news of events concerning soldiers.

The following is a list of most of the published sources consulted.

Adams, Charles W. *Civil War Reminiscences Interestingly Told.* Greenfield, Ohio, n.p., [1917?].

Armes, George A. *Ups and Downs of an Army Officer.* Washington, D.C., n.p., 1900.

Army and Navy Journal, 1864-66.

Atwood, Evans. Diary, edited by W. J. Lemke. *Arkansas Historical Quarterly,* vol. 12, 1953, pp. 340-69.

Bailey, W. F. *The Story of the First Transcontinental Railroad.* Pittsburgh, Pa., Pittsburgh Printing Co., 1906.

Beach, James. "Old Fort Hays." Kansas State Historical Society, *Collections,* vol. XI, 1909-10, pp. 571-81.

Bowles, Samuel. *Across the Continent.* Springfield, Mass., S. Bowles & Company, 1865.

Butler, Benjamin F. *Private and Official Correspondence.* Norwood, Mass., Plimpton Press, 1917. 5 vols.

Crawford, Lewis F. *Rekindling Campfires.* Bismarck, N.D., Capitol Book Co., 1926.

Davis, Theodore R. "A Summer on the Plains." *Harper's New Monthly Magazine,* vol. 36, 1868, pp. 292-307.

Dixon, Olive K. *Life of Billy Dixon.* Dallas, Tex., Southwest Press, 1927.

Dodge, Grenville. *The Battle of Atlanta and Other Campaigns.* Council Bluffs, Iowa, Monarch Printing Co., 1911.

Drips, J. H. *Three Years Among the Indians in Dakota.* Kemball, S.D., Brule Index, 1894.

Easterwood, T. J. *Lights and Shadows on the Big Horns.* Dundee, Ore., Dundee Printing Co., 1881.

Ellison, Robert S. *Fort Bridger, Wyoming.* Sheridan, Historical Landmark Commission of Wyoming, 1938.

Frederick, J. B. *Ben Holladay, the Stagecoach King.* Glendale, Calif., A. H. Clark, 1940.

Frontier Scout, 1865.

Gallaher, William A. "Ho! for the Gold Mines of Montana; Up the Missouri in 1865," edited by James E. Moss. *Missouri Historical Review,* vol. 57, 1963, pp. 156-83.

Garfield, Marvin H. "The Military Post as a Factor in the Frontier Defense of Kansas, 1865-1869." *Kansas Historical Quarterly,* vol. 1, 1931, pp. 50-62.

Gatchell, T. J. "Life of John Ryan." *Annals of Wyoming,* vol. 31, 1959, pp. 48-52.

Gleed, Charles S. "Eugene Fitch Ware." Kansas State Historical Society, *Collections,* vol. XIII, 1913-14, pp. 19-41.

Goss, Warren Lee. *The Soldier's Story.* Boston, Lee and Shepard, 1871.

Gray, John S. "Will Comstock—the Natty Bumpo of Kansas." *Westerners Brand Book,* Chicago, vol. 18, 1962, pp. 89-96.

Grigsby, Melvin. *The Smoked Yank.* Chicago, Regan Printing Co., 1891.

Grinnell, George B. *The Fighting Cheyennes.* Norman, Okla., University of Oklahoma Press, 1956.

Hafen, LeRoy R. *The Overland Mail, 1849-1869.* Cleveland, Ohio, A. H. Clark, 1926.

Hafen, LeRoy R., and Ann W. Hafen. *Powder River Campaigns.* Glendale, Calif., A. H. Clark, 1961.

Hagerty, L. W. "Indian Raids Along the Platte and Little Blue Rivers, 1864-65." *Nebraska History,* vol. 28, 1947, pp. 176-86, 239-60.

Harlow, Alvin F. *Old Wires and New Waves, the History of the Telegraph, Telephone and Wireless.* New York City, Appleton-Century, 1936.

Hebard, Grace R., and E. A. Brininstool. *The Bozeman Trail.* Cleveland, Ohio, A. H. Clark, 1922. 2 vols.

Holley, Frances. *Once Their Home; or Our Legacy from the Dahkotahs.* Chicago, Donohue, 1891.

Holman, Albert M., and C. R. Marks. *Pioneering in the Northwest.* Sioux City, Iowa, Deitch & Lamar Co., 1924.

Hull, Lewis B. "Soldiering on the High Plains, 1864-1866," edited by Myra E. Hull. *Kansas Historical Quarterly,* vol. 7, 1938, pp. 3-35.

Humfreville, J. Lee. *Twenty Years Among Our Hostile Indians.* New York City, Hunter and Co., 1903.

Hyde, George E. *Pawnee Indians.* Denver, Colo., University of Denver Press, 1951.

Jones, Robert H. *The Civil War in the Northwest.* Norman, Okla., University of Oklahoma Press, 1960.

Keiley, A. M. *In Vinculus, or the Prisoner of War.* New York City, Blelock and Co., 1866.

Kingsbury, George W. *History of Dakota Territory.* Chicago, S. J. Clarke, 1915.

Mackey, William H. "Looking Backwards." Kansas State Historical Society, *Collections,* vol. 10, 1907-8, pp. 642-54.

McMurtrie, Douglas C. "Pioneer Printing in North Dakota." *North Dakota Historical Quarterly,* vol. 6, 1932, pp. 221-30.

Malone, Bartlett Y. *Diary.* Chapel Hill, N.C., James Sprunt Historical Publications, University of North Carolina, vol. 16, no. 2, 1919.

Mattison, Ray H. "Fort Rice—North Dakota's First Missouri River Military Post." *North Dakota History,* vol. 20, 1953, pp. 93-104.

Meline, James F. *Two Thousand Miles on Horseback.* New York City, Hurd and Houghton, 1867.

Minnich, J. A. *Inside of Rock Island Prison, from December 1863 to June 1865.* Nashville, Tenn., Publishing House of the M.E. Church, South, 1908.

Mokler, Alfred J. *Fort Caspar.* Casper, Wyo., Prairie Pub. Co., 1939.

Montgomery, Mrs. Frank C. "Fort Wallace and Its Relation to the Frontier." *Kansas State Historical Society, Collections,* vol. 17, 1926-28, pp. 189-283.

Musgrove, Richard W. *Autobiography.* n.p., n.d.

Myers, Frank. *Soldiering in Dakota Among the Indians.* Huron, S.D., Huronite Printing House, 1888.

O'Reilly, Harrington. *Fifty Years on the Trail.* New York City, Warne, 1889.

O'Rielly, Henry. *Memorial of . . . Concerning Military Roads.* New York City, January 8, 1858. Broadside.

Palmer, H. E. "History of the Powder River Indian Expedition of 1865." Nebraska State Historical Society, *Transactions and Reports,* vol. 2, 1887, pp. 197-229.

Pattison, John J. "With the U.S. Army Along the Oregon Trail, 1863-66." *Nebraska History,* vol. 15, 1934, pp. 79-93.

Perkins, J. R. *Trails, Rails and War; the Life of General G. M. Dodge.* Indianapolis, Ind., Bobbs-Merrill, 1929.

Reid, James D. *The Telegraph in America.* New York City, 1886.

Richardson, Albert D. *Beyond the Mississippi.* Hartford, Conn., American Pub. Co., 1867.

Rogers, Fred B. *Soldiers of the Overland.* San Francisco, Calif., Grabhorn Press, 1938.

Root, George A. "Reminiscences of William Darnell." Kansas State Historical Society, *Collections,* vol. 17, 1926-28, pp. 479-513.

Rusling, James F. *Across America.* New York City, Sheldon and Co., 1874.

Ryus, William H. *The Second William Penn, a True Account of Incidents That Happened Along the Old Santa Fe Trail in the Sixties.* Kansas City, Mo., Frank T. Riley Pub. Co., 1913.

Spring, Agnes Wright. *Caspar Collins.* New York City, Columbia University Press, 1927.

Stanley, Henry Morton. *Autobiography.* London, Sampson, Low, Marston and Co., 1913.

Sturgis, Thomas. *Prisoners of War, 1861-65.* New York City, Putnam's, 1912.

Taylor, Joseph H. *Sketches of Frontier and Indian Life.* Bismarck, N.D., the author, 1897.

Union Vedette, 1865-66.

U.S. Congress, 39th. 1st sess. House Executive Document 58. Washington, D.C., 1866.

U.S. Congress, 39th, 2nd sess. House Executive Document 20. Washington, D.C., 1867.

U.S. Congress, 39th. 2nd sess. House Executive Document 23. Washington, D.C., 1867.

Walker, George M. "Eleventh Kansas Cavalry, 1865, and the Battle of Platte Bridge." Kansas State Historical Society, *Collections,* vol. 14, 1915-18, pp. 332-40.

Ware, Eugene F. *The Indian War of 1864.* Topeka, Kan., Crane & Co., 1911.

Waters, William E. *Life Among the Mormons and a March to Their Zion.* New York City, Moorhead, Simpson and Bond, 1868.

Watkins, Albert. "History of Fort Kearney." Nebraska State Historical Society, *Collections,* vol. 16, 1911, pp. 227-67.

Welty, Raymond L. "The Army Fort of the Frontier." *North Dakota Historical Quarterly,* vol. 2, 1928, pp. 155-67.

Welty, Raymond L. "The Frontier Army on the Missouri River, 1860-1870." *North Dakota Historical Quarterly,* vol. 2, 1928, pp. 85-99.

Young, Charles E. *Dangers of the Trail in 1865.* Geneva, N.Y., Press of W. F. Humphrey, 1912.

Index